THE COMPLETE IDIOT'S GUIDE® TO

Coaching Youth Soccer

W9-AHJ-240

796.33 MUC
Muckian, Michael.
The complete idiot's

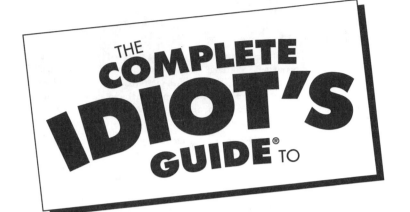

Coaching Youth Soccer

by Michael Muckian with Dean Duerst

ALPHA

A member of Penguin Group (USA) Inc.

Copyright © 2003 by Michael Muckian

All rights reserved. No part of this book shall be reproduced, stored in a retrieval system, or transmitted by any means, electronic, mechanical, photocopying, recording, or otherwise, without written permission from the publisher. No patent liability is assumed with respect to the use of the information contained herein. Although every precaution has been taken in the preparation of this book, the publisher and authors assume no responsibility for errors or omissions. Neither is any liability assumed for damages resulting from the use of information contained herein. For information, address Alpha Books, 201 West 103rd Street, Indianapolis, IN 46290.

THE COMPLETE IDIOT'S GUIDE TO and Design are registered trademarks of Penguin Group (USA) Inc.

International Standard Book Number: 1-59257-057-7
Library of Congress Catalog Card Number: 2003100771

05 04 03   8 7 6 5 4 3 2 1

Interpretation of the printing code: The rightmost number of the first series of numbers is the year of the book's printing; the rightmost number of the second series of numbers is the number of the book's printing. For example, a printing code of 03-1 shows that the first printing occurred in 2003.

Printed in the United States of America

Note: This publication contains the opinions and ideas of its authors. It is intended to provide helpful and informative material on the subject matter covered. It is sold with the understanding that the authors and publisher are not engaged in rendering professional services in the book. If the reader requires personal assistance or advice, a competent professional should be consulted.

The authors and publisher specifically disclaim any responsibility for any liability, loss, or risk, personal or otherwise, which is incurred as a consequence, directly or indirectly, of the use and application of any of the contents of this book.

Most Alpha books are available at special quantity discounts for bulk purchases for sales promotions, premiums, fund-raising, or educational use. Special books, or book excerpts, can also be created to fit specific needs.

For details write: Special Markets; Alpha Books, 375 Hudson Street, New York, NY 10014.

Publisher: *Marie Butler-Knight*
Product Manager: *Phil Kitchel*
Senior Managing Editor: *Jennifer Chisholm*
Senior Acquisitions Editor: *Mike Sanders*
Development Editor: *Jennifer Moore*
Senior Production Editor: *Katherin Bidwell*
Copy Editor: *Cari Luna*
Illustrator: *Marsha Richter*
Cartoonist: *Chris Eliopoulos*
Cover/Book Designer: *Trina Wurst*
Indexer: *Heather McNeill*
Layout/Proofreading: *Megan Douglass, Becky Harmon*

Contents at a Glance

Part 1:   **Suiting Up**   1

1 Getting Started   3
*You've already made the commitment to coach your son
or daughter's soccer team. Now what?*

2 Understanding Soccer Culture   17
*More than a sport, soccer is a culture and way of life
for millions. Understanding its history and culture will
give you a winning edge.*

3 The Coach in You   27
*The ability to coach lies hidden deep inside almost everyone.
We just have to find it.*

4 Developing Your Coaching Skills   37
*Once you've found your inner coach, it's necessary to hone
the skills necessary to make that coach successful.*

5 The Elements of Team Building   49
*Soccer is a team sport, and team sports mean teamwork.
You can't win without it.*

6 Dealing with Soccer Parents   55
*Soccer moms and dads can sometime be a coach's biggest
obstacle, especially for those coaches who want to stay sane
for the season.*

Part 2:   **Training Daze**   67

7 The Four Pillars of Soccer Wisdom   69
Take the time to learn about the foundations of soccer.

8 Principles of Play and Practice Design   79
*First you plan, then you practice, practice, practice. And if
that all works out, you'll be ready to play and win.*

9 Tools of the Player's Trade and How to Teach Them   87
What every soccer player needs to know to master the game.

10 Skills and Drills   103
*Success means training, training, training. Here are skills,
drills and a few frills to get you going.*

11 Athlete Health, Conditioning, and Safety   117
*Sports can mean injuries for the unprepared. Are your kids
ready for the game and do you know how to handle those
who aren't?*

Part 3: **Playing the Game** **127**

12 Understanding and Applying Strategies 129
Soccer is a game of strategies, and they're more effective than you'd ever imagine.

13 The Characteristics of Defense 147
Goodbye, passive defense; hello, aggressive play. The best defenders are in your face and never let up.

14 A Good Offense 161
A good offense involves a whole lot more than just kicking the ball into the net.

15 The Care and Feeding of Goalkeepers 173
They're a rare breed and the team's recognized leader. Treat them as you would any other lynchpin of success.

16 Restarts 185
When the ball goes out, how do you get it back in, strategically speaking?

17 Understanding Match Analysis 201
How do your strategies measure up against the opposition?

18 Team Tactics: Attack and Defense 209
Teams that function as single units, both in offense and defense, have a better chance of winning the game. Watch for those characteristics that tell you when your players are on track.

19 Preventing Goals 217
The last thing you want is for the opposition to score. The right strategy will keep them at bay and help you win the game.

20 Beyond the Game 225
Once you've mastered the skills and concepts behind coaching, where can you and your young players go next? The soccer world is wide and here's a starter's guide.

Appendixes

A Glossary 231

B Youth Soccer Organizations 239

C Soccer Resources 245

Index 253

Contents

Part 1: Suiting Up   **1**

1 Getting Started   **3**

Putting Your Team Together 4

New Experiences 5

Responsibility and Reward 5

Exercise, Exercise, Exercise 5

Let's Get Social! 5

A Stronger Sense of Self 6

Getting Started 6

You Need a Place to Play 6

You Need a Ball 8

Shirts, Shoes, and Shin-guards 8

Cones, Whistles, and Coaching Supplies 9

The Basics of the Beautiful Game 10

Playing the Game 10

Playing the Right Positions 13

By the Numbers: How Age Affects Play 14

Under 6 14

Under 8 14

Under 10 15

Under 12 15

Age 12 and Beyond 15

Coaching the Future 16

2 Understanding Soccer Culture   **17**

America Before Soccer 17

Give Me Your Tired, Your Poor … Your Soccer Players 18

Your Gym Teacher Was Ahead of the Times 18

A Little Soccer History 19

Soccer Mania 20

The Biggest Cup in the World 20

Make the Most of the Differences! 20

Who's Who in Youth Soccer 21

Where You Fit In 23

Good Coaches Care About Their Teams 23

Good Coaches Know What They're Talking About 23
Good Coaches Train with Empathy and Intelligence 24
Good Coaches Are Enthusiastic 24

3 The Coach in You   27

What Is a Coach, Anyway? 28
Finding the Coach Within You 29
Pedaling Back in Time 29
Cultivating Your Inner Coach 30
Know the Game 31
Lead by Example 31
Remember Who You're Dealing With 31
Teach Skills and Strategy 32
Keep Everyone Involved 32
Developing Your Coaching Style 33
The Cheerleader 33
The Tactical Technician 34
The Commander 34
The Builder 35

4 Developing Your Coaching Skills   37

Your Coaching Philosophy 38
Taking the Developmental Approach 38
Know Your Team 39
Take It Slow 40
Show and Tell 40
Train to Compete 40
Make It Easy! 40
Sign on the Dotted Line, Coach! 41
Developing a Player "Contract" 43
Putting the Finishing Touches on Your Coach-ness 44

5 The Elements of Team Building   49

Teamwork by Definition 50
Applying the Teamwork Process 51
Commandment 1: Teamwork has physical and intellectual
  components. 51
Commandment 2: Teamwork is sometimes as difficult to
  learn as it is to teach. 52

Commandment 3: Teamwork begins early and never ends. 52
*Commandment 4: Even very advanced players need to
understand and appreciate the team concept.* 52
Commandment 5: Without teamwork, there is no team. 52
Teamwork Training Drills 53

6 Dealing with Soccer Parents **55**

Harnessing Mom and Dad's Energy 56
Anatomy of a Soccer Parent 56
Defining Your Parental Strategy 58
First, Have a Plan 58
Your Team's Budget 61
Drafting Your Parental "Team" 62
Developing Your Coaching Staff 63
Writing a Playing Contract with Parents 64

Part 2: Training Daze **67**

7 The Four Pillars of Soccer Wisdom **69**

The Philosophy of Play 70
The Philosophy of Sports 71
Sports level the social playing field. 71
Sports let us get physical. 71
Sports cultivate self-esteem. 72
Sports cultivate self-fulfillment. 72
Defining the Four Pillars of Soccer 72
Technical Aspects of Play 73
Tactical Mastery of the Game 74
The Psychological Characteristics of Performance 75
Physical Traits of the Players and Their Efforts 76

8 Principles of Play and Practice Design **79**

Plan, Then Practice 80
Designing the Practice 81
1. Pre-Practice Activity (10–15 Minutes) 82
*2. Coach's Introduction and Practice Concept Discussion
(About 5 Minutes)* 82
3. Warm Ups and Stretches (About 10 Minutes) 83

Practice A: Skills Development 83
Practice B: Playing the Game 84
Cool Down and Wrap Up (10 Minutes) 85
It's Game Day! 86

9 Tools of the Players' Trade and How to Teach Them   87

The Fundamentals of Teaching Fundamentals 88
Learning the Skills 90
Dribbling 90
Take It Step by Step—Literally! 92
Follow the Curve 93
Passing and Receiving 94
Put Your Whole Body into the Kick 94
Foot Positions Are Key 94
Receiving the Pass 95
Juggling the Ball 96
Heading the Ball 98
Shooting the Goal 100
Combination Drills 101

10 Skills and Drills   103

Warm-Up Exercises 104
Hurdler's Stretch 104
Tripod Stretch 105
Toe Touch 106
Keeping Warm Ups Fun 106
Relay Tag 107
Stoplight 107
Rotation 107
Dribbling Drills 108
Zigzag 108
Zigzag Tag 109
Crablegs 109
Foxes and Rabbits 109
Passing and Receiving 110
Basic Catch 110
Triple Play 110
Round Robin 111

Juggling or Mastering Ball Control 111
   Up the Ladder *112*
   Double Ladders *112*
Heading 112
   Basic Headball *112*
Shooting the Goal 113
Cool-Down Exercises 114

11 Athlete Health, Conditioning, and Safety   117

Get a Physical Before Getting Physical 118
   Health Problems You Should Know About *119*
   It's Gotta Be Pain Free *120*
Understanding Athletic Stress 120
Promoting Healthy Lifestyles 121
Young Players Are What They Eat 123
   Balance Your Diet Effectively and Completely *123*
   Stay Hydrated *124*
   Be Wary of Nutritional Supplements *124*
Pre-Game Meals 125
   Three or More Hours Before Exercise or Game *125*
   Two to Three Hours Before Activity *125*
   One to Two Hours Before Activity *125*

Part 3:   Playing the Game   127

12 Understanding and Applying Strategies   129

Got Plans? 130
Getting to Know the Field 130
Know Your Players 133
Systems of Play 134
   The 4-4-2 ....*134*
   The 4-3-3 ....*136*
   The 4-2-4 ....*137*
   The 3-5-2 ....*139*
   The 3-6-1 ....*140*
Defining Your Youth Soccer Strategy 142

13 The Characteristics of Defense   147

It's Time to Get Defensive! 148
Defensive Positions and Play 148

Zone vs. Player-to-Player Defense 151
Factors in Defense 152
  Pressuring the Offense *152*
  Providing Defensive Support or Cover *153*
  Tracking Your Opponent *154*
  Attacking the Ball *154*
Taking Control of the Ball 155
A Closer Look at Tackling 156
  Toe Pokes *157*
  Funnelings *157*
  Block Tackles *157*
  Sliding Tackles *158*
Defense Comes Into Its Own 159

14 A Good Offense **161**

Assuming the Forward Position 162
  The Forwards *162*
  The Midfielders *163*
Systems of Play = Offensive Strategies 163
Tools of the Offense 165
  Moving the ball toward the goal is an important part of
    the offense, making dribbling skills crucial. *165*
  Good passing and receiving skills will mean greater success. *165*
  Basic Passing Shots *167*
  Putting the Ball in the Air: The Chip Shot *169*
  Teach Passes According to Skill Level *170*
Shooting the Goal 170

15 The Care and Feeding of Goalkeepers **173**

What Sets Goalkeepers Apart 174
Catches and Saves 175
  Catch Me If You Can *176*
  Other Ways to Make a Save *180*
Don't Just Stand There! 181
  Goalkeeper Positioning *181*
  The Near Post Save *182*
Supporting the Defense 183
Giving It the Boot! 183

16 Restarts **185**

When the Ball Goes Out of Bounds 185

Identifying Restart Opportunities 186

Corner Kicks 186

Free Kicks 189

Goal Kicks 191

Throw-ins 192

Offensive and Defensive Strategies 192

Executing a Corner Kick: The Flood 193

Defending a Corner Kick: Zone in the Goal 194

Executing a Direct Free Kick: The Peel Out 195

Executing an Indirect Free Kick: The Castle 196

Throw-ins: Isolation and Triangle 197

Practice Makes Perfect! 198

17 Understanding Match Analysis **201**

Analyzing the Field Options 202

Scouting the Opposition 203

Checking Out Their Defense 203

Looking Over Their Offense 205

Teaching Change 207

Demand Concentration 207

Practice Hard and Well 207

Set Goals 207

Conserve and Direct Energy 208

Stay in the Day 208

18 Team Tactics: Attack and Defense **209**

Mounting a Team Offense 210

Offensive Teamwork 210

Offensive Strategies and Field Positions 211

Developing Team Defense 212

Attack Aggressively and Unremittingly 212

Funnel the Position to Protect the Goal 213

Protect the Space Goalside 213

Watch for Tackle and Passing Options 214

Force the Opposition into Predictable Patterns 214

The Value of Teamwork 214

19 Preventing Goals   **217**

Make No Mistake 218

The Problem with Goals 218

Giving the Ball Away 219

Design and stick to an offensive strategy. 220

Think two or three steps ahead before taking advantage of
unexpected opportunity. 220

Learn to recognize the characteristics of opportunity. 220

Pressuring the Ball Carrier 221

Make sure the defender sticks close to the ball carrier. 221

Make sure the defender is between the ball carrier and is in
position to block shots on goal. 221

Supporting the Challenger 222

Tracking Your Opposition 222

The Perils of Restarts 223

20 Beyond the Game   **225**

Now What? 226

Did I do the right thing by my players? 226

Did I coach my team developmentally, helping them learn
the techniques in ways that they could master? 226

Did I expect the best from my players
and teach them to expect the best from themselves? 226

As coach, did I lead by example? 227

Don't Forget Your Role 227

Beyond Play 228

Encourage players to follow the pro teams. 228

Encourage their involvement in professional soccer groups
and associations. 228

Create an appreciation for soccer as a lifetime recreational
activity. 229

Appendixes

A Glossary   **231**

B Youth Soccer Organizations   **239**

C Soccer Resources   **245**

Index   **253**

Foreword

No excuse!

No one is born to coach soccer. But thanks to this book, almost everyone can learn.

As a professional soccer coach who has devoted his life to the game, I'm excited by the continued interest in the sport worldwide. When I see some of the well-meaning attempts by parents and others to coach youth teams, however, I want to tell them to pack up their cones and whistles and go home.

Soccer isn't nuclear physics, but a little knowledge is still a dangerous thing. A lot of kids start young and want to go on to high school and even college teams. Some have been coached well enough to succeed. Others have to unlearn the bad habits they picked up and start over. We lose too many of those kids along the way.

Michael Muckian and Dean Duerst have done exactly what needs to be done in writing *The Complete Idiot's Guide to Coaching Youth Soccer*. As an amateur and professional coach, respectively, they have gone out of their way to write a guide that's both complete and accessible. This is the coaching guide that youth soccer coaches everywhere have been waiting for.

The Complete Idiot's Guide to Coaching Youth Soccer isn't some quick little book of tips and techniques that answers only the easiest questions. Sure, the basics are here, but this book takes a more comprehensive approach to the sport—one that will build a coach's appreciation for what needs to be done and why, rather than just telling him or her how to do it. And the better the coaches are, the better the players and teams will be.

The best thing about this book is that it's written at an easy-to-read "kick the ball" level that merges tactics and strategies in ways both novice and experienced coaches will find valuable. As either a new or an experienced coach, you can't help but benefit from its approach.

If you coach youth soccer and you don't have professional training, you need this book. Even if you're an experienced professional, you'll still want this book in your library. It's the quickest and cleanest explanation of the ins and outs of soccer I've ever seen.

With Michael Muckian and Dean Duerst on the job, there's no excuse for poor youth coaching anymore. As a professional, I'm looking forward to the high quality of youth soccer players who will be running down the field in the future.

—Anson Dorrance

Head Coach, Women's Soccer
University of North Carolina-Chapel Hill
Author, *Training Soccer Champions*

Introduction

If you've picked up this volume, chances are it's because:

You're a professional soccer coach and are interested in seeing how the other half lives.

You're a parent who's been drafted—either willingly or against your will—to coach little Britney or Justin's youth soccer team and you don't know the first thing about the sport.

You're a parent of little Britney and Justin, who have just become new members of the neighborhood soccer team, and you need to find out what the heck you're in for.

You *are* little Britney or Justin and you want to know what your coach is doing and why.

You're any one of a dozen peripherally interested parties—a grandparent of a youth player, sponsor of a youth team, a teacher of kids more enthusiastic about their soccer team than your class—who needs to know more than you already do about the world's most popular sport.

If you fit into any of those categories, then this is the book for you. *The Complete Idiot's Guide to Coaching Youth Soccer* draws on a lifetime of learning, creating the ultimate guide for coaches, parents, teachers, players, and anyone else interested in tuning in and turning on to this exciting pastime that has caught the fancy of kids of all ages, races, creeds, and countries. Even if you're not a coach, this guide explains the game in a way everyone can understand.

It's just a darn good resource on the sport, even if you don't even know little Britney or Justin.

How to Use This Book

We've broken down your soccer education into three sections to set you on the right road.

Part 1, "Suiting Up," discusses the game itself, its history and culture. We also look at what it takes to be a good coach and how to unlock those elements within yourself before you ever pick up a clipboard or blow a whistle. Coaching is not to be taken lightly, but neither is it to be feared. Our tips will help you master the basics.

We also talk about team building, an entirely new concept for many youth players but one critical to their mastery of the game. Finally, we explore the care and feeding of soccer parents. Moms and dads can be a coach's biggest headache, but we have some solutions we think will channel their "enthusiasm" constructively while helping manage the business side of your team.

In **Part 2, "Training Daze,"** we talk about all the basics necessary for safe and effective play. Beginning with the four pillars of soccer wisdom, we move into play and practice planning and design to further hone your developing coach's skills. We throw in some skills and drills for good measure, although we know you'll soon be developing many of your own.

In addition, we've consulted with a pediatric nurse practitioner to discuss the necessary conditioning, nutrition, and other factors of safe play. Soccer is a sport, and in sports kids sometimes get injured. Here's how to be prepared for the challenges of on-field and off-field player health.

By **Part 3,** we're ready to begin **"Playing the Game."** Defense, offense, and goalkeeping strategies each get their own chapters. Knowing *how* to play a position and, more importantly, *why*, will help your young players succeed more often. And that's what we all want.

We also delve into more sophisticated strategies, such as match analysis, team tactics, and preventing goals. Take some time with these chapters because even if your players aren't quite ready for them yet, you can plant the seeds of these fairly sophisticated strategies in their minds.

Finally, we close with a quick look and list of resources for beyond your youth team. There's even a glossary designed for easy access if you run across a term you're not familiar with.

Extra Help

Throughout this book you'll see terms, tips, boxes, and breakouts designed to supplement the information presented in the text. Pay attention to them because that's where we've buried some real nuggets of wisdom.

Time Out
Here you'll find tips and ideas relevant to successful coaches, as well as other bits of information worth taking the time to read.

Yellow Card

Just like they do in the game of soccer, these yellow cards will warn you about things to avoid and other problem areas.

Playing Tip

Players *and* coaches will find additional information, tips, and tricks for being more effective on field and off.

Dedication

This one goes out to my sons, Brian Muckian and Sean Muckian, who slogged through many muddy afternoons and Saturday mornings trying to prove that it was just as hard to play soccer as it was to coach it.

They may not have gotten as much as they hoped for from the experience, but the old man got all that he expected and a great deal more from the time spent together on the field.

Thanks, guys! MM

To my beautiful wife, Nancy. She truly is the inspiration to all my efforts. For my children: Jacob, Marley, and Reggie. They are the love and fun of my life. And finally to my family for they all inspire me, and to Mel whom I once told, "I am going to write a book on soccer someday."

"Dino"

Acknowledgments

Numerous ideas, thoughts, and input go into preparing a volume like this, and the sources of that inspiration deserve to be acknowledged.

Mike Sansone and Rick Volkman were my early coaching mentors in soccer and wrestling, respectively, and I appreciate the experiences they shared, both on field and off, that helped me understand there are coaches hiding inside each of us just waiting for the right time to come out.

Dean Duerst, of course, gets big thanks for his enormous contributions to this book. He's one of the few people I know who has lived and breathed soccer most of his life. If there is such a thing as inspiration on two feet—and swift feet at that—it most certainly is him.

My wife, Jeanie Muckian RN MS APNP, deserves credit for many things, including production assistance with the manuscript. As a certified pediatric nurse practitioner, however, her big contribution to this volume was the development and creation of the information on young athlete health, nutrition and injury issues. As a former elementary school teacher and mother of two former soccer players, Jeanie has a lifelong commitment to kids' health and well-being, which comes through many times throughout this work and her life.

Finally, many thanks to my agents Marilyn Allen and Bob Diforio for helping make this project happen, as well as to Mike Sanders, Jennifer Moore, and all the other people at Alpha Books who believed that Coach Duerst and I were the right pair to write this volume. We hope you think so, too.

—Michael Muckian

I am very proud to have collaborated on a book of this nature and most importantly thank Michael Muckian for his teamwork to pull this project off. Obviously, I am gratefully indebted to the support of our publisher for making this project possible. And very importantly to all of the people, male and female, who I have played with and coached; you are the reason I was involved.

—Dean Duerst

Trademarks

All terms mentioned in this book that are known to be or are suspected of being trademarks or service marks have been appropriately capitalized. Alpha Books and Penguin Group (USA) Inc. cannot attest to the accuracy of this information. Use of a term in this book should not be regarded as affecting the validity of any trademark or service mark.

Part 1

Suiting Up

Maybe it was the pair of big, brown eyes that looked up at you over the black-and-white ball that roped you into it. Maybe it was the desire to make a contribution in return for the help you had received yourself as a child. Or maybe it was just a healthy interest in what has long been the world's most popular sport. No matter what the reasons, you've joined the growing legion of professional and amateur youth soccer coaches. Congratulations!

For many, saying yes to a pleading son or daughter was the easy part. Now it's time to perform, and you're not even sure where or how to begin.

This part is designed to introduce you to the basics, both of soccer and how to coach its youthful players. As you'll see, the fun has only just begun.

Chapter 1

Getting Started

In This Chapter

◆ Getting your youth coaching career underway

◆ Understanding young athletes

◆ Balls, cones, and whistles

◆ How the game is played

Becoming the coach of a youth soccer team may not have been your idea. As a matter of fact, you may have taken on the task at the request of a son, daughter, friend, or neighbor. Maybe you're getting paid for doing this, but you're in the minority if you are. It's much more likely that you're a volunteer coach who will, from time to time, feel overwhelmed by the task and under-trained for the challenge as you run down the field chasing a bunch of brightly clad kids who, in turn, are chasing a black and white leatherette ball.

Welcome to the club—you're not alone! A lot of well-meaning adults end up pitching fits or turning prematurely gray because they've agreed to do something they're not sure they know how to do: coach a youth soccer team. And did we mention that a dozen eager young hopes rest on the success of the endeavor? Yet, when it comes to personal satisfaction, little will rival the joy and fulfillment of being a youth soccer coach. It may be the last time you, as a parent, will be able to interact meaningfully—and *playfully*—with your child before peer pressure erodes your influence. At the very least, you'll help a group of young athletes prepare themselves physically, psychologically, and socially for the future by mastering the skills of the game that's played on the world's stage.

Not quite up to the challenge? Read on and prepare yourself. Then lace up your cleats—you may also hear them referred to as "boots"—because there's a lot of work to be done!

Putting Your Team Together

The beauty of youth soccer is that recruitment is rarely a problem. As coach, you may be able to decide who will be goalkeeper, who will play forward, and who will defend. You may even decide the number of players in each of these positions. (Except, of course, for the goalkeeper—there's never more than one of them) But chances are you'll be given the team as a single unit and will be expected to make the best of it. Maybe it's a church youth group or a scout troop. Or neighborhood kids or a pickup squad from local city leagues. It doesn't matter, because you'll be expected to make serious and committed soccer players out of them, no matter what their level of interest, skill, and motivation.

And if you know anything at all about working with kids, you know that taking the game too seriously is a dangerous and slightly wrongheaded approach to what, done correctly, could be an invigorating exercise and a delightful pastime. Too many coaches—and, for that matter, players' parents—take the game far too seriously. This can result in occasionally unpleasant behavior on their part and discouragement for the kids. Statistics show that the vast majority of youth soccer players lose interest in the game by the age of 13. Too often, poor or misguided coaching is at the root of the problem.

> **Playing Tip**
>
> One of soccer's greatest advantages is that, unlike most other sports, physical size doesn't really matter. Youth soccer requires only two attributes in its players: (1) they like to run and (2) they are enthusiastic about the game. Some of the best youth players are built close to the ground and can fix their eyes on the goal and then run like rabbits.

Playing soccer is, at its most basic, just that—*play*. And it should be treated as such during practices, games, tournaments, and championships. Mom and Dad may see soccer success as the vehicle for young Justin to learn future leadership skills or the means by which little Tiffany will break the bonds of male-female stereotypes. The young players, on the other hand, are there for completely different reasons. Let's take a look at those reasons.

New Experiences

Soccer provides kids with a new experience that allows them to develop valuable training skills, including athletic conditioning, teamwork development, and confidence. As a goal-directed form of play, it adds meaning to children's play.

Responsibility and Reward

As part of a team, each player has a role to play and tasks to perform, and doing them benefits the whole team. They will feel valued when their efforts are acknowledged by their teammates and coaches. By being rewarded for performing their role, they also develop a sense of responsibility.

Everyone cheers the forward who scores the goal that wins the game, but there can be only so many heroes in life. Through good coaching, players learn the critical role each plays in contributing to that goal, whether its covering the opposition or providing the setup that leads to the winning kick. Understanding how such things work in soccer will teach kids to value their contributions in other aspects of their lives.

CAUTION **Yellow Card** _____

You may have to work hard to engage your youthful players, pushing them beyond what they think they can do. But be careful not to push them harder than they can go. Generally, the younger the team, the lighter the coaching touch should be. Pushing them beyond what they realistically can be expected to do may result in discouragement, disinterest, and even injury. And that will turn them off to the game faster than anything else.

Exercise, Exercise, Exercise

Physical activity is as necessary as breathing and sleeping for young kids. The running and kicking involved in soccer is reward in and of itself. If that running and kicking results in a goal … well, for many kids, that's a bonus.

 Playing Tip _____

Too many American kids are overweight, in part because of lack of physical activity. As a purely aerobic activity, soccer can get those young potatoes off the couch and out onto the playing fields.

Let's Get Social!

As part of a soccer team, kids get a chance to interact with others their own age outside of the classroom in a meaningful and structured way. This gives youth players a sense of who they are and how others see them, and teaches them appropriate ways to express themselves. Learning to become part of team in soccer will ultimately benefit them in other life situations.

A Stronger Sense of Self

At a typical youth soccer practice, you'll see a group of kids out on the field with one or two coaches. This close interaction between the kids and the adults (while other adults and parents are off on the sideline or not even in attendance), often makes kids feel like they're on equal social footing with those involved adults. Practicing and succeeding in an activity they enjoy that is respected and perhaps even revered by adults can give kids a better sense of self-worth. That may be reason enough for some kids to slip on those cleats!

Yellow Card _____

Be very careful, in your well-meaning attempt to bring your young team pride through winning the league victory, that you don't undermine the sport's intrinsic and more valuable benefits. Winning may have been the only thing to the great football coach Vince Lombardi but, to these kids, it's probably nothing other than a happy byproduct of a joyful activity.

And if that's the case, those kids may have you to thank. Never underestimate your role in making their youth soccer careers, no matter how short, a valuable and worthwhile experience.

Getting Started

As a child, Brazilian soccer superstar Pele learned to play soccer in the back streets of Rio de Janeiro, using a bundle of rags as a ball. Sure, it was primitive, but Pele had all he needed: a place to play and a ball. We'll touch on other things in a minute, but as long as you have those two basics, you can get the game underway.

You Need a Place to Play

A regulation soccer field is 75 by 110 yards, far too large for younger players. Even official youth soccer rules allow fields to measure between 50 to 100 yards in width and 100 to 130 yards in length (for more on the parts of a soccer field, see Chapter 12). When first teaching kids soccer, you should size your field according to their age, strength, sophistication, and skill level.

The under-six crowd will benefit from playing on fields as small as 25-by-20 yards, increasing to 50-by-30 yards for up to 8 years old, 70-by-50 yards for up to 10 years old, and the standard adult size after age 12.

By making these adjustments, you're bound to wind up making the experience more fun, and thus more successful, for the players.

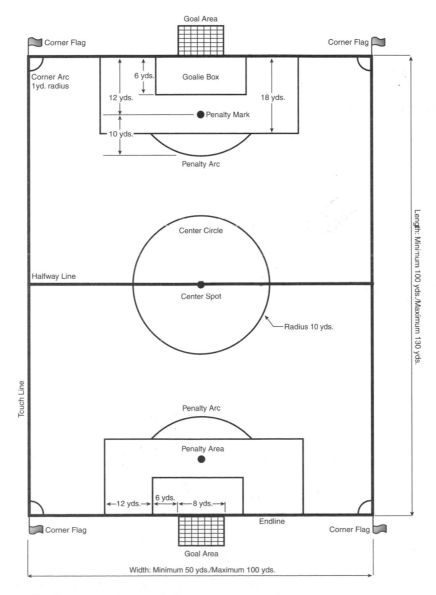

The dimensions of a soccer field.

You Need a Ball

The familiar black-and-white soccer ball comes in different sizes and with different types of coverings. Just as when sizing your field, choose your ball based on the age, size, and sophistication of the players as well as your team's budget. If you can, provide a ball of some kind for every young player. It need not be a regulation ball—that will probably be too expensive. Cheap plastic or rubber balls will be just as good for allowing kids to get the feel and size of the orb. By having their own balls, the kids will also be more committed to the game.

Starter balls—the kind most youth teams play with—have a rubber bladder surrounded by processed rubber, similar to that used to make automobile tires. They retain their shape and hold air, but they can be a little hard, especially on younger players' heads. Choose your ball based on cost and durability, but also with the kids' comfort in mind.

> **Time Out**
>
> Top-of-the-line professional soccer balls cost from $75 on up and tend to be covered with stitched leather or, more likely, polyurethane, giving them a softer cover and aerodynamic superiority. Mid-quality balls cost in the neighborhood of $35 to $40, with low-end balls as cheap as $15.

Balls come in a number of sizes. The number 3 ball, a 10-ounce model, is best used by players between 5 and 7 years of age. It's light enough so that the youngsters can practice their skills while preparing them for larger models as they grow and develop.

The number 4 ball, generally about 12 ounces, is good for players between 7 and 12 years old, while the 14-ounce number 5 ball, the equivalent of the professional model, is suitable for players age 13 and older.

Shirts, Shoes, and Shin-guards

As a young player, Pele was probably dressed in raggedy shorts and went shirtless and barefoot. Although their needs are still simple, today's youth players require a little more than that:

- **Matching shirts or jerseys** are necessary for identifying the team, with an alternate color scheme for the goalkeeper. Unlike basketball, even many pro soccer teams don't consider shorts part of the uniform, but coordinated shirts are a must, with an alternating color or pattern for away games against teams with the same color scheme as yours. Light, colorful jerseys designed for soccer work the best, but even generic t-shirts with iron-on numbers will do in a pinch.

> **Time Out**
>
> When it comes to outfitting players, soccer is one of the least expensive team sports.

◆ **Cleated soccer shoes** give players extra traction, which comes in handy particularly on wet fields. Because children's feet grow so fast, parents often buy inexpensive vinyl shoes with hard rubber cleats. That's fine as long as the shoes fit well, allowing the player both flexibility and mobility. Shoes that are too small can damage young feet, while shoes that are too big can cause players to trip and fall. They don't have to look good, but they do have to perform as well as the young athlete wearing them.

Playing Tip

At the rate kids grow, keeping them equipped with gear that fits them can be a wallet-busting endeavor! A variety of discount and secondhand sporting goods stores, such as Play It Again Sports, are good sources for quality gear that has only been slightly worn. Local soccer leagues and organizations that sponsor gear exchanges also can sometimes be a good resource.

And remember to have players bring an alternate type of footwear to put on after the game. Cleats worn on hard surfaces, such as asphalt or concrete, can be unduly hard on young players' feet and legs, especially after a game.

◆ **Shin-guards** are a necessity. All players, no matter what their age, must wear them under their knee socks in order to be allowed to play. Young bones can be seriously damaged if left unprotected, and the shin is the one spot that runs the repeated risk of being bruised, cut, and even broken if left unprotected. As coach, it's your responsibility to minimize the possibility of injury for your players, no matter what their age. Start at the knee and work down.

Playing Tip

Goalkeepers need all of the supplies just mentioned, as well as gloves and elbow pads. They're the only ones allowed to touch the ball with their hands, which means they'll be diving for those balls. Basic protection will help them do their job better. Consider, too, hats, brims, or eye protection for those goalkeepers forced to stare into the sun for long periods. Once again, it's a matter of protection *and* performance improvement.

We discuss what gear the team is usually responsible for and what gear the players' parents are responsible for in Chapter 6.

Cones, Whistles, and Coaching Supplies

You'll need bright orange cones to mark the boundaries of the playing field. These rubber cones are also useful for drills and exercises. Count on needing a minimum of six—two to mark each end zone and two to place at midfield. If you're playing without formal goal cages, then you can put two more at each end to help identify the goals, for a total of 10 cones.

You'll also need coach "stuff," such as a whistle to call the plays and periods and a stopwatch to time games and drills. So you can keep up with the team, you'll also want your own set of cleats to wear. (You'll thank us for this advice the first time you coach in the rain.)

Yellow Card

Many coaches carry supplies of aspirin or pain reliever, mostly for themselves but sometimes to administer to injured players. However, *make sure you know players' medication allergies before administering anything. And never administer anything— even an aspirin—without prior parental approval.* There will be nothing in your first aid kit to address anaphylactic shock should a player take a med that he or she is allergic to.

Other supplies you'll probably want on hand include the following:

◆ **First aid supplies**   these are critical to treat the inevitable bumps and bruises incurred in practices and games. The basic drugstore kit, supplemented by ice packs and wraps, should be enough.

◆ **Food and drinks**   Bring an ample supply of fluids, especially if practicing in warm weather, and a snack to replenish the team's energy. Water is still the best drink, but kids may prefer lemonade or some other noncarbonated beverage. Crackers, energy bars, even fruit are good snack choices. For some players, after-scrimmage snacks are the highlight of any practice, and there's nothing wrong with that!

◆ **Miscellany**   There is a mountain of miscellaneous items, some of which include a cell phone in case of emergencies; towels for a variety of purposes; and blankets that tired or injured players can rest on. Choose your gear based on your needs and remember that, no matter how much you load into the van or SUV, you'll always forget something—and that something is probably the thing you will need the most that day.

The Basics of the Beautiful Game

The beauty of soccer—and player Pele did describe it as "the beautiful game"—lies in its simplicity. Therein, too, lies the game's appeal. It's the simplest of all team sports to play and to understand, making mastery of its rules easy as well.

Playing the Game

Although there's more to soccer than simply running and kicking, it's not so much more that young players can't grasp even its subtler points.

The goal of soccer is to move the ball down the field and kick it past the opposition's goalkeeper and into the net to score a point. The team with most points at the end of the game wins. Easy as that may at first sound, remember that while your team is attempting to score, the other team will be doing its best to prevent you from doing so. The secret to soccer is to figure out the right strategy, enabling you to cover the ground you need to cover to score enough points to win.

Each team is comprised of 10 players assigned to forward, midfield, and defensive positions based on the team's prevailing strategy. (We'll talk more about those strategies in Chapter 12.) In addition to 10 fielders, each team also has 1 goalkeeper, whose role doesn't change regardless of the strategy employed. The goalkeeper's job is always to keep the opposition from scoring.

It may be self-evident, but soccer is a game played primarily with the feet. Players advance the ball down the field mostly by kicking it, but they may also rebound it off the torso, legs, and even heads of other players. The only parts of the bodies players may not use to advance the ball are the arms and hands.

The other exception to the no-hands rule is, of course, the goalkeeper, who may use any part of his or her body to block the shot or seize control of the ball as it enters the penalty box (the area around the goal). Once the goalkeeper picks up the ball all play stops until that ball is put back into play, which may be done by kicking or throwing the ball downfield.

Yellow Card

Should a player touch the ball with hands or arms, even accidentally, play is stopped and a penalty called against the team of the offending player. A player from the opposite team may then put the ball back into play with a direct kick.

How Long?

Most adult soccer games consist of two periods—halves—of roughly 45 minutes each, with a 15-minute break in between. You'll want to scale the length of your game based on the age, sophistication, and stamina of your players. For very young players, 45 minutes may seem like a lifetime, and they won't be able to keep up, either physically or mentally. For very young players aged seven to nine, you may want to keep the time down to 20 to 30 minutes halves, increasing the time as the players grow in stamina and skill.

Playing Tip

Make sure you know the average game times used by your league. They will determine both practice and play times for your young athletes.

Unlike American football, soccer does not have what might be considered a formal kickoff. In a soccer kickoff, a forward midfielder stands at the midline and kicks the ball in the direction he or she wants it to go. The ball must move forward one revolution, then the ball becomes fair game for anyone to go after.

How Many?

As a rule of thumb, the younger the team, the fewer the number of players, which maximizes the exposure of each of them to the ball in play. Very young teams may have as few as three players on each side for practices and scrimmages. That number can increase as players age as long as each side remains balanced.

Keeping the Ball in Play

The ball must actually *cross* the line in order to either be a goal or out of bounds. Touching the line or ricocheting off the goal bar and back into play doesn't constitute a goal or a foul. Even dribblers can dribble along the line and not be out of bounds, provided the ball doesn't fully cross the line.

Time Out!

Timeouts for injuries is time often added at the end of the game to make sure it reaches the required length of play. At more advanced levels, there also may be extra time or overtime to resolve a tie. In competition, ties are resolved by a penalty-kick tiebreaker.

Let's Call It Even

Tiebreakers consist of five players from each team who line up to kick from the penalty spot 12 yards from the goal. If the game is still tied after each team has executed its five shots, then it goes into sudden death, meaning that the process continues 5-kick round by 5-kick round until one team or the other comes out ahead.

Time Out

Players are penalized for fouls, with the penalty increasing with the severity of the foul. Accidental tripping or personal fouling, such as roughing the player, generally is amended with a free kick for the injured team. The kick will be indirect—from the kicker to another teammate—for less serious fouls, or directly at the goal (called a direct kick) for more serious ones. Deliberate acts of abuse or mayhem earn either a yellow card or a red card, depending on the seriousness of the foul and the referee making the call. A yellow card is essentially a warning; if a single player is awarded two yellow cards one game, it's the equivalent of a red card. A red card means the player is ejected from the match. When punishable fouls are committed in the penalty box, the ref may award the guilty player a red card *and* give the fouled team a free kick.

Playing the Right Positions

From a distance, all soccer players look alike and look like they're simply running all over the field after the ball. But the game is far more strategic than that, and players occupy positions for a reason. We'll talk more about positioning strategies in later chapters. For the moment, we'll simply list the basic positions on any soccer team:

◆ **The goalkeeper** occupies the penalty area and is dedicated to keeping the other team from scoring. The goalkeeper rarely ventures from the penalty box and can kick, head, throw, punch, or use any other method at his disposal to remove the ball from the goal area and put it back into play. The goalkeeper's primary job is to distribute the ball to his teammates—and away from the goal.

◆ **The defenders** vary in number—anywhere from one to four—and their job is to protect the goal and support the goalkeeper. Their primary role is to make the goalkeeper's life as easy as possible and to keep the ball out of the penalty area. Conservative strategies play a high number of defenders, while more aggressive teams tend to send more players up field. Defenders may range as far as midfield when the ball is far downfield, but never so far away that they can't quickly return to their primary tasks of defending their goal.

◆ **Midfielders** occupy the middle portion of the field and alternate between defensive and offensive action. They tend to range farther from their own goal than defenders, but rarely beyond the middle third of the field.

◆ **Forwards** are usually the fastest players. Their job is break through the opposition's defenses and score goals.

Playing Tip

The basic formation 4-4-2 refers to four defenders, four midfielders and two forwards. The more aggressive 4-2-4 strategy (four defenders, two midfielders, and four forwards) puts greater emphasis on offense.

Playing Tip

Many coaches believe every player should play each position at least part of the time to get a better feel for the game. This includes the position of goalkeeper, a job that tantalizes some players and terrifies others. Even those kids who don't want the job should spend at least a little time protecting the goal so they know what it's like. Improved team performance—as well as increased camaraderie among players—will be the result.

Once you start drilling and scrimmaging, you'll begin to get a sense of who will perform best in which position. Site those players accordingly, but be careful not to lock players into positions where they don't get to see the amount of action they need (which varies player to player) or, conversely, fail to successfully support the team due to lack of speed, skill, or some other performance shortfall.

By the Numbers: How Age Affects Play

Soccer leagues are typically organized by age group, with common age breaks for players under 6, 6 to 7, 8 to 9, 10 to 11, 12 to 13, and so on. You will need to tailor every aspect of your coaching to the age group you're dealing with. To give you some idea of what you can expect players of each age group to be capable of, we've adapted the following list from one created by Jeff Pill (see the full list at www.eteamz.com/soccer/pills/jpill.htm).

Under 6

Close your eyes and imagine a classroom full of kindergartners. It's likely that at least one of them is crying, half of them aren't listening to the teacher, and three of them have their hands up because they really "gotta go." It's the same thing out on the soccer field.

This lovable group of munchkins has a very short attention span and very little understanding of the game. They haven't yet developed the coordination necessary to play more than a rudimentary version of the game. Don't throw up your hands in frustration, though, because they've got one huge thing going for them: These kids love to be active! They will run and play for as long as you let them. All you need to do is put a ball in front of them and let them romp around. Sure, you should teach them the basics of the game and spend time working on their footwork and attitude, but don't, we repeat *don't*, expect too much. No matter how much you practice positions or passing, they probably not really grasp these concepts enough to apply them in a game situation.

> **Time Out**
>
> If something off the playing field distracts them, by all means, try to get them refocused. But don't be afraid to stop the play for a while if it's something worth watching!

The important thing is to keep it fun and keep it simple. Don't be a stickler for rules, and *always* be positive.

Under 8

By this time most kids can ride a two-wheel bike without training wheels, a sign of developing coordination. At the same time, however, their bodies are growing rapidly, and so they may appear to be a little klutzy.

Although they will have longer attention spans than their under-six counterparts, don't expect them to really grasp more than a few simple concepts at once. You might, however, be surprised to see that they can actually pass the ball from one teammate to another. Don't count on it, though.

Playing Tip

Seven and eight year olds love to dribble the ball and shoot for goals, but they won't spend much time passing. That's okay for now.

Under 10

Coaches who have only dealt with players under the age of 8 before will be shocked to find that 8 and 9 year olds really "get" the game. After all, by this time many of the kids have been at the game for three or more years. Not only are they capable of understanding simple strategies and tactics, they might even be able to employ them during a game. As a matter of fact, they might even care about *winning* the game. That's not to say that play won't still be unpredictable, but it's at this age that coaches can really see their work paying off.

Under 12

With developing skills and appreciation for the beauty of the game comes developing attitudes—some of them negative—including fierce competition, intentional fouling, and yelling at teammates and referees. Nonetheless, they will also have an increased sense of teamwork and will be able to think abstractly about play situations.

Differences in size and ability start becoming very noticeable in kids around this time, with some players who look old enough to drive cars and others still looking like they should be in car seats. It's important to be supportive of the under-developed, less-skilled players, as they can get easily discouraged and might drop out of the sport. You can really make a difference in this regard.

Yellow Card

Kids of all ages are sensitive to criticism. Don't think that just because your players are older they won't mind harsh words directed at them. You're a role model for them, after all, and they care about what you think of them. Keep all comments constructive and as positive as possible.

Age 12 and Beyond

Most teenage soccer players are seasoned veterans. By this time, they should be comfortable with the basic skills described in this chapter and can start focusing more intently on more specialized defensive and offensive strategies.

Coaching the Future

Soccer is a wonderful youth sport, and one that loses 20 times as many players as it keeps. As we mentioned previously, much of this has to do with the way coaches—even well-meaning amateur coaches—treat their players, often expecting them to act like miniature professional athletes. The goal of any coach should be to provide a safe and enjoyable soccer experience for his team. A secondary, but no less important, goal is to create a love of and appreciation for the game that will extend well beyond those formative years, leading to the development of a true soccer player and athlete to the degree each player is capable.

As we'll see in the next chapter, the soccer culture is, indeed, global, as vast in its opportunities as the cultures that embrace the game. Mis-coaching young players deprives many of them of wonderful opportunities to continue their own personal growth as players, advocates of the game, and perhaps, one day, even coaches themselves.

Fostering that growth and development is a significant and critical responsibility for any coach, either amateur or professional. Mastering the coaching of youth soccer teams means understanding and embracing those responsibilities with the right level of commitment. In the same way we entrust the intellectual growth of our children to our teachers, we entrust their physical and psychological growth to our coaches.

Your impact is more powerful than you can imagine. It may at first seem like an obligation, but it's also an honor and an opportunity. Take the time, make the effort, and don't blow it. Too many young athletes are counting on you.

The Least You Need to Know

- Soccer can help prepare young athletes physically, psychologically, and emotionally for future challenges.

- Both fields and balls are critical to play, but they should be sized to the age and skills of their players. For younger players, use smaller fields and lighter balls.

- Cleated soccer shoes are optional, but shin guards are a necessity. It's the coach's responsibility to make sure the team has adequate protection.

- Most adult teams consist of 11 players, but younger teams typically use fewer players to allow each more time with the ball.

- The basics of the game are easy to understand and to teach.

- The goal of any coach is to provide a safe and enjoyable soccer experience for the young team. A secondary, but no less important, goal is to create a love of and appreciation for the game that will extend well beyond those formative years.

Understanding Soccer Culture

In This Chapter

- ◆ A brief history of soccer
- ◆ What motivates players, teams, coaches, and fans
- ◆ Developing attitude along with aptitude

The older you are, the more likely it is that when you were growing up the aura surrounding the world's most popular game was more of a rumor than a fact, at least in middle-class American households. It wasn't that long ago, after all, that soccer wasn't a popular sport in the United States. To most Americans one more game involving a ball really didn't matter much at all.

America Before Soccer

Post-World War II sports fans were generally baseball nuts who cheered the New York Yankees, cried when the Dodgers left Brooklyn, and prayed for the Chicago Cubs. (In the later case, many are still praying and will be for the foreseeable future.)

In the meantime, a certain subsection watched the growth of a sport known around the globe as "American football," and city kids on concrete playgrounds cheered the formation of the National Basketball Association. Northern kids realized that sharpening those boring old ice skates their parents gave them was the secret to something called hockey, while others knocked smaller spheres over tennis court nets and down fairways toward greens. Whether it was round, flat, or ovoid, if it could be manipulated and moved quickly and competitively by a reasonably healthy man or, less frequently, woman, then someone built a sport around it.

But in the case of soccer—in the minds of many a simplistic substitute for a more familiar form of football (a game that now has more rules, penalties, and performance criteria than most countries' foreign policies) there was little evidence of the game being played stateside. Soccer was something that people played overseas, in Europe and South and Central America primarily, and was as foreign-sounding and odd-looking as cricket. America had its own roster of athletes and teams. Did we really need to add soccer to that list?

Part of that reluctance may have been due to the country's traditional isolationism, a geographic and psychological separation from the rest of the world that lasted right up until the bombing of Pearl Harbor and America's entry into World War II. But when Mohammad doesn't come to the mountain … well, you know the rest.

Give Me Your Tired, Your Poor ... Your Soccer Players

Although we're taking some creative license with the quote etched on the Statue of Liberty, it was immigrants who brought the game of soccer to the United States. As different cultures and ethnic groups who prized the sport began to grow in size and influence over America's social and athletic landscape, their favorite game grew in stature. These days, wander past any city park on Sunday afternoon and the chances are good you'll see brightly clad Latino, Indian, or Eastern European kids—as well as adults—kicking a soccer ball around. And that's just the tip of the ever-growing iceberg!

Your Gym Teacher Was Ahead of the Times

But what a lot of people forget is that almost everyone who was ever in a physical education class in the United States has played some form of soccer. It's been a formal or informal part of schools' P.E. curricula from kindergarten on up. Thanks to the simplicity of its premise and kids' natural ability and penchant to execute the sport's foundation activities—running and kicking a ball with other kids—soccer of some type is a natural form of physical education.

Think about kickball, crab soccer—which even uses the name—and any of a dozen versions of the same basic concept you probably played in gym class. All are based on the principles and practices of soccer. That means kids are put into soccer training before they've even heard the word. Once you, as youth soccer coach, get your hands on them, chances are they've already been practicing soccer skills for at least the past few years.

And as coach, that gives you an advantage enjoyed by none of the other popular team sports. Could you really ask for anything more?

Time Out

Interest in soccer has increased enormously in the past few years and so has participation, particularly in youth soccer. According to the Soccer Industry Council of America, nearly 20 million Americans of both sexes and all ages play soccer. That includes formal team and league involvement as well as kicking the ball around the yard with friends and family. Roughly half of those 20 million tend to be more heavily and routinely involved in the sport. Sixty percent of the participants are males and 40 percent female, a balance better than just about any other team sport.

A Little Soccer History

As far as anyone knows, there is no Abner Doubleday—the man credited with inventing baseball—or James Naismith—the inventor of basketball—of soccer. It appeared in many ancient and tribal societies in some form from Greece and Rome to Japan and the South Pacific. Some ancient societies used elements of the game as a ritual dance to celebrate great victories in battle. (In place of a ball, however, the severed head of the rival tribe's best warrior or chieftain was kicked around.)

Records also show that as early as 1700 B.C.E., Chinese emperor Huang-Ti invented a game called tsu-chu, played by kicking a leather ball. Soccer continued to evolve throughout the ensuing centuries, the growing dearth of rival chieftains' heads notwithstanding, until the English began developing rules, guidelines, and variations of the game. By 1863, the first *Laws of the Game* were published by the London Football Association. Those rules, in turn, were used for the first game on American soil, a match in 1869 between teams from Princeton and Rutgers universities.

Monumental as that match may have been, accounts also show that some form of what we now called soccer had been played by the pilgrims in Jamestown, Massachusetts, almost 250 years earlier. The fever was overtaking the new world even then, fueling the momentum to bring us where we are today.

Playing Tip

Say the word "soccer" to players and fans from other countries and you might get a polite smile and nod of recognition, especially if they know you're a well-meaning American. But outside U.S. borders the game you know as soccer is simply called "football" and the game you know as "football" is called "American football." For the record, American football is considered by most non-Americans to be a rather curious, unnecessarily complicated, and often time-consuming exercise.

There's no way around it. A game played primarily by kicking the ball with only one player allowed to handle it should be called "football." A game played primarily by passing and running while holding the ball, with only one player allowed to kick it … well, that should be called something else.

Soccer Mania

For many people, soccer's image too often is colored by reports of violence and hooliganism during play-off games; of grandstands collapsing under the weight of mammoth crowds assembled to see their national teams; and of riots that spill out of stadiums and onto the streets of the host city.

It's true that such things have happened, and such actions never can be excused. But they're only the dark side of what otherwise is a worldwide love of the sport.

The Biggest Cup in the World

American football has its Super Bowl, baseball its World Series, professional hockey its Stanley Cup. Soccer has the World Cup. World Cup matches attract more attention and generate more excitement worldwide than the other three sports combined ever could. The reason for the difference is as obvious as it is profound: In the three U.S. sports just mentioned, the conflict is team against team. In world soccer, however, it's country against country. A win for the national team of Brazil, for example, reflects not only on the team and its players, but on Brazil as well, engendering enormous pride among the country's citizens.

Make the Most of the Differences!

Is it any wonder that the occasional grandstand collapses? The jubilation and energy that accompanies any soccer match, while not quite on par with the World Cup, is just as exciting and meaningful for the players involved and, in turn, those involved with the players. At the youth league level, this includes coaches, parents, sponsors, schools, and everyone else who forms the team's social infrastructure. Understanding how to work within that social culture is central to your success in coaching youth soccer.

As a coach, you need to understand the nature and orientation of the kids on your team and realize that, just because they all wear the same color jersey, it doesn't mean they all understand the game the same way. You'll need to develop a cohesive and consistent strategy that doesn't skew to one particular ethnic group, no matter how culturally diverse your team may be. You can only do this by figuring out the different strengths players bring to the game and using them to the team's advantage.

So even though the basics of soccer are easy to teach, the international aspect of the game makes it far more complex than many other sports. As a coach, you must recognize that cultural complexity. Brazilians, for example, may favor a more aggressive approach, while the Northern Europeans tend to build defensive fortresses that the opposition finds difficult to penetrate.

Take the time to learn the perspective each player brings to the team (as well as your own perspective) and how they impact your team's efforts. If you're coaching a multicultural group of kids who bring many different ways of playing the game, don't force them all into the same mold. Instead, utilize their strengths while minimizing their weaknesses. Done right, this strategy will help you develop a more multifaceted, higher performance team.

Who's Who in Youth Soccer

Now that you know how global the game of soccer really is, let's focus on the youth soccer culture in the United States. Consider the following pecking order by which the youth soccer world defines itself:

- **First, there are the players.** Whether we're talking about members of school teams, city youth leagues, or church or synagogue groups, the players themselves are the foundation of any organized soccer effort, and there are millions of them of both genders and all ages. Soccer kids are everywhere, clad in oversized jerseys and kicking balls around parking lots. Without the players, none of the rest of this would exist.

- **After players come teams.** You generally need to be part of a larger entity—a club or a league at least—to have a successful team. Otherwise, who would your team play? The teams, of varying sizes and sophistication, serve as the homes for those millions of players we just mentioned. No player, no matter how good, can win (or lose) a game by him- or herself. It takes a team to take the field and score the goal.

Time Out

Kids play for the love of the game, because they like being active with other kids their age, or simply because some well-meaning adult told them they had to do it.

◆ **Teams beget clubs.** At more organized levels, and especially in the higher age groups, come clubs. These are groups of teams, usually from the same area, town, or geographic region. Clubs provide the opportunity for teams to practice and scrimmage more frequently without excessive travel. They also provide a familiar social fabric for the teams and their members.

◆ **And clubs beget leagues.** Just as clubs are groups of teams, leagues are groups of clubs. Most states have several leagues, designed to facilitate play wherever there is adequate participation. There is no limit to the number of clubs in a league. Generally speaking, it's however many make play practical.

◆ **State associations come next.** There is at least one state association for most states. In the case of California, New York, Ohio, Pennsylvania, and Texas, there are two associations just because the states are so large and/or densely populated. Associations set the standards for play and serve as an organizing hub to bring together teams from the various regions. (See Appendix B for a list of state soccer associations.)

◆ **Finally, the national regions.** Because of the sheer numbers of players, teams, clubs, leagues, and associations, soccer is divided into the following regions:

> **Region I** is known as the Eastern region and extends from Maine in the north to Virginia in the south.

> **Region II** covers the Midwest. It's range travels west from Ohio and north from Kentucky, reaching as far as the Dakotas, Kansas, and Nebraska.

> **Region III** travels south from the Carolinas in the east and Oklahoma in the west, covering all points in between.

> **Region IV** is the West, from the Rocky Mountain states all the way to the West Coast.

These four regions are the official designees of the United States Youth Soccer Association, based in Richardson, Texas. Other national associations include the Soccer Association for Youth, headquartered in Cincinnati, Ohio; and the American Youth Soccer Organization, located in Hawthorne, California. The mission of all three is to promote soccer growth and development among kids. To a greater or lesser degree, all three espouse an "everybody plays" mentality to better promote the joy of the game and an appreciation for more than just its competitive nature.

Where You Fit In

At the hub of the youth soccer culture we just described stands the coach, whose job it is to make this all possible by providing instruction and support for the young soccer players. Feeling a little dizzy? Don't worry—by the time you're finished reading this book, you'll have the tools you need.

But first, you should take some time to think about whether you have the personal attributes that are required of any coach. We begin with the most important attribute of them all.

Good Coaches Care About Their Teams

Even if you don't have the background, you're not sure of the ability, and you don't really even know what it means to motivate kids to succeed, you've got to care enough about those kids to make the effort to learn.

Saying that coaches must care about their teams might be stating the obvious, and there isn't a coach in the world who wouldn't agree that he or she cares about the team. But it's important to understand what caring means before making a commitment

If you care about another person, you come to his or her aid in time of need, making sure you both are able to move forward, or neither moves at all. If you care about being the best at something—be it soccer or sewing—you do it as often as you can; and when you're not practicing it, you're reading about it, thinking about it, perhaps even dreaming about it. It envelops you. If you care about a cause, you're willing to sacrifice time, effort, energy, and opportunity to make sure that its goals are accomplished. The idea of turning your back on it never enters your mind and you never stop until you succeed.

Now apply those standards to coaching youth soccer. Would you be willing to do any and all on behalf of the kids without a second thought? If not, perhaps you should hang up your cleats.

Good Coaches Know What They're Talking About

Coaches are the only source most youth players have for authoritative information about the game they devote hours of energy and effort to master. The coach is the person they turn to for answers to their hundreds of questions and to make things right when there is any kind of dispute, on field or off. If Coach doesn't know something, they reason, then it can't be important. In that case, Coach better be sure that what he or she doesn't know doesn't come back to bite the team during a game.

Good Coaches Train with Empathy and Intelligence

Novice coaches make the same mistake novice employee managers do. They step forward, tell the team what to do, perhaps even showing them the moves. Then they step back and expect it to happen. Meanwhile, team members step back, scratch their heads, and say, "So, now what?"

Knowing what to do and telling the team how to do it is the easy part. Real coaching comes in when you see your entire team as 20 or so different learning opportunities waiting to happen. All players should be operating at as close to the same level as possible, but good coaches know that such miracles only happen after a concerted effort on his or her part. The coach must cultivate and train every individual *as an individual* with the idea of making that individual a more effective part of the team.

Sound challenging? It can be absolutely exhausting, especially when you realize that both intellectual and emotional elements come into play even before physical training and skills development begins. But that's what it takes and, if you're good, that's what you'll do.

Playing Tip

It's true, no one can know everything. But good coaches know nearly everything about the game of soccer, and they study hard to make sure that what they don't know comes as close as possible to truly being unimportant. In the cases of the best coaches—well, they do know everything. We don't how, but they manage.

Good Coaches Are Enthusiastic

A coach without a love of or enthusiasm for the game might as well not suit up. A disinterested or frustrated coach makes for disinterested, frustrated players. The young athletes take their cue from you, and unless your message is upbeat and energetic, you won't get to first base with them. (Sorry to mix sports metaphors, but in this case, it fits.)

A lack of enthusiasm signals a failure to appreciate the opportunity.

Good coaches may be the hubs of the wheels of activity around which the team turns, but they also are the driving force behind cultivation of the effort to make the team a success. A team will perform effectively with the right mix of players. But with the right coach, someone who believes in what he or she is doing and communicates that commitment, that same team will succeed admirably.

Do you have what it takes? We hope so.

Yellow Card

Not everyone can or should coach youth teams. It's an honor and privilege that should be given only to those who fully appreciate the weight of the commitment and have the capability to execute it successfully. If your heart's not in it, that lack of interest will show, and then your team won't be interested, either.

The Least You Need to Know

- ◆ Soccer began its ascendancy in the United States as different cultures and ethnic groups that prized the sport began to grow in size and influence over the social and athletic landscape.

- ◆ Nearly 20 million Americans of both sexes and all ages play soccer.

- ◆ Soccer is played differently in different countries. Understand the nature and orientation of the kids on your team and realize that, just because they all wear the same color jersey doesn't mean they all play the game the same way.

- ◆ The player is the heart of soccer.

- ◆ Not everyone has the skills, the intelligence, and the sensitivity to coach youth soccer.

The Coach in You

In This Chapter

- ◆ A working definition of coaching
- ◆ Understanding your impact on others
- ◆ Cultivating your inner coach
- ◆ How different styles make an impact
- ◆ Defining your approach

There's a chance that you're coming to youth soccer with academic coaching credentials and significant professional experience. That's something that happens all the time. High school and college-level soccer coaches with a vested interested in the sport—perhaps even a child who's old enough to become involved—or who just want to extend their involvement and serve their community in the way they know best, frequently end up coaching youthful athletes.

For some, in fact, it's a matter of due diligence. By giving kids a good coaching experience when they're young, the professionals keep fewer of them from dropping out of the sport in later years, thus assuring a larger talent pool when they're ready to recruit for high school and college teams. If part of coaching is to build an appreciation for the sport, thus a longer sports life for the athletes involved, then who better than a pro to make sure the whole thing gets off on the right foot?

However, many more youth soccer coaches find themselves recruited from the parental ranks, individuals who usually have minimal coaching background. In addition to dealing with the shortcomings and learning curves of young athletes, some coaches may find they're not that much better off than their players. If you fall into these ranks, then you have a lot of work ahead of you before ever taking the field.

What Is a Coach, Anyway?

We all have an idea of what a coach is. We've all seen the movies and many of us have played sports and remember who inspired us to victory or chastised us in defeat. Remember Pat O'Brien in *Knute Rockne, All American?* There was a coach whose affability and dedication just made you want to go out and win one for Gipper. He didn't even have to say anything. He just pasted on that big ol' Pat O'Brien smile and you immediately knew his heart would just break for you if you didn't score that winning touchdown.

Of course, those are the movies. More often than not coaches inhabit the opposite end of the spectrum, walking the sidelines and chewing antacids when they're not chewing you out for fumbling or losing the ball. For every Pat O'Brien wannabe, there are a dozen Bobby Knights. "We don't play with injury, but we learn to play with pain," a former coach we knew was fond of saying. "And pain only becomes injury when the jagged end of the bone breaks through the skin."

Well, sic semper tyrannus back atcha, bub!

Too often, even well-meaning amateur coaches slide dangerously close to that do-or-die mindset, primarily because that's how they had been coached when they participated in sports. They don't mean to be gruff, noisy, and abusive. It just happens. And then the youthful players lose their initiative because Coach doesn't like them anymore. One by one, his or her players begin to drop out of the sport, no matter how much backpedaling Coach tries.

Time Out
Webster defines "coach" as "the person who is in overall charge of the team and the strategy in games." Note that the reference to "the team" comes first. When coaching youth sports, never sacrifice the welfare of the team in pursuit of the strategy to win.

If you take only one thing from this chapter, make it this: Youth athletes become involved in sports for different reasons and with different motivations than adults. Your ability as coach to adjust to those needs and wants will determine not only the success of the team, but of the individual players involved. And at least among the younger ranks, the team and the game exist to serve the developmental needs of those players.

In other words, you have a responsibility to the kids first and the sport second. True, there are championships for almost every age group, and kids love to win just as much as anyone else. But more important to those kids than winning is the play itself and all the benefits of being a member of a team. Concentrate on cultivating those benefits first. It's very likely that a cohesive team will follow. Try it the other way, however, and you're doomed to fail. And when you fail as coach, chances are your team will fail, too.

Finding the Coach Within You

Anyone who participates in team sports will probably think back to his or her high school or college athletic experience as a foundation for understanding coaching. Those who had a good experience will be able to transfer some of those talents to the soccer field, while those who didn't may inadvertently transfer some of that experience anyway. In either case, these would-be coaches are making a mistake.

By the time athletes reach higher levels of achievement, it's no longer so much a matter of the game as it is of the role, performance and, yes, even the politics of prep and college sports. At this level, there's more at stake than merely the score of a game and there's certainly more at stake than the well being of individual players. Older players know this; younger players, on the other hand, don't know it, nor should they.

Pedaling Back in Time

If you need a personal coaching model to follow and you don't have significant experience—and by significant we mean working with the age group you will be coaching—start with your memories of riding a bike and teaching others how to do so.

If you were like most kids, riding a bike was something you really wanted to do, but you were also afraid to do it. Riding a bike meant transferring from the safety of tricycle to a bigger, more mature world with more difficult challenges. You also ran the risk of not being able to do it, which might make you look and feel stupid. In addition, if you couldn't do it, you might fall down, skinning your knees and banging up your body. Kids with really active imaginations might even have seen themselves falling off their bikes and sliding under the wheels of a truck or a bus. Not a pleasant experience, even if it was only imaginary.

Playing Tip

If there's a guiding principle that governs any youth activity, especially elective activities like sports, it's keep it friendly and keep it fun. Keeping it friendly and fun draws kids in to the activity and helps them overcome any anxieties they may have. For a kid, anything that's fun is worth doing—not bad advice for those of us who no longer are kids.

But once you managed to stay on that bike for more than a few feet, pedaling under your own power and maintaining your own balance, you experienced a rush like the one the Wright Brothers must have felt when they stayed aloft at Kitty Hawk for the first time. You had become free of the limitations of childhood, riding farther, faster, and freer than you ever did before. You had moved on, leaving one world behind for a new adventure. At the time, nothing felt better.

Chances are you experienced that feeling all over again if you taught your son or daughter to ride a bike. You had those same tentative fears, watching them teeter on their first two-wheeler, afraid that they were afraid, afraid they would fall and hurt themselves, afraid they would give up in frustration. You remembered how you felt, but you could do little more than give guidance and hope for the best.

Then it happened. With your help, your son or daughter figured it out, maintaining balance and taking off as if they had been born to ride. You thought you were exhilarated when you learned to ride, but now suddenly your heart nearly leaps out of your chest. A whole new world of fears and perhaps loss may have opened, but it paled in comparison to watching your child enjoying his or her success. And you helped that young person achieve that goal.

That's the coach within you at work, remembering your own experiences and transferring them successfully to your child. Now you must do the same thing for your young soccer players and remember that what you do is a means to the next step, not an end in itself. Your goal is to help them move forward. If you've done it right, they will reward you with joyful performance and never look back. And that's worth more than any victory.

Cultivating Your Inner Coach

Once you've got the right mindset, it's time to cultivate that attitude so that you're not only talking the talk, but walking the walk—or in this case running the run—as well. There's also an element of "coach-ness" required so that you are accepted by your young team members as the ultimate authority you are—or should be—when it comes to team direction and game strategy. Coaching is more than a whistle, a clipboard, and a playbook. You also need to master a body of knowledge and mode of behavior that communicate—kindly—that you are in charge.

Here is some, but not all, of what you need.

Know the Game

Soccer isn't a difficult game, but it does have its challenges. There are a wealth of strategies and procedures involved in coaching a winning team, many of which we'll get to later in this volume. You need to be the be-all and end-all when it comes to the game, knowing a little about its history and a lot about how to play it. This will come in especially handy when dealing with parents, who will expect more out of you—or at least different things—than the kids will.

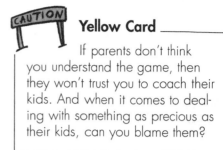

Yellow Card

If parents don't think you understand the game, then they won't trust you to coach their kids. And when it comes to dealing with something as precious as their kids, can you blame them?

Lead by Example

You don't have to be Pele or Mia Hamm, but you do need the basic ability to demonstrate a corner kick or teach someone how to dribble. Chances are, your players won't remember what you told them, but they'll remember what you showed them.

Demonstrate in slow motion to begin with, gradually increasing your speed to their speed. Examples of professionals or at least older players executing the skills also will help. The important thing is to demonstrate in a way that encourages them to try it, rather than discourages them into thinking that they will never be able to do it as well as you.

Time Out

Studies show that students retain a third less information when they're not shown how to perform.

Leading and teaching by example goes beyond mere skills into your very presence on the field. We'll talk about coaching styles later in this chapter, but rest assured that how you act will be mimicked by your players, both on-field and off. If you yell during practice, your players will come to accept yelling as an appropriate way to give direction.

Remember Who You're Dealing With

We've already stressed this point, but it's worth repeating. Coaching is essentially an educational function. Making demands beyond the skill levels of young players can be destructive. At the same time, under-coaching also can be damaging, but in a different way. In both cases, you can undermine the ability and interests of young athletes, driving them from the sport.

A good coach discovers and hits a stride that keeps his or her players interested, but doesn't create hurdles too high to surmount. The younger they are, of course, the lower those hurdles and more basic those skills need to be. But remember that, as coach, you are responsible for teaching them something. Allowing them to learn within their own limits can be part of the fun that you provide. Stretching those limits to reasonable extremes will make it fun for you as a coach. That's when you know that you're really doing your job.

Teach Skills *and* Strategy

Young athletes quickly discover that soccer is more than just running back and forth down a grassy field randomly kicking a ball. There is a reason for doing what they do. It may be a simple strategy at first, but it will get more complicated. By teaching your players this strategy, you will help them develop and maintain interest in the sport.

When kids understand strategy, then the purpose of skills training will also make more sense to them. Likewise, when a player knows how to execute a particular skill, then the purpose of that skill is all the easier to understand. It's important to know how to take the ball upfield and avoid the goal defenders from a conceptual point of view, but without being able to execute the motions to fulfill that mission, that strategic understanding quickly fades. Keeping players stimulated by strategy *and* skills keeps them interested and active in the game.

Keep Everyone Involved

Including every player in every practice *and* every game may not be practical among pro, college, or even high school teams. For your purposes, however, it's a necessary component of skill and team development. The best way to develop players is to get them out there on the field and in contact with the ball as often as possible.

Part of this has to do with the simple fact that kids learn best by doing, and so the more soccer they "do," the better they'll become. Kids also have short attention spans, and the longer they have to wait for their turn, the less interested many of them will be when that turn finally comes around.

Time Out
Many young players have significant anxiety about getting out on the field and performing. This can be true even of experienced players when in a new group or situation. It's the coach's job to relieve that anxiety and let the players know it's important just to be active and out there. Once they've overcome their concerns about how good or how poor their natural skills may be, coaches can begin the delicate task of individual and team training.

Developing Your Coaching Style

Let's face it; some of us simply shouldn't coach. Our natural tendencies under situations of stress won't allow it. For those of us who have what it takes to be a good coach, we must find a coaching style that's comfortable and fits our personalities. Trying to be someone you're not won't work. When we try to appear sincere when we're not, we come off as affected and ineffective.

On the other hand, there are different ways to coach successfully. Just as there are different styles and strengths of players, not all coaches are made from the same mold. Those who figure out how to marshal their natural abilities and augment them with a background in the sport and its techniques can't help but succeed.

What kind of coach are you? There are many successful types, and you're probably a blend of several of them. But here are some of the foundation styles from which you can build your own coaching persona.

Yellow Card _____

No one can smell insincerity better than a group of kids. Stop being yourself and you may as well stop coaching.

The Cheerleader

You might call this one the Gipper, the one who inspires and excites, motivating players through a rush of personal energy that never flags and always fuels the flames of play, no matter what the circumstances.

> **Strengths:** Coaches who act as cheerleaders can energize a game. Their enthusiasm is infectious and can bring a team to life.

> **Weaknesses:** Sometimes that energy can take a wrong turn. If their highs are very high, chances are their lows are very low, and they may apply the verbal strop just as forcefully as they cheer the winning team to victory. Cheerleaders also sometimes gloss over individual shortcomings and player or team problems in favor of promoting the team's energy, only to find that the old charm no longer works. Then they get mad.

If you're a cheerleader, don't let the energy flag as long as it can deliver a positive result. And don't let it get in the way when the team or an individual player needs something other than a "rah-rah-rah" to solve a problem.

The Tactical Technician

The tactical technical could also be called the Strategic Thinker. This is the type of coach who sacrifices energy for cool logic and an almost chesslike approach to the game. The Technician knows the game inside and out, studying his or her team as if it were a complex machine. It is, of course, but that's not always the best way to manage it.

Strengths: The nice thing about Technicians is that they can inspire confidence with their cool, levelheaded approach and encyclopedic knowledge of the sport. This works better with older teams, who can understand or at least appreciate the human thought process. But younger teams also can gain confidence from the Technician's serene command of the problems at hand. In some cases, a level head and sedate manner is exactly what a team of young players needs.

Playing Tip

In addition to figuring out your coaching style, make sure to take time and get to know your individual team members. Your kids may be forwards, midfielders, or goalkeepers, but they're kids first and foremost, and they want you to *like* them as well as coach them.

Weaknesses: Technicians have to be careful that, while they're busy planning, their team doesn't completely lose its energy and strength. The evident lack of outward enthusiasm can come off as arrogance, boredom, or disinterest, causing players to respond in kind. Too often the Technician forgets that, hey, these are kids who just want to play the game. Your plans may be grand or grandiose, but the kids may need something other than a rocket scientist at the helm.

Emotional control is as critical as physical control for mastering soccer. Mastering skills is one thing—as a superior technical coach you have those down cold. Now master the emotions, ratcheting them to the right level at the right time.

The Commander

We used to call them natural born leaders, but they're also sometimes ruefully referred to as "Type A's." There's a good chance you either work for one now or have in the past. You may have adored that person or loathed him or her; either way, chances are you were in the presence of a Commander, someone who could make you "step to" and accomplish difficult tasks.

Strengths: The Commander personality, when compassionately displayed, often works well with youth teams. Whether they admit it or not, most kids simply want to be told what to do to succeed. Most are too young to figure it out for themselves and many possess what Eastern mystics often called "monkey minds," brains so full of chatter that they can barely concentrate much less make the right decisions most of the time. Temper command with compassion, balance firmness with fairness, and you may have a winning combination.

Weakness: If you don't think you have any weakness, then chances are you have Commander tendencies. The most obvious, of course, is the "Damn the torpedoes and full speed ahead!" mentality that will sacrifice all individual issues in favor, if not of victory, then of the execution of process. Commanders are most dangerous when they lose sight of both humanity and purpose, letting commands exist for their own sakes rather than the sake of the team.

Commanders are the strongest characters in some ways, the weakest in others. By being the most in control, Commanders also are the ones who need the greatest amount of self-control. Take a strong will to your strong-willed tendencies and you may wind up with a winning combination.

The Builder

Finally, there are coaching types who use an almost deductive style of team development. They take the characteristics and roles of the individuals on the team and, through analysis and assembly, construct the definitive performance vehicle for delivering the ball to the opposition's goal net. Not surprisingly, these coaches are called Builders.

Strengths: In other social settings we might refer to this type as consensus builders, those who arrive at an opinion or goal through the construction of agreement with others. From a coaching standpoint this attribute may also be effective, provided the Builder works hard to get all team members involved in the decision and then works harder still to make sure follow-through occurs. Effective Builders coax strong, dedicated performances from their young teams.

Weaknesses: Building, by its nature, fosters decentralization, and the old adage, "When all are leaders, no one leads," is painfully possible here. In addition, lack of decisive leadership, if not matched with a successful response, may be seen as weakness by team members, parents, and opponents alike. Once that happens, little can be done to reverse it.

To master the technique of the Builder, especially among young teams, you must pay close attention not only to facts but also to challenges yet to come and head problems off before they fully blossom by involving everyone. Being a Builder can work, but it takes effort to succeed.

No matter what your coaching style—Cheerleader, Technician, Commander, Builder, or some combination of styles—do the right thing by your players based on your own personality and strengths.

The Least You Need to Know

- ◆ Your ability as coach to adjust to player needs determines not only the success of the team, but of the individual players involved.

- ◆ If you need a personal coaching model to follow, start with your memories of riding a bike and teaching others how to do so.

- ◆ Coaches must have a comprehensive knowledge of the game and lead by example.

- ◆ Coaches need to adjust to the age and sophistication of their players, stimulating interest and action in the game.

- ◆ As often as possible, make sure that everyone practices and everyone plays. Constant motion and involvement is best.

- ◆ No matter what your coaching style, always do right by your players.

Chapter 4

Developing Your Coaching Skills

In This Chapter

- ◆ Formulating your coaching philosophy
- ◆ Taking a developmental approach
- ◆ Developing a coaching "contract"
- ◆ Developing a player "contract"
- ◆ Putting the finishing touches on your coach-ness

Most successful coaches have a personal philosophy, something around which they build their program, guide their team, and use to determine their level of success. Part of this philosophy is based on the rigors and demands of the activity they coach, the rest on personal goals, characteristics, and style.

The most famous and oft quoted sports philosophy probably belongs to legendary Green Bay Packer coach Vince Lombardi, who is best known for saying that "Winning isn't everything, it's the only thing."

When it comes to pro football as played by millionaire professional athletes, few would challenge that sentiment. But that type of philosophy is inappropriate for youth soccer coaches whose developmental obligations don't generally include squeezing the life's blood out of every young athlete. We admire the great Green Bay coach, but think there may be a more constructive philosophy for coaching youth soccer.

Your Coaching Philosophy

Your philosophy will be up to you. No matter what you choose to write down—and that philosophy should always be written down as a reflection of your personal commitment to it—we recommend that it be some variation of the following:

> Victory is nothing more than the combined consequences of a game played well.

This captures a very important point that Coach Lombardi's personal ethos lacks:

> Victory is more about process than end results.

Playing Tip

When you're coaching young kids, one popular technique is to liken the movements to familiar images or animals. For example, describing the ball as moving slowly forward like a snail or darting from opposing players like a rabbit provide young minds with a useful image, which they can then emulate.

As coach, you're responsible for helping your team master the process as a means to the goal. If you remember Webster's definition from the previous chapter, you know that's exactly what coaching is. Too many amateur coaches, with Lombardi's words ringing in their ears, know where they think they want to go (victory), but have no idea how to get there (process).

And failing to map the route is the quickest way to get lost. Developing a coaching philosophy is your first step. Write it down, and you'll be ready to begin developing the skills you'll need to coach your team to personal and group victories.

Taking the Developmental Approach

Think of yourself as a teacher, because that's what coaching really is. Even at the pro level, the coach's role is to guide the team and develop strategies to help them grow and develop, both as a team and as individual athletes.

Development is especially critical among younger athletes because they are still maturing physically, emotionally, and intellectually. As their coach, you can be either an asset or roadblock to these processes.

Time Out
Although not usually called for among youth teams and leagues, some coaches are committed enough to get licensed through the U.S. Soccer Association's National Coaching School. The school, which has several facilities across the United States, offers training courses that result in class A, B, or C licensure. Coursework involves field instructions in tactics and training as well as classroom work on team management and sports psychology. If you're serious about youth coaching, you might consider pursuing a license. Each state also has its own youth soccer coaching office, and the National Soccer Coaches Association (NSCAA) provides coaching clinics, symposiums, and courses. They can be reached at www.nscaa.com or by email at info@nscaa.com

Early childhood development is a science and discipline unto itself, and we don't have time to delve into it thoroughly here. For our purposes, it's enough to know that infants begin with reflex movements until eight or nine months of age, then move on to rudimentary movements until age three. Fundamental movements and motor skills kick in at age three and last until age six or seven. It's during this latter stage that children begin to kick, throw, and do other basic sports movement. For the most part, they're not yet very good. But they understand the concepts and can execute basic movements that they will be able to develop.

It's at this point that many volunteer coaches find themselves with a wide-eyed bunch of urchins in oversize T-shirts drooping down to their knees who couldn't give a hang about soccer but might really enjoy running around and kicking a ball with their friends. Now that you're on the job, how do you proceed?

Know Your Team

The younger your charges, the more developmental coaching you'll be doing. Presumably they're motivated to some degree; otherwise they wouldn't be there. Even if the kids are basically from the same background, you'll begin to see the seeds of what will be a wide array of skills and understanding. Do your best to get everyone's thinking running along the same track. That may be enough work to last you an entire season.

Simple exercises and drills work best, such as basic kicking and dribbling exercises (see Chapter 10). Once you find the level of competence and relative maturity of the team, that becomes your baseline. Once everyone has mastered those foundation skills, you can begin working with various players to cultivate individual talents.

Playing Tip

Progress will be determined by a combination of your coaching abilities and your players' maturing processes. Often, those maturing processes will win out.

Take It Slow

Among the youngest players, you'll start with basic skills such as kicking and dribbling, and create games and exercises that reinforce those skills.

One effective tool is to combine aerobic exercise with skill training. For example, before each game, have the kids run down the field (exercise) while dribbling a ball (skills training).

Show and Tell

Remember, children learn best when something is demonstrated to them and they then are given an opportunity to try it themselves. Demonstrate kicking and dribbling techniques first. This gives them a visual imprint of what it is you want them to do. Once they see you do it, allow them to feel it through practice. The two steps taken together will go a long way to helping them develop mastery.

Train to Compete

Despite what we've been emphasizing all along, actual games are part of what soccer is all about—even the youngest players will compete against other teams. We practice so we can play our best during a game. Make sure your players understand the connection between training and competition

Make It Easy!

Soccer loses a lot of young players. Some of that's a function of changing interests on the part of the kids, but it's also the result of burnout or a soccer experience that becomes a real drag. To keep as many kids playing as possible, you've got to keep things fun and make sure everyone is improving. Kids—or anyone, for that matter—don't like to do what they don't do well. Helping them master the basics is a start to greater soccer enjoyment for the whole team.

The same goes for the coach. If you're not having fun, then you shouldn't be doing it.

Playing Tip

One of the best supplemental techniques coaches can use is taking their teams to actual soccer matches. Sure, it may be the local college or even high school, but the kids won't care. The important thing is that they'll be able to see well-trained and conditioned athletes in action. Not only will this provide role models for them, they'll get to enjoy the excitement of a real game. At the very least, have them watch soccer on TV.

Sign on the Dotted Line, Coach!

Anyone who has ever attempted to master a task, be it rock climbing, ballroom dancing, or quantum physics, knows that the worst to achieving success is usually ourselves. We complain that we don't have the time, the resources, the energy, or the purpose to do it. But all we're really lacking is the commitment to get the job done. Once we have that commitment, everything else will come with time.

One of our favorite philosophers, Jedi Master Yoda from *Star Wars*, said it best:

Do or do not. There is no try.

The same holds true for coaching youth soccer. Make the commitment and then follow through until you achieve success. Anything less is merely an excuse.

By signing a soccer "contract," you'll be making a record of your commitment to the team to do what's necessary to create a positive experience and, with any luck, a winning team. If anyone asks, you'll have the document handy as a way to demonstrate your personal commitment. But the purpose of the document is primarily to articulate that commitment to the person who should be your toughest critic—you. Putting your soccer commitment in writing is like a putting a business plan in writing. When it exists in black-and-white, it's more likely to get done.

To what, then, will you be committing when you write out and sign the coaching contract with yourself? (Put it in writing; otherwise it's simply no more than a nice idea.) You may have your own list of principles, but here are some foundational elements that should appear in every coach's "contract":

- ◆ **Commit to learning as much as possible about the sport and its coaching principles.** As we said earlier, you're the ultimate resource for the majority of your team members and their parents when it comes to soccer knowledge. Your commitment to coaching, first and foremost, means that you know what you're doing and why.

◆ **Commit to the welfare of your team members.** Kids of all ages are vulnerable physically as well as emotionally. A good coach commits to providing a safe environment that fosters growth in athletic skills as well as physical, intellectual, and emotional well-being. A great coach makes it happen day in and day out.

◆ **Commit to creating a disciplined environment that promotes developing, learning, and growth.** Despite what some may think, we're not talking about army boot camp here. But we are talking about creating realistic expectations for your youth athletes—and their parents—that can be easily achieved, fun to execute, and will ultimately benefit the kids involved. That discipline begins with the coach, but extends down the line to everyone involved.

◆ **Commit to developing a winning attitude.** Developmental coaching is good, but even the most disinterested kid knows that the team practices and plays to win. While winning should be the ultimate goal, it should not be pursued at all costs. Soccer teams can "win" at multiple levels, including …

Winning games and perhaps even the league championship.

Showing significantly improved skills and abilities on the part of the team and/or its young athletes.

Overcoming the struggle we all have with skills training and personal discipline.

Improvements in teamwork that lead to the development of social and interactive skills and abilities;

Commitment to a cause—specifically the team and its sport. This can and probably is one of your team members' first forays into social development and responsibility.

◆ **Commit to fostering an appreciation for soccer.** As coach, it's critical that you support the continued growth and welfare of the game.

◆ **Commit to your own personal development and that of your coaching assistants.** Read books, go to professional soccer matches, rent videos, and watch the World Cup. It all adds to your own development as a soccer coach and "expert."

In the world of soccer, a practicing coach is just one more link in the chain. To his or her team, however, he or she is the most important link.

CAUTION

Yellow Card _____

We can't say it enough: It's your job to keep your team members safe. But because accidents do happen, we recommend that you always record even the slightest twist of the ankle. You can create a special form, or simply record the mishap in a notebook. That way, if necessary, you can provide medical professionals with some background on the injury. And you will know you took the time to make the notation and provide appropriate treatment.

Developing a Player "Contract"

Just as creating and signing your own coaching contract lends weight to your commitment to the team, having your players sign their own contracts helps keep them committed.

It may seem odd at first, when facing a field of after-school 10-year-olds, to think in terms of a contract. Getting them to sign any piece of paper means nothing in a court of law. But in many cases it will mean something to them—it'll probably be the first "contract" they've ever been asked to sign.

There are a few secrets to successfully writing and negotiating a youth soccer contract:

◆ **Make the contract as clear as possible.** Anything that doesn't immediately appear to relate to the players or their world will be lost on them.

◆ **Explain the contract.** Despite what some grownups still think, kids aren't dumb. If you tell kids to do something, they'll want to know why. If you can't tell them why, they're not going to do it.

◆ **Keep it brief.** No "party of the first part" here. Take the most important points, explain the reasons for doing them, then ask the kids to sign on the dotted line. That may not sound like much, but it doesn't have to be much to be enough.

So what do you include in your contract with your team members? Options may vary based on the nature of your group, whether they're boys or girls, and what part of the country you're in, but the following foundational elements should find their way, in some form, to most contracts:

◆ **Players must commit to attending practice and games.** Explain that you understand there will always be conflicts, but that the players need to attend practice in order to play. Soccer is a team sport and, as such, requires that the players be able to depend on each other.

Playing Tip

As Woody Allen says, 90 percent of success in life is just showing up. The same holds true for soccer practice and play.

◆ **Players must commit to a healthy lifestyle that will give them the strength they need to play.** That means eating right (including vegetables), getting enough sleep, and avoiding the stress that comes from bad grades and not getting their homework done. (Parents will like that you slipped in that last one.) Bad habits, such as fighting or smoking, are, of course, out of the question.

◆ **Players should commit to a positive, winning attitude toward teamwork.** In some ways, this will be the most difficult for youth athletes to follow. But by fostering the interdependency that is natural to the sport, you can help build a better social consciousness and commitment on the part of your players.

◆ **Above all, players need to commit to themselves, to giving their best to the sport so they can, in turn, get the most out of it.** This may be "out there" for most youth players, but many parents will understand and appreciate its inclusion because that's the primary reason they want their kids involved in the first place.

The idea of having kids sign a document that includes such lofty goals may seem unnecessary. But by having them do so, you take them one step closer to understanding and agreeing to the principles upon which sports participation is built.

It's up to you whether you want to take this step, since many parents may not understand its importance. But for those who see the true value of youth sports, who perhaps had been involved themselves as kids, it shows that you have a clear understanding not only of what's at stake, but also what can be gained beyond a jersey that too soon will be too small and a few afternoons a week in the fall and the spring out in the fresh air.

Putting the Finishing Touches on Your Coach-ness

Now that you know a little bit about coaching styles (from Chapter 2) as well as the foundational elements every good coach needs to build on, it's time to talk about some finishing touches you'll need to put you in the best possible position to coach.

At the risk of seeming redundant, let us point out again the coach is the turnkey to youth soccer success. You are the connecting tissue between your team and others in your conference and league, among team members and even between team members and their parents, at least when it comes to all things soccer-related. Never take that responsibility lightly nor let your vigilance flag when it comes to making sure that connective tissue is strong and healthy. Your ability to master the technical aspects of coaching soccer is extremely important, but your ability to master the administrative, interpersonal, and political aspects of the team and its various related parties is equally critical.

Here are some aspects to consider when putting the final touches on your coaching persona:

- **Look and act the part.** You're not only a coach, but the head of the enterprise. Avoid raggedy cut-offs and dirty T-shirts. Look smart and efficient, because that's what parents will expect and team members appreciate.

- **Keep a positive and winning disposition.** Nothing skews a practice more than when the coach is in a bad mood or preoccupied with some other issue. There may be times when you want to use anger or disappointment as a tactic, but do so only in limited doses. You should focus on making practice and games fun and enjoyable.

- **Be on time and efficient.** Young players will waste enough practice time. They can't afford to have a coach who has forgotten the corner cones or arrives late. Remember that you set the pace. Make sure your standards are high, so you can demand the same from others.

- **Like a good scout, always be prepared.** Have a good supply of extra clothes in the car in case the weather changes or clothes get wet or dirty during play, as well as blankets and first aid kit in case of an emergency. Get a very good waterproof jacket and sweatpants. Many times the coach is the last one left on the field when all the players have been picked up. Don't forget the extra socks and sunscreen!

- **Be sincere in your comments, lavish in your praise, and follow through on your promises.** That's good advice for anyone in a leadership position, but especially valuable to youth coaches whose young players may be too used to adults who don't treat them with respect.

- **Make a sandwich of your feedback.** The first words (top slice of bread) are always positive; the middle portion (the meat) is critical and constructive; and the last words (bottom slice of bread) are positive and reinforcing. You can always vary this with just one critical point and then a positive reassuring message next.

Playing Tip

When giving players information, sometimes it's appropriate to put them in their positional groups and break down the instruction for them. For example, bring all defenders in and remind them of the safety first credo while playing near their own goal. That will help them understand and appreciate their roles.

Yellow Card

Remember also that too much information can cause the dreaded "information overload"— meaning that players won't remember any part of what you said!

◆ **Repeat Yourself. Repeat Yourself.** Always repeat key points and make them very clear and concise. It never hurts to say things twice or even three times, even when you're dealing with adults. Similarly, when performing key exercises, repeat them. This helps your team absorb and process the information. Repetition is often the secret of coaching success!

◆ **Take responsibility for team losses and give them credit for victories.** This is a simple technique that shows you're part of the team, but it doesn't undermine their motivation to win. Help your young athletes do the best they can and give them credit when they do.

◆ **Stress the need for constant improvement.** Don't let young players rest on their laurels. (But make sure you congratulate them on their successes!) Even things done well can stand to be done a little better. Establish a philosophy that stresses improvement, and it will come as no surprise when you ask for more from them.

◆ **Stay flexible, fluid, and professional.** New situations arise and plans change. Be ready to take advantage of those opportunities. Your ability to do so sets a good example for players who face a field with constantly changing situations.

◆ **Be open to others' ideas.** In addition to being courteous and improving communications, you never know where the next great suggestion may come from. Being a leader involves developing the best possible plans, and all suggestions should be welcome, even those you don't act on.

◆ **Remember that your "team" is larger than 11 players.** You may have backup players and parental volunteers, sponsors and assistant coaches. Even your opponents may be considered part of the soccer team that supports the growth and development of the sport. All have a vested interest and all may be considered resources. Use them.

◆ **Appreciate your effort.** You're providing children with an invaluable growth experience. You deserve a pat on the back for that, even though you may occasionally get a kick in the pants from players' parents! Make sure you understand and appreciate the sacrifices you're making. They are anything but small.

Now let's get going. There's work to be done!

The Least You Need to Know

- Develop a coaching philosophy.

- As a coach, you're responsible for your team members' physical, emotional, and intellectual growth.

- Teach skills incrementally and demonstrate them graphically. Kids learn best by watching others perform the skill.

- Develop a coaching "contract" with yourself to help support the commitment you'll need to do the job right.

- Develop a player "contract" for your young athletes so they know that joining a team requires their commitment.

- As Yoda says, do or do not. There is no try.

Chapter

5

The Elements of Team Building

In This Chapter

- ◆ Defining teamwork
- ◆ Applying the teamwork process
- ◆ The five commandments of teamwork
- ◆ Some teamwork training drills

Ask anyone unfamiliar with the sport to watch a few minutes of a soccer game and describe it, and they'll probably tell you about a large field littered with 22 players aimlessly chasing a ball back and forth. To that observer, there will be little rhyme or reason to the players' movements other than to drive the ball to the goal of the opposing team in hopes of scoring a point.

But there is very little about soccer that is aimless. The game has a very strong strategic foundation behind what appears to be a set of very rudimentary skills. The running and kicking are all a part of the action, of course, and are central to executing that strategy. Those who know the game can see the patterns forming on the field, patterns that lead to the set up, the shot, and, with a little luck, a goal.

Our naive observer probably will also fail to notice the teamwork involved. That apparently random running up and down the field (while admittedly sometimes aimless) is often the direct result of strategy. And for any strategy to work, there must be teamwork.

For some coaches, teamwork is the hardest concept to teach. It can be especially difficult for kids who are just themselves learning to master skills not only for the sport, but also for life in general. To ask them to perform in tandem with others, who themselves really don't know which end is up, can be a real challenge. But every coach knows that teamwork is what makes a team. Without it, that coach merely has 11 individuals running around on the field trying to get things right and only succeeding by happenstance.

The younger the players are, the tougher it is to teach them teamwork. In this chapter—and throughout the rest of this book, we'll share techniques you'll be able to put into play to foster teamwork.

Teamwork by Definition

We don't always go back to Webster's classical assessment, but in this case, a little says a lot. And, we might add, these are some of Mr. Webster's better definitions.

Let's first consider the word "team." We'll bypass all of Webster's references to draft animals and focus on those definitions that relate to young soccer players:

> **Team**   a) a group of people constituting one side in a contest or competition; b) a group of people working together in a coordinated effort; c) to join in cooperative activity of or done by a team.

Now let's look at the word "teamwork":

> **Teamwork**   a joint action by a group of people in which individual interests are subordinated to group unity and efficiency; coordinated effort, as of an athletic team.

Yellow Card

Kids, especially younger ones, tend not to think in terms of "WE," only in terms of "ME." Turning those 11 ME's into a team is a challenge for every coach. Just remember that the younger the player, the more rudimentary that concept of teamwork will be in his or her mind. You'll have to adjust your coaching expectations to fit.

The definitions lay out some of the foundational elements that, while very evident to many of us who've been involved in sports, are still new concepts for the kids on your team.

You won't find much written about teamwork at the youth sports level because it's difficult to apply the standards of teamwork and expect consistently good results. But cultivating teamwork will be critical to the success of your team.

How you teach teamwork will depend on the age of your players. Like many educational strategies, the best way to teach teamwork is when you're teaching specific skills. When we get to the chapters that discuss skills teaching, we'll point out exercises where teaching teamwork is particularly useful.

Playing Tip

In your lessons about working together, use the old acronym T.E.A.M.—Together Everyone Accomplishes More. It's a tired old chestnut, to be sure, but it's probably new to the kids and says exactly what needs to be said.

Applying the Teamwork Process

Teamwork principles can and should be meted out at all levels of play and practice. Once the kids get into the right teamwork rhythm, teaching it becomes no more than a maintenance job. It will be a constant maintenance job, to be sure, but not an intellectually challenging one.

You want them to kick the ball and make a goal, right? They know they'll make you and the rest of the team happy if they score. That is what they will try and do … by themselves because they don't yet realize that it's even more fun when more people are involved. Until you teach them otherwise, involving someone else in the play only diminishes their own role and value to the process. You have to teach them there is even greater glory when that goal results from teamwork.

Playing Tip

Anything that builds teamwork improves play. Some of the most effective strategies include things like team songs or chants to build camaraderie. Nicknames, especially if they involve animals or familiar imagery that promotes playing success, will also have a positive impact. The idea behind all this, of course, is to build identity and community among the members of the team. That will lead to increased teamwork and greater success.

So what do you do? Consider the five commandments of teamwork as a possible process for reaching that difficult goal.

Commandment 1: Teamwork has physical and intellectual components.

Ask parents to teach the concept of teamwork at home just as you do on the field. Even if player performance is very good, it becomes that much better when those skills are considered as part of overall teamwork. Be prepared to practice the physical and intellectual aspects of the teamwork.

Commandment 2: Teamwork is sometimes as difficult to learn as it is to teach.

It doesn't matter how good the individual players on your team are. If they aren't a strong team, then teams with better teamwork will beat them. That obliges you to make an extra effort to teach teamwork, not only as part of the individual skills and strategies, but almost as a separate discipline in itself.

Commandment 3: Teamwork begins early and never ends.

No matter what level your players are at, introduce some elements of teamwork. Skills drills involving ball handling, for example, should include some group exercises (see Chapter 10).

Commandment 4: Even very advanced players need to understand and appreciate the team concept.

Top drawer players—and some hot dogs—are sometimes capable of executing amazing plays, running the ball up to the goal mouth and snaking it past the goalkeeper in a jaw-dropping show of dexterity. But the really good ones know that they couldn't make the play without the effort of their teammates, who are keeping the field open for them and providing the protection they need. That's where the true pros concentrate their efforts.

Time Out
When teaching the concept of teamwork and cooperation to very young kids, consider having them run a three-legged race. Have pairs of kids stand side-by-side, and tie their inner legs together. Then, have them race against other pairs of kids in the same position. Competing in those races requires teamwork in its most elemental form.

Commandment 5: Without teamwork, there is no team.

Painfully evident? Yes, but still often misunderstood by players more interested in grandstanding for their friends and family. This statement should be the coda of your coaching administration. We'd be hard pressed to find a plainer way to say it.

This is by no means a comprehensive conceptual list, but it should be enough to get your team underway. So, go team!

Teamwork Training Drills

When it comes to teaching teamwork, you have to give verbal as well as physical instruction. The first drill should be a verbal one, in which you instruct the team on the importance of teamwork. The players may not look like they're listening, but they're logging the information away for future reference.

Then, try to involve the concept of teamwork in as many skill drills as you can (not all drills will be appropriate). That way players learn both the skills as well as how to work with others.

Consider, for example, passing drills in which two players are required to pass the ball back and forth as they advance up the field. Pretty simple stuff, right? Maybe, but that simple exercise involves the following elements:

- The players are building their stamina and aerobic capacity as they run.

- Eye-foot coordination is increasing with each step as they learn to control the ball's motion and direction with their feet.

- Strategic thinking develops as they negotiate reception of the ball being kicked to them as well as judging the direction and trajectory of the ball as they kick it.

- Personal judgment is being exercised as they decide on the speed and force with which they will kick the ball.

- Teamwork skills are honed as the players learn to depend on each other's successful execution of the task to move forward.

- Personal responsibility is learned as the players work to execute their part of the task.

- A personal relationship is forged through the successful sharing of a task.

It really is more than running and kicking a ball.

The same analysis may be done for any exercise during practice and any play during the game—and sometimes the list of benefits gets even longer—but the point remains the same. Team skills form the hub around which everything operates. The team may not realize that and may not need to, but as coach it helps for you to understand the complexity—and value—of teamwork.

Make teaching teamwork one of the pillars of your coaching administration.

The Least You Need to Know

◆ Teamwork is the foundation upon which soccer strategy rests.

◆ Classically defined, teamwork is a joint action by a group of people in which individual interests are subordinated to group unity and efficiency. It's a coordinated effort that's exercised by an athletic team.

◆ Using the old acronym T.E.A.M.—Together Everyone Accomplishes More— may be a good way to get kids to remember the concept behind the word.

◆ Good coaches teach teamwork as a physical and intellectual activity.

◆ Without teamwork there is no team. Make this the coda of your coaching administration.

Dealing with Soccer Parents

In This Chapter

- ◆ Making sense of soccer parents
- ◆ Defining your parental strategy
- ◆ Creating your team's "business plan"
- ◆ Drafting your parental "team"
- ◆ Writing playing contracts with parents

Ask most novice youth soccer coaches what their greatest fear is, and it will be young players who have breakdowns or go ballistic on the field from pressure. Ask experienced coaches, however, and it's not the players they're worried about …

It's the players' parents. Really.

All coaches have horror stories about parents who are so involved in their child's sports career that they become impatient, unruly, and downright hostile to the opposing team, the coach—either theirs or ours—and even the young players themselves. At that point, it's no longer a matter of just taking care of the team and its problems. Suddenly there's a whole new factor involved, and it's a factor that conceivably could take a poke at you.

Sports moms and dads have alternately been supporting and plaguing players and coaches since the dawn of youth sports. The classic tales of belligerent Little League dads, violent hockey parents, and yes, hostile soccer moms and dads, have their basis in fact.

As coach, you're responsible for the well-being and growth of your young athletes. Unfortunately, that means you've inherited their parents, too, and in a way are responsible for them as well. It wasn't in the coaching job description, we know, but it does become a fact of life. Don't say we didn't warn you.

Harnessing Mom and Dad's Energy

As horrific as some of those tales and their bloody descriptions may be, there's a bright side to the whole thing. Aggressive response on the part of parents is almost always born of support for their child and commitment to the team, the sport, or at least the experience. Let's face it, soccer parents yell, scream, and make scenes because they love their kids and are just trying to make an impact on their lives.

A savvy coach knows how to put that energy to good use. A parent who's involved in his son's performance might make an excellent line judge, for example, or be an effective part of a campaign to drum up corporate sponsorships. It's like harnessing a hurricane. All you have to do is figure out how to make that energy function on the side of good rather than evil.

That's your job. You're the coach. And with enough planning and insight, a good coach can accomplish almost anything. Even when those things involve soccer parents

Anatomy of a Soccer Parent

It takes all kinds to make the world go round, and that same cross-section is represented in the ranks of soccer parenthood. That means a little diplomacy and a lot of psychological assessment of the players, the parents, and their relationship will help you not only avoid unpleasant scenes, but also improve your relationship with everyone.

Here are some of the more difficult denizens of the sidelines that you'll run into, both in practice and in play:

- **The Screamer.** This is a little like a deranged version of the cheerleader and morphs into two varieties: Old Yeller (usually male) and Hysterically Yours (usually female). In both cases the M.O. is similar, resulting in much the same outcome. They prowl the sidelines, yelling at their player, the team, the opposition, the coach(es), the referee(s) and, sometimes other parents. Sometimes they're upset with a play or a call; sometimes the pressure is too much for them; sometimes that's just how they are.

- **The Pacer.** These are parents who are screaming on the inside, but we don't hear it because they keep their angst bottled up, choosing instead some form of physical expression. It isn't always pacing, but pacing can be the most unnerving. In addition, they may pace right into the way of the action, either on field or off, making your job even more difficult.

- **The Critic.** The first thing you learn as coach is that (a) everyone knows a little something about the sport you coach; and (b) they all think you would benefit from their input. The critic can be public, yelling suggestions and directions from across the field, or he can be more subtle, coming to you during breaks and halftime to give you the sum total of his knowledge on a repeated and unasked for basis.

> **Time Out**
>
> If a parent gets too far out of line—yelling, screaming and, especially, swearing—it's not inappropriate to stop the practice and give the offending parent a yellow card, signifying that they have committed an error egregious enough for you to make an example of them. Present the yellow card with enough formality and one time should be enough.

- **The Chatterer.** Soccer play and practice are and should be social occasions. However, there should be a limit or at least some respect tied into that sociability. Every so often someone steps over that boundary line, assuming that the playing field is his or her private parlor, talking loudly and nonstop throughout the action. Private conversations tend to be the business of the people having them but, in this case, private become public, usually thanks to volume, distracting both the players and the coach. Additional demerits are awarded to those who combine chattering with eating, drinking, and/or smoking.

- **The Phantom.** This is the most elusive and, in some ways, most destructive type of parent, more because of what they don't do than what they do. They don't get their kids to practice or the games promptly or with any regularity. They're tardy with any team dues, payment of fees, and/or provision of equipment. They arrive late or leave early, sometimes with their young players in tow, but often leaving that duty to a fellow parent. Children of phantoms will be the first to drop out because their parents' apparent apathy eventually takes it toll.

So what do you do with this asylum of parental types? Don't worry—you're the coach. You'll think of something. We'll also have some ideas for you later on in this chapter that will minimize the damage from these usually well-meaning, albeit ill-mannered, adults.

Playing Tip

One of the areas we stress throughout this volume is team etiquette. It's not enough merely to master the sport. Your players also have to know how to function as a team, and a certain portion of that has to do with courtesy and the respect with which they treat themselves, their teammates, the opposition, and their coaches.

By stressing behavior and sportsmanship with them, you're subliminally creating allies, who then will show their parents the proper way to act (most of whom deep down don't want to be an embarrassment to their kids). In the end, it's one more way to stress positive behavior, both on the field and off.

Defining Your Parental Strategy

We purposely didn't offer solutions for dealing with problem parents in the afore-mentioned scenarios because no incidental reaction will be as effective as a sound strategy developed beforehand. In a way, that strategy is simply a part of the develop-mental steps you'll take to cultivate and grow your team, but will emphasize the organizational and social elements of coaching and *team management*.

This is where parent volunteers come in, and this is where it will be easiest to rein in the over-eager parents.

We said earlier that most of the people reading this volume will be volunteer coaches. That means, then, there also will be no paid staff to schlep equipment and tote lemonade for the after-practice snack. In addition to coaching your team, you also will have to build a team of parents and other adult volunteers to help you with the complex task of turning their sons and daughters into young athletes.

Time Out

Team management involves the administrative aspects of being a coach, including such mundane tasks as scheduling games, managing equipment, and otherwise making sure everything is in place to play the game.

The upside is that in most cases those who volunteer will have a vested interest—namely, offspring involved in the team—and will already be available for you to put to work, considering that they already have to haul Junior and/or Missy to practice and games. The bonus is that it can be an effective way to corral difficult adults into channeling their energy for constructive purposes. Do it right and you'll be able to chalk up a double victory.

First, Have a Plan

All effective "doing" by parents begins with planning by the coach. Here are some of the tools at your disposal:

◆ A complete schedule of games, which you will build a complete schedule of practices around. The game schedule often is provided by whatever league your team is part of. In order to accommodate all teams, the dates quickly become fixed and are not subject to the whims of individual coaches, players and, especially, parents.

Playing Tip

Twice a week tends to be the practice norm, usually after school from 4:00 to 5:30 P.M. or some similar slot. There may also be the occasional Saturday practice, but Saturdays are often game days, so frequent weekend practices may not be practical.

It's up to the coach, then, to create a schedule of practices that is sufficient to meet the needs of that roster of play and share that schedule with parents as soon as possible.

◆ A statement of coaching and team philosophy that lays out basic requirements.

Don't get too long-winded or philosophical, but say enough so parents all have the same level of understanding and feel good about your coaching "administration." In most cases, the parents don't need to approve the coach, but it sure helps to have them on your side.

A sample statement might read as follows:

> The purpose behind the Fighting Blue Devils is to give young athletes an opportunity to explore the fun and enjoyment of playing soccer while, at the same time, developing teamwork skills that will serve them in other endeavors as they grow older.

Team involvement also will help your young athlete develop strength, physical fitness, self-respect and respect for others, and sense of community. I hope you will do what you can at home to foster these skills and cultivate this growth.

Your help and assistance is greatly appreciated!

◆ The rules of play in a format convenient to consulting during practice and play (and did we mention for proving a point during discussions with parents?).

◆ A list of critical contacts to help you throughout the season. Your league contacts will be the first entries on this list—names, titles, affiliations, and telephone numbers will be important. Your soccer directory also should include any

Time Out

A good rulebook or authoritative reference is critical. We touch on virtually all you need to know in the game of soccer throughout this volume, but you'll also need a rulebook. Any good-sized bookstore will have one or more in stock.

contact info for individuals whom you may need to reach throughout the season, including the following:

◆ Groundskeepers or authorities for the field(s) you practice and play on. You'll want to know who to call in the event the field has been rained out or is unusable or another team mysteriously shows up to practice at the same time you do.

◆ Expert resources such as coaching friends and perhaps someone a little higher up in the soccer world with whom you can share ideas. You may run into problems or challenges you hadn't anticipated and it would be nice to have someone in the know to go to for advice.

◆ Any individuals or organizations who have given money to support your team. You never know when you may need more support or when the opportunity might arise to recognize and reward that support publicly.

◆ A supply source for the balls, cones, and other equipment you may need. That need could arise quicker than you might think.

◆ Complete information for all the parents, guardians, and other family members for every player you coach. You'd be surprised how many people fail to have the right information handy when a player gets hurt and needs to have a ride home or to the hospital.

◆ All appropriate emergency numbers, including ambulance services and hospital numbers. No matter how careful we are, injuries do occur, and as a coach you need to be prepared for them.

Time Out

It's not unusual to ask local businesses to sponsor sports teams. That usually involves asking the community bank, corner tavern, or even a business owned by a parent of one of the players to pay for jerseys, gear, snacks, or even league membership fees. An assertive soccer parent with good contacts in the business world will be a coach's best salesman here!

Yellow Card

Having the right tools at your disposal will be critical for the success of your team. That goes for information as well, including health information. Know what your kids' health profiles are lest you be unpleasantly surprised. Got kids with asthma? Then know that August and September will be especially difficult for them because of all the pollen in the air. Someone allergic to bee stings? Make sure you have the right first aid supplies with you and be prepared to call the EMTs if the child goes into anaphylactic shock. Knowledge is the first step toward preserving their safety. Make sure yours is complete.

Your Team's Budget

Managing your team's budget is also an important part of overall team management. We'll assume for the sake of this section that we're not talking about a group of street kids playing with a ball made from a bundle of rags. Instead, let's take the standard urban or suburban team that either has (a) a sponsoring business; (b) dues and fees that are used to offset expenses; or (c) a combination of the two. Although the amount won't be much, it should be enough working capital to see you through the season.

That income, usually delivered up front at the beginning of the season, will serve as your operating revenue. The expense side will likely include the following fixed costs:

♦ Dues, fees, and other expenses for being part of the league.

♦ Fees and costs for field rental and other facility-related costs.

♦ Balls, cones, and other basic supplies.

♦ In the case of sponsorship dollars, jerseys (at least two) and other uniform items (see Chapter 1).

♦ A first aid kit with a reasonable amount of medical supplies, including elastic bandages, cold packs, and other medical necessities.

Time Out
A simple fundraiser held some time during the season might be another source of support money.

Time Out
In addition to jerseys, which are often included as part of the team dues, players will need cleats, shorts, socks, and shin-guards. Players' parents are responsible for purchasing these items.

We describe these costs as "fixed" because (a) they are usually borne by the team and/or league "administration"; and (b) you really can't operate without them.

The variable expenses may surprise you because, in most cases, they should be considered must-haves. But if the team budget can't cover the costs, team parents might have to kick in additional funds. We chose to separate them out because you can practice and play without them. The experience won't be as pleasant, but at least it's not a ball of rags.

Yellow Card _____

Make the snacks as healthy as possible and try and avoid salty foods like chips. The salt will make players even more thirsty than they probably already are. And make sure there's always some extra for the siblings of the players who show up.

Variable expenses include …

♦ After-practice refreshments, including a noncarbonated beverage like lemonade and a high-energy snack, such as fruit or granola bars.

♦ An end-of-season banquet or pizza party.

♦ Plaques, awards, and/or certificates to recognize the contributions of each player. Usually, everyone receives something.

Drafting Your Parental "Team"

If we can make lemonade out of lemons, we can certainly make positive contributors out of difficult parents. At least that's the theory, and you'll be surprised to find how often it actually works. It may not handle all situations for you, but with the vast majority of adults on your side, the few dissenting voices likely will fade into oblivion.

There's a practical method to the madness as well. To successfully "manage" the team environment, you're going to need a "staff" of interested adults who can help execute tasks. Of course, none of them will be paid, but few will expect it and even fewer would want to be.

Volunteers can be eager and energetic while at the same time being uncontrollable and undisciplined. They can be loyal and committed, while still being ignorant of what's expected and unreliable in its execution. Volunteers have their own management challenges, and understanding them is your challenge as coach. But there are tools at your disposal that can help:

Time Out

Older siblings sometimes make enthusiastic and energetic supporters as well, sometimes functioning more effectively than parents. It's not only the number of volunteers, but who fills the positions as well. They also may be more willing to volunteer time because they have more time available.

♦ Job descriptions for each volunteer position that includes performance expectations.

♦ You guessed it! Contracts the parents sign that commit them—conceptually, at least—to the goals, objectives, and execution strategies of their kids' teams.

We touched on contracts for players and coaches in an earlier chapter. In this chapter we're going to execute one for parents as well. It could prove to be the most difficult and most effective contract of the three.

But first, let's talk about the various positions played by volunteer supporters of the kids' team. For the sake of simplicity, we will have all positions "report" either to the head coach (presumably that's you) or the team manager, who has been recruited by the coach to handle support services, such as lemonade detail.

And, given that these are volunteer positions, neither coach nor manager can afford to take too heavy a hand. But you already knew that, didn't you?

Developing Your Coaching Staff

Let's start with a position description for the person in charge of everything:

- **Head Coach**   In his or her role as leader, the head coach sets the tone for team performance and professionalism with a commitment to providing young soccer players with a learning experience that's safe, enjoyable, and worth the time and energy all present are putting into the game. For more information, see *The Complete Idiot's Guide to Coaching Youth Soccer* (ahem).

Of course, each coach needs support on the field as well. Those positions include the following:

- **Assistant Coach** (2–3 opportunities available)   Assistant coaches form the second line of command, standing in for the head coach in case of injury or illness and executing the agreed upon strategies of the coach and team. Assistant coaches may work with small groups of players or specific positions (such as midfielders or goalkeepers). Individuals with previous coaching experience are preferred, but not essential. Strong commitment, inherent athleticism, and previous experience playing team sports will suffice.

- **Line judges** (2–4 positions available)   During practice and play, line judges are the individuals who follow the team up and down the field, signaling when the ball is kicked out of bounds and identifying which team committed the foul. A keen eye and enough energy and stamina to follow players up and down the field is all that's required.

On the administrative side, the opportunities to help are no less important. Those positions include:

- **Team Manager**   In the same way the coach manages the sports efforts of the players, the team manager oversees support function and volunteer contributors who provide that support. That includes any and all functions that aren't (a) determined by league rules and decisions, and (b) not related to the developmental efforts of the sport itself. That means making sure the oranges are ready for after-practice snack and calls are made in the event a practice has been rained out. These can either be done by the manager or delegated to other volunteers. Thus, it helps if the manager is diplomatic and has some previous administrative and/or people-management experience.

- ◆ **Refreshment Captain(s)** This is a rather high-falutin' title for someone who makes sure the jugs are filled with beverages and supplies are well in hand. When the team pays, this person may have to do the shopping. When parents are responsible, this person may have to call to remind people it's their week to bring "snacks." As a rule, parents of either gender are effective in this position.

- ◆ **Gear Wrangler** This may end up the job of the manager, but someone has to be responsible for making sure the balls, cones, first aid supplies, blankets, and necessary equipment besides the food makes it to practice. This usually falls to the person with the largest mini-van or SUV.

Yellow Card

Make sure that if tasks are shared, each person knows his or her responsibility and when it needs to be executed. Then write it down, because what gets written down gets done.

- ◆ **Phone Tree Leader** Invariably, games and practices get rained out, which means calls have to be made to tell parents so they don't needlessly show up. This usually takes the form of a telephone tree that is created and managed so that each person calls just two other people, thereby sharing the responsibility and reducing the burden. One individual must be responsible for building the tree and managing the calls.

There are other tasks, but they all fall under these general categories. In the unlikely event that you have too many good volunteers, tasks can be shared among parents. Just remember that when there are too many leaders there are, in effect, no leaders.

Writing a Playing Contract with Parents

If you're reading chapters in sequence, you've already drafted two contracts—one for yourself as coach and one for your young players. Now comes the time to develop one for players' parents. And that may be the most difficult one to execute.

Some parents may see your soccer practices and games as a form of babysitting, while others know it's just what Meagan and Bennett happen to be into *this* year. That means their commitment to what you are trying to accomplish, even in the most well-meaning cases, may be secondary to other demands of life. If that distraction becomes, well, too distracting, those parents are going to start letting their kids down by not doing what they promised and failing to get their players to practice. And that lets everybody down.

That's the reason for the contract.

What you include in the contract will depend on what you want parents to do. You may or may not include the aforementioned position descriptions, knowing they won't refer to everyone. If at all possible, have a general meeting with the parents to explain the contract's concept and purpose. Some coaches prefer to do this without the players present, but having them there hearing their parents agree to support their sports efforts can be extremely valuable, building a new bond between parent and child.

Time Out
Like the contract with the players, it should be to-the-point. Kids won't do something for which they see no value in the outcome. The same goes for parents.

No matter what else you put in your contract, you'll definitely want parents to do the following:

- ◆ Commit to supporting the child's participation in the team throughout the entire season. That includes providing the proper gear and making sure kids get to all practices and games.

- ◆ Commit to improving the child's ability through support of a healthy lifestyle. That includes proper nutrition, limited junk food, no alcohol or tobacco, proper warm ups and exercise—including skills practice if possible—and the right amount of sleep every night. Ask parents to support that commitment by modeling this behavior themselves.

- ◆ Help the child learn the value of teamwork, good sportsmanship, and a winning attitude. These will do more to promote the game among young athletes than most of the other exercises combined. Once again, modeling good behavior will be critical to success.

- ◆ If possible, make yourself available for one of the volunteer positions. At the very least, make provisions that the child can get to practice and game regularly and in a timely manner.

- ◆ Even if you have no interest in soccer whatsoever—hard to believe, we know—be positive about the experience and understand its overall developmental value to the young athlete and his or her future.

A parent would be hard-pressed to find reason not to sign such a document. Some will fail to either sign or observe the tenets of the contract. But just by asking them to read it, you've made it clear to them what youth soccer is all about.

The Least You Need to Know

- Soccer parents' bad behavior is sometimes no more than misdirected efforts to support their kids. Savvy coaches can harness that energy and make good use of it.

- In addition to being coached, teams also must be managed, and that's where parental volunteers can be put to good use.

- Tools like schedules, a coaching philosophy, and a digest of soccer rules all help bring order to the chaos.

- Budget team resources to cover the basics and as many additional costs as possible. Parents may have to make up the rest.

- Opportunities exist on both the coaching and administrative side for parents to make a difference.

- Signing parents to a simple "contract" is an effective way to get them to commit the necessary support for their kids' successful participation.

Part 2

Training Daze

As with any sport, the key to success comes down to three words: training, training, and training. The purpose of training, of course, is (a) conditioning, (b) skills mastery, and (c) the ability to respond to situations that arise without having to think, "Now, what is it I should be doing?"

That may sound a little daunting when it comes to youth sports, but it doesn't have to be and, in fact, it shouldn't be. Playing youth soccer is just that—play—and kids like to play. If you've guided them effectively, then practice becomes play and, since play is what they like to do, then getting them to practice shouldn't be a problem.

Of course, getting them to do things right may be another matter entirely. That's what this section is about and that's what we'll concentrate on for the next five chapters. It's not always easy, but it certainly isn't impossible and can be very enjoyable.

The Four Pillars of Soccer Wisdom

In This Chapter

- ◆ The philosophy of play
- ◆ The philosophy of sports
- ◆ Defining the four pillars
- ◆ Technical aspects of play
- ◆ Tactical mastery of the game
- ◆ Psychological characteristics of performance
- ◆ Physical traits of the players

A lot of coaches get by without delving too deeply into the guiding principles behind what they're doing. They're content to rely on a playbook they've cobbled together from things they've seen and read, hoping that the talent on their team is good enough to help bridge the conceptual gaps they overlooked. For some, that approach is more than enough; for us, however, it doesn't quite cut it.

The sport of soccer is built upon key elements—a philosophical foundation. Sure, you can go a long way just by kicking a ball around, but if you want to excel, you must know and appreciate that there's more to the sport than that.

The purpose of this chapter is to explore what that "more" is in ways that you can put to good use. Call this chapter, "The Philosophy of Soccer" if you like. It forms the foundation for the next section of the book and, like it or not, for all the games you choose either to play or coach from this point forward.

The Philosophy of Play

Next time you're near a field of kids at play—it doesn't have to be soccer and, in fact, maybe it shouldn't be—step back and watch the action as if you were a scientist examining creatures in their own habitat. The younger the kids, the more naturally they play, the freer and less inhibited their movement. Few adults can watch kids at play and not want to shed their burdens and join them. Fewer still understand what they're really seeing and why they're yearning for it.

As adults we longingly watch kids at play, not because we want to be gangly, pimply youths who don't know which end is up. We watch those kids because we want to be able to let go of all our cares and simply act and react. We don't want to worry about what the right thing to do is, or what others will think of us. And we want this primarily because we know that, in the balance of it all, that's how we were designed to operate in the first place.

The lure of play is escape, of course, but it's less of an escape *from* something—a job, a task or anything else pulling on our time and energies—and more of an escape *to* something—to pure pleasure and fulfillment. Kids know this, but they eventually lose this knowledge as adults train it out of them, conditioning them with a task (your job) and reward (your paycheck) system.

If there's a higher purpose to your coaching—your own philosophy, if you will—it's to understand and appreciate the purpose of play. Creating a strategy and executing moves (your job) that allow you to score points and win the game and perhaps the championship (your reward) is important, but so is the act of simply *playing* the game.

Make that part of your coaching philosophy. It's more important than you think.

The most important thing to remember, as we launch into the chapters devoted to skills training and development, is that we must preserve the aspect of play for kids. Kids first learn to "play soccer" not because of the "soccer" part, but because of the "play" part. Play already is something they know how to do. It's the soccer part that it's up to you to teach, but never at the cost of sacrificing play.

Make the credo for your youth soccer team the same one that many coaches use, one that's well known in the sport:

> We lost. We won. Either way, we had fun.

Sounds a little like the chorus to a camp song, doesn't it? Nevertheless, it makes the point clear: Above all, have fun.

Keep play at the heart of soccer and you'll have an enthusiastic, joyful team. Since attitude is the key to success in anything, a joyful team quickly becomes a winning team. And that makes everyone happy.

Time Out
Some people say I'm the best [female] soccer player in the world. I don't think so and because of that some day I might be.   —Mia Hamm, the best female soccer player in the world

The Philosophy of Sports

Why do we go out there to run, kick, yell, sweat, and take a chance on injury when we know we don't have to? Sport makes play acceptable for adults. Sports have more rules than straight play, of course, and humankind has found ways to make obscene amounts of money at it, but sport has its basis in play nonetheless. Positive results include the following:

Sports level the social playing field.

Sure, every team has coaches and every game referees to tell you what you're doing wrong. Each team has a captain, but that person is rarely empowered to hire and fire other players. Instead, the players learn to rely on each other, based not on rank but on skills. In terms of a social fabric, each person has a designated job that only he or she is empowered to do at any one time. The person must perform that task or risk jeopardizing everyone else on the team.

Sports let us get physical.

Running and yelling, doing things that are physical first and intellectual second (or maybe third) is rare in polite society if it doesn't fall into an organized framework in pursuit of a specific goal. Sports provide that outlet for athletes of all ages. That, in fact, is a large part of its appeal.

Time Out

In the West, at least, most of us lead sedentary lifestyles tied to computers, cash registers, or other forms of technology. Even those who do engage in physical labor find themselves armed with power tools, if only to save the company time and man-hours. We don't have the chance to develop the lung capacity and instinctual eye-hand coordination that saved the lives of our ancestors and for which our bodies really were designed. Sports are a socially acceptable substitute for that missing link in our development, which is another reason for its popularity.

Sports cultivate self-esteem.

As kids and adults learn skills and become healthier and more joyous, they develop greater self-esteem, which gives them more self-confidence. At the same time, their success as the member of a goal-directed social organization—the team—gives them the social graces and personality that make better members of society. All of this is a very, very good thing.

Sports cultivate self-fulfillment.

There's an inner benefit—one that's difficult to articulate—that comes with sports participation. It's a self-awareness and, in the best cases, a sense of wholeness. Perhaps it's a matter of completing the intellectual-emotional-spiritual-physical loop that so many of us don't have the opportunity to do in today's automated society. Or maybe it's something more. Either way, there's an internal benefit, a form of fulfillment that comes through participation that's part of the activity's philosophical underpinnings.

And that's enough philosophy for anyone.

Time Out

As long as you're coaching youth soccer, you'll never really have the chance to communicate the soccer philosophy to your young charges. They will be too busy enjoying the game to sit back and think deep thoughts. You'll have to do it for them. And you do this by preserving, supporting, and pursuing the philosophical principles behind the sport and making sure that those who don't understand don't get in the way of the real purpose of the game.

Defining the Four Pillars of Soccer

This section is devoted to what we call the four pillars of soccer, and the rest of this chapter will be spent defining them, setting the stage for what's to come in the next four or five chapters. Don't worry. The heavy stuff soon will be over.

What's important in any philosophy is the application of its principles. It's less important what you believe in than it is how you act on that belief and how the principles behind that particular school of thought guide your daily life or, in this case, your soccer life. If you understand and accept the principles, then you stand a better chance of mastering the skills you need as coach and that your athletes need as players.

Here are the pillars on which you should build your coaching program. We'll get into the particulars in greater detail in future chapters. Consider this part an introduction.

Technical Aspects of Play

Any athlete at any level knows you have to understand and practice the technical aspects of the sport in order to succeed. This includes technical superiority in skills and judgment, as well as the ability to execute positions, plays, and performance at the best level possible.

The mastery of technical aspects of play—what the rest of this book is devoted to—is the foundation on which performance is built. And performance consists of the following elements:

- Technical mastery of the necessary performance skills.

- Instinctual judgment regarding when to apply those skills.

- Ability to perform those skills in such a way so as to enhance and complement, rather than restrict and compromise, the performance of team mates.

- Capability to augment and evolve those skills so they advance as needed by the player's age and by the growing skills of the team.

Technical mastery extends to the coach as well and becomes an even heavier burden when you consider the coach has to be a master of sorts of every position and under every condition. His or her skill needs include all of the above as well as an additional set of requirements that include:

- Extensive knowledge of the game and the ability to answer questions that may be raised.

- An understanding of each of the positions and how they interact on the field.

- The application of coaching skills and the responsibilities that come with them.

- Knowledge and ability to execute or assign the myriad administrative details that come with running a team.

Upcoming chapters will offer a lot more information along these lines. Be prepared to take notes.

Playing Tip _____

There's a wonderful line in the film *Chariots of Fire*—arguably the best sports film ever made—that's uttered by a coach to one of his runners: "You can't put in what God's left out." Most coaches feel that way about their young athletes, some of whom simply shouldn't be there. The genius in coaching comes in finding ways to augment those shortcomings and provide a beneficial experience, no matter what the natural ability of the athlete, for all the reasons mentioned so far. That's the heart of your job as coach.

Tactical Mastery of the Game

If technical aspects of play are ultimately up to the players, then tactical mastery of the game is usually left to the coach. Of course, as players mature, they can shift tactics and strategies as the situation warrants. But especially for younger kids, strategy and tactics become almost the sole responsibility of the coach.

The game of soccer consists of the following tactical situations:

◆ The opposing strategies as designed by the coaches and players of the two teams on the field.

◆ The tactical skills of the players in an attempt to execute those strategies.

◆ The field set-up of forwards, midfielders and defensive players and how effectively those positions are played.

◆ The random circumstances that result when the two strategies come together at tactical points of play.

Tactics are the means by which strategies are executed and goals are accomplished. And just like any battle plans, there must be flexibility or at least the painful recognition that A + B doesn't always equal C. You want to score goals. The opposing team doesn't want you to score; moreover, they want to score goals against you. The struggle that results is called soccer.

When it comes to strategic execution, the successful team plays the opportunities that lie in between the two teams' strategies. It's a "run between the raindrops," if you will, in which well-trained players see opportunities that arise and take advantage of them. Good tactics are designed to create such opportunities, and sometimes that even works. Many times, however, holes in the other team's defensive fabric occur spontaneously and well-trained players are able to take advantage of them.

That means mastery of tactics operates at two levels:

♦ Developing strategies and tactics that will result in the opportunities to score goals.

♦ Developing the ability to adapt to changes and opportunities on the field, which will also result in the opportunity to score goals.

As the youth coach, you have the wonderful opportunity to integrate tactics and techniques into the practice plan. In many practice exercises, you can work on tactics and techniques at the same time—without the need for any long-winded explanations. For example, develop a game with six goals that players must dribble through to score a point. This will force them to dribble quickly and possibly change directions when finding one goal to be blocked they can go to the most open goal.

For very young teams, such games may be challenging. But as teams—and their coaches—mature in skills and abilities, activity and play can be successfully augmented by strategies and tactics to bring even greater value to the athletes and others involved with the team.

Playing Tip

It was Henry Ford who said, "Whether you think you can or you think you can't, you're right." No team can win if it doesn't believe with all its heart that it will win and then plays to make that happen. Learning a winning attitude is as critical as learning the right moves.

The Psychological Characteristics of Performance

There are no such things as born winners or, for that matter, born losers. But there is such a thing as having the right attitude in order to succeed. That's true of anything, of course, but is absolutely critical in sports.

Think of the times you've watched a sporting match in person or on TV—any sport will do but American football probably has the most frequent examples—and the tables turn in the last minutes or even seconds of the game. A team comes from behind, sometimes through the execution of sound strategies but more often due to errors made by the other team or unusual and unanticipated circumstances that allow the underdog to seize control and win the day. They're able to do this for no reason other than they had the right attitude and brought it to bear when they needed it most.

Knowing how to play the game, understanding and pursuing the right strategic and tactical approach, and then being conditioned to perform (we'll get to that one in a moment) are all critical elements to success. Failing to understand the psychological characteristics of performance and embrace the right attitude can seriously undermine success at all those other levels. The team that wins believes it can win. The team that believes it will lose usually doesn't have a chance.

The psychology of soccer players is as complex as that of anyone else, and coaches of all age groups constantly battle personal fears, bad habits, self-esteem issues and a host of other human characteristics that have the ability to undermine success. Several characteristics stand out as being especially critical to success when it comes to sports:

♦ A teams wins because they enter the field believing they will. Players will work harder if they believe the end result of those efforts will be success. Those who don't believe they'll win are just marking time on the field and shouldn't play.

♦ A team wins because individual players do their best in support of their team and the team, in turns, operates in support of individual efforts. That's called team psychology, and no team will be successful if one or more players think everything rests only with them and operates accordingly.

♦ A team wins because individual players believe in themselves and their abilities. Team success must come first, but teams are made up of individuals, each of whom plays a critical role. Players confident in their own skills and abilities will create a team successful in its efforts. That, too, is the result of training and attitude.

♦ A team wins because the coach believes it will and the team, in turn, believes the coach can help make victory happen. As coach, you're one of the largest and strongest links in the chain, or should be. Your influence exceeds that of all others including, in many cases, players' parents, teachers and friends. Don't make the mistake of taking that responsibility lightly. Just about everything you say and do has an impact.

Time Out

Just about anyone you talk to will tell you that the Green Bay Packers' recent years of success are due mostly to quarterback Brett Favre. And if Favre were honest, he might admit to feeling like he was carrying more than his share of responsibility. Yet Favre never plays like anything other than a member of that team. That recognition and commitment strengthens the team fabric, making all of them play a little better. That's what makes teamwork an important psychological factor to success.

Physical Traits of the Players and Their Efforts

Think of any discipline you like, from sports to art to music, and you will quickly realize that the seeds of success are found in practice, practice, and more practice. "How do you get to Carnegie Hall?" the old musicians' joke goes. "Practice, man, practice." The same is true for soccer.

In Chapter 11, we'll talk at length about how to condition young players, what to do and what not to do, what to expect in terms of performance and what to forget about. Right now, however, we're going to talk more broadly about conditioning and training as it relates to performance. Like the other three pillars, without this crucial element, there is no hope of success.

Professional teams practice five times as much as they play, if not more. There are several reasons for this:

◆ Players need to be in condition to play. Their bodies need to build up the stamina to withstand 90 minutes of constant running, kicking, and other forms of physical exertion.

◆ They need to be steeped in the technical skills of their position with the ability to execute them without thinking about them while at a full-tilt run.

◆ They need to be trained to such a fine level that they're capable of making instantaneous changes in plans as opportunities present themselves. Knowledge of the need to make those changes has to come from within; they don't have time to step back and weigh the pros and cons.

◆ They need to be sufficiently conditioned so the extended conflict of play doesn't result in illness or injury. In cases when it does, their general health must be such so as to speed recovery, both for their own good and that of the team.

◆ Finally, their conditioning must be sufficient so that playing soccer enhances rather than inhibits the other aspects of their lives. If the rest of their day and week after a game is spent recovering from the effort of play, then they need to be in better shape.

As a volunteer coach, or even if you coach a high school or college team, you have limited ability to monitor their lifestyles. You can make suggestions or perhaps even demands of parents or older athletes in regards to maintaining a healthy lifestyle. In the end, however, your influence may extend only so far as the field. Providing the right guidelines and monitoring performance so that it cultivates good habits while driving bad habits out is important. In this case, doing your best may have to be good enough.

We'll explore each of these at length in future chapters. For right now, let this be your guide as we move to the more technical chapters and skills development.

The Least You Need to Know

- ◆ Understanding the philosophy of soccer, or any sport, aids in your ability to coach that sport effectively.

- ◆ Creating a coaching strategy that understands, appreciates, and rewards the aspects of play in soccer, not just the ability to score points.

- ◆ Both players and coaches need a comprehensive understanding of the technical aspects of play and how to execute skills intrinsically.

- ◆ If technical aspects of play manifest most evidently with the players, then tactical mastery of the game is usually left to the coach to engineer.

- ◆ A team must believe it can win to be successful.

- ◆ Player conditioning and practice are essential to team success. Players unfit to play will compromise the rest of the team and its efforts.

Chapter 8

Principles of Play and Practice Design

In This Chapter

- ◆ Planning your practice
- ◆ How practice is organized
- ◆ Scenarios for success
- ◆ Getting ready for game day

To this point we've discussed a variety of basic elements to set the stage for your coaching efforts. We've labored long and hard discussing proper coaching technique, although not as long and hard as you will labor throughout the actual season exercising that technique. At this point you should be ready to hit the field with your soccer balls, cones, whistles, playbooks, ice packs, parental "helpers," and gaggle of eager young players.

So, there you are. Now what?

In this chapter, we're going to outline the format of some actual practices to get you set on the right course of action. There are many ways to practice, and sometimes you just want to keep things simple and fun. That's okay as long as you don't neglect the actual training you're obligated to do. Your young athletes should come out of the other end of this more knowledge-able about and skilful in the sport of soccer than they were when they arrived.

Plan, Then Practice

For most coaches, soccer has two seasons. (Sometimes it's three seasons if you include indoor soccer, but that's often with a different group of kids.) In many cases, it's two halves of the same season. There is a fall half and spring half, with just enough time in between for young players to lose their edge.

In most cases, there are 10 to 12 games per seasonal half. You should practice twice as often as you play in a game. More practices would be better, but probably won't be practical either for the coaches or team members. If your team regularly plays on Saturday mornings, you may want to schedule practices on Tuesdays and Thursdays after school. That way, they'll have regular exposure to soccer with time to rest in between. The actual practice time will depend on when school lets out and when team members can make it.

 Yellow Card _____

No matter how young or how experienced your players are, warm ups and stretching exercises are critical to safe practice and play. Fail to warm up your team and they risk stiffness, even injury when they try to exert themselves. Young kids, especially, hate the idea of warming up, and coaches get tired of prodding them. Make it into a game and identify each exercise with an animal and you may have better luck stretching those young muscles and avoiding injury.

Once you establish a practice time, create a practice schedule and put one into the hands of every player and every parent. Youth players, especially, likely won't make it to practice under their own steam, which means parents or older siblings will have to bring them. They'll need to know when and where if you expect the players to show up.

Time Out

Practice and game time also may depend on when the field is available. A youth hockey coach we knew had to practice his team at 6 A.M. twice a week because the rink was so crowded. We hope you won't face similar rigors in scheduling your practices.

With the exception of inclement weather—and then only to the degree that it makes the field unusable—practice times have to be firm. Not every player will be able to make it every time, but you and your coaching assistants will. That puts a burden on you, of course, but presumably you have the time to make the commitment to the sport. Your attendance will be mandatory.

If someone else is responsible for hauling the equipment, that person will have to be there, too. Otherwise, you also get to be the cone roadie.

Taking a practice break around mid-season might be a good idea to give everyone a needed break—coaches, parents, and especially players.

Playing Tip

Consider assigning practice "homework," especially during your mid-season practice break and between seasons, to keep players sharp and motivated. Homework can include dribbling the length of the backyard several times or chipping into a plastic bucket.

Building a solid team that creates a positive experience for its players is the best way to ensure continued participation. If the kids want to come, Mom or Dad will bring them. They all have to care about the experience, but you have to be the one to care the most. Your commitment and enthusiasm will be contagious, resulting in a good response from your players.

Designing the Practice

Practices generally begin when the coach's whistle sounds and end when he or she dismisses the players for the day. In between quite a few things happen that should be plotted out in a logical fashion and over which the coach must exercise control. We've already talked about having a seasonal plan. Later on we'll talk about developing the right strategic and tactical game plans. But you should also design your practice plan to make the most out of the limited time the team has together to practice.

A lot needs to be accomplished during those practices, and there never seems to be enough time to do everything you want to. Rather than over-plan and then fail to do what you set out to do, pick one or two specific things to work on and concentrate on them. If you try to do too much, then you'll diffuse and confuse the effort and not accomplish anything.

In the following sections, we explain two practice schemes you can follow. Both serve different needs and can be used to develop your own models. Steps 1 through 3 are the same for both plans. From step 4 on, the plans vary based on what you want to practice that day.

Time Out
Just as teachers have lesson plans, coaches need practice plans.

Playing Tip _____

Practices need to be structured and designed to teach the skills necessary to make both players and the team successful. For the first practice of the season, however, it's enough just to kick the ball around and have some fun. The kids need to become comfortable with the concepts of the game and you as coach, not to mention each other. Stress the fun part of the game and allow them to get a little familiar with what's coming up in the weeks ahead. That will be effort enough for the first time out.

1. Pre-Practice Activity (10–15 Minutes)

Kids will arrive at practices at different times. Rather than have the early arrivers stand around and wait for everyone else, have something for them to do. If you don't they'll find their own means of occupying themselves, which is a potential coaching opportunity gone to waste.

Such activities could include setting up the cones or hauling gear from the car or van of whomever is carrying it. Kids will enjoy doing these things, and it will make them feel useful. It also may be a good way to get shy or inexperienced kids more involved.

You might also begin with an early practice of the skills you're stressing that day, or reviewing from the previous practice. Since the kids won't have warmed up, whatever they do will have to be done at an easy level.

Playing Tip _____

One way to coax players to arrive earlier might be to allow a little two-on-two or three-on-three game. If you have a capable assistant who could work with the small group, so much the better. It's an excellent way to promote skills development as well as get a little more of the fun part of practice. It shouldn't be anything too aggressive, mind you, but something to get them energized.

This part of practice will last as long as it needs to, but probably will run in the range of 10 to 15 minutes.

2. Coach's Introduction and Practice Concept Discussion (About 5 Minutes)

Kids learn best when they're given a routine to follow. That consistency can help them build a greater comfort level and enables them to learn more effectively. To that end, each practice should start with the coach's introduction and brief discussion to set the tone for the day's practice.

You can use the time to share information about upcoming events, to talk about areas that need work, or to set the stage for the day's practice. Never skip this step—it gives an official feel to the practice and establishes your authority and leadership for the next hour or so.

Time Out

If you have critical information to share—schedule changes, for example—this information will have to be communicated to those who don't make it to practice.

3. Warm Ups and Stretches (About 10 Minutes)

The secret to a successful warm up is to make it fun!

You can start with leg stretches, jumping jacks, and other familiar forms so the players feel like they've "worked out." This also is the time you may want to practice a few drills that promote teamwork as well as raise their heart rates. Be careful not to confuse this with skills training. No matter how you couch it, this always should be presented as a warm-up activity that is fun as much as it is anything else. (See Chapter 10 for some exercise ideas.)

From this point, practice can take one of two basic directions:

Practice A: Skills Development

As the name implies, this is designed to allow players to practice dribbling, passing, or any other skills they need to concentrate on. Try the following regimen:

Small Group Exercises (15 Minutes)

Team exercises and activities are often most effective when they start with small groups. There are fewer people, which gives many kids the sense they can master these exercises more effectively. And indeed they can, if only because the "team" exercise often is brought down to the smallest possible combination, namely one-on-one drills and exercises.

The practice of set-up drills and tactical strategies also can be effectively managed with small group sessions. Passing skills can be combined with shooting on the goal, for

Playing Tip

Bringing two players together to practice dribbling, passing, or some other drill can be very effective when the two serve as a mutual support system and help each other learn to perform more effectively. Pairing a novice with an experienced player may be an excellent way for one to mentor the other and, in turn, learn more about the skill by having to teach it.

example, as the same group of players repeat the exercise in rotating fashion, each playing another position in the formation so they can get the feel of what's required from each part of the set up.

While small groups can be ideal ways to learn certain aspects of the game, care should be taken to combine them with larger group exercises that are a more realistic part of the game. Not every player or group of players has to practice the same skill at the same time, but everyone should become familiar with all the varieties drills and techniques.

Coaches and their assistants should make themselves available to guide the players as they practice. That may involve moving among the groups or working with a certain group attempting to master skills they may find challenging. Sometimes the coach has to be everywhere at once, but that's something you're probably getting used to.

Larger Group Exercises (15 Minutes)

Team exercises give all players the chance to interact. This, of course, more closely replicates the challenges of a real game, but also can be seen as a developmental opportunity to broaden the skills everyone just practiced in small groups.

Large groups can consist of smaller groups put together like pieces of a puzzle, with each group practicing some aspect in the larger arena. If each group was practicing the same thing, they may take turns doing what they learned in a broader, more team-like environment.

The larger groups tend to function best when the emphasis is on team development or more strategic activities, once again because it comes closer to more realistically replicating the game scenario.

Practice B: Playing the Game

Once again, the coach's introduction and warm-up exercises precede this type of practice, which is focused on skills development and strategy in a more realistic setting.

Playing a Mock Game (15 Minutes)

Just like it sounds, the group is divided into two teams to play a game against one another. The coach blows the whistle and the teams compete just like they would on game day.

As a training exercise, what you observe during the game will set the stage for the next portion of the exercise. You and your assistants should keep a keen eye open for areas of weakness and things that the team is doing wrong—or perhaps not doing at all—for review during the next segment or practice. Also note what the team is doing right and where strengths lie. You should discuss strengths and weaknesses with the team during evaluation period, but these observations will also help you devise appropriate game-day strategies.

Sometimes it's okay to let things pass. Other times, you may want to whistle practice to a halt and offer special session on some skill that appears lacking, complete with drills and special emphasis. Do so constructively, not punitively, and turn a problem into a coaching opportunity.

> **Time Out**
>
> During mock games, you'll want to have teams wear different colored shirts so players can identify their teammates.

Reviewing the Game Results (15 Minutes)

Once the game is over, the coaching staff should sit down with the team and evaluate it. Strengths and weaknesses both should be evaluated and skills and abilities should be identified as well as areas in need of improvement.

For the sake of simplicity, focus on no more than two key areas in need of improvement. Anything more than that, and the lessons won't stick, not to mention generating a potential drop in morale.

Wrap up the group evaluation with a few specific areas that need to be worked on in the near future as well as a few strengths.

> **Yellow Card**
>
> Care should be taken not to embarrass any players. Rather than blame players, think of team or player weaknesses as areas where you, as coach, may not have done as good a job coaching the team as you could have.

Play the Game Again (10 to 15 Minutes)

This time around, those areas of strength and weakness should be observed even more closely to see what, if anything, players have done to correct shortfalls and build on existing strengths.

Under ideal circumstances, of course, there should be signs of progress or at least attempts in that direction. Of course, that doesn't always happen, indicating a need for more practice.

Cool Down and Wrap Up (10 Minutes)

No matter which scenario you choose to follow—drills or a practice game—the final step should be a cool down period followed by a wrap up activity.

Time Out

Effective coaches have separate folders with different practice plans and strategies tucked away inside. Another folder will contain actual play strategies. The contents may be at times interchangeable, but the folders help the coach organize thoughts, ideas, and plans.

Despite the fact that the kids have been running for the past hour, many coaches have their team take a lap around the field. This is less important for its aerobic benefit than it is for tying up the practice for the day.

Teams may also chant the team chant or sing the team song, if they have one, again closing practice and promoting team spirit. This last bit is more valuable than you might realize because players need to carry that spirit with them wherever they go so they don't have to recreate it with each and every practice or play date. The last thing you want to do with something as important as team spirit is start over every time.

It's Game Day!

Game day is the time it should all come together. This is where the strategies that have been built around practices all week come to play. This is where the coaching staff can see the benefit of all their and the team's hard work.

Stress positive thoughts and offer encouragement prior to and throughout the game. Part of what you're coaching is their spirit, their drive, and abilities in the face to opposition.

Don't forget to show team spirit by repeating your chants and songs, pep talks and cheering. There's a good chance players might be nervous, and such activities will help them relax. Make sure that the team is warmed up and confident. Sure, they may be nervous, but if they believe in themselves, that's a big first step to victory. And that, of course, is what game day is all about.

The Least You Need to Know

- The more carefully you design your practice, the more value that practice will have for you and your players.

- Make play a part of your practice. In fact, play may be the most important thing you do during that first practice.

- Warming up before practice is critical to enhancing performance and reducing injuries.

- Scheduling practice days and times and sticking to that schedule is important.

- No matter which practice methodology you follow, open each session with an introduction and directions from the coach and warm-up sessions.

- When it comes to game day, emphasize team-building activities like songs and chants to maximize the comfort level and build team spirit.

Chapter 9

Tools of the Players' Trade and How to Teach Them

In This Chapter

- ◆ Soccer's fundamental moves
- ◆ Learning the skills
- ◆ Dribbling
- ◆ Passing and receiving
- ◆ Juggling the ball
- ◆ Heading the ball
- ◆ Shooting the goal

Soccer is a game that relies on skills, strategies, and knowledge. So far, we've spent a lot of time concentrating on your skills as coach, offering advice on how to approach the world's greatest sport, how to prepare yourself as coach, and the steps to take to get ready to teach the game to players of varying ages.

Now that you know *how* to coach and teach soccer, it's time to focus on *what* to teach. There are distinct skills involved that players need to practice to be successful. In this chapter we're going to look at the foundation skills and how you might best teach them to your players and coach them in their use.

The fundamentals of soccer are simple. Only so many steps are needed to master the dribbling, passing, kicking, and heading that go into making a good soccer player. Once players understand those steps, it all boils down to practice, practice, and more practice. There's no way around it. That's how athletes of any age master a sport, and that's what your team members will have to do as well.

But when it comes to soccer, practice not only comes closer to making perfect, it also can be the most enjoyable part of the game.

The Fundamentals of Teaching Fundamentals

Because soccer skills are not complex and, outside of advanced strategies, there aren't that many of them to learn, they should be easy to teach, right?

Yellow Card _____

Unless you're the goal-keeper, never, ever touch the soccer ball with any part of your hands or arms. You already know this, of course, and most of your players will, too. However, that should be the *first* instruction you give to young players. Make them stick to that rule regardless of what happens.

Not necessarily. Unless you take the right developmental approach, you can turn kids off to soccer quickly and permanently. Patience is the key here. And practice. Remember that as coach you are guiding their development. That means you have to do whatever it takes to bring them along and help them advance their skills. Push too hard or too fast and you will lose them for good. And that's not good.

Even though you'll ultimately tailor your approach to variables such as the players' ages and the conditions, it will still boil down to communicating with your players on an intellectual, emotional, and physical level:

◆ Players have to be able to understand what it is the coach is trying to say. In order to learn how to head the ball, for example, they must first know what heading is.

◆ Players have to be emotionally prepared to accept direction and perform the task. Because of its nature, heading the ball is intimidating to many inexperienced players who fear getting injured. The coach must overcome that fear in order to teach the skill.

◆ Players have to perform the task so they understand how the action relates to them physically and can build a sensual "memory," if you will, of how the task feels. Once players are taught how to head the ball, for example, they're less likely to fear the move because they have a series of sensual memories showing them that heading can be done without sustaining injury.

In order to reach your players on all three levels, follow these steps:

1. Describe the activity and its purpose within the game. Dribbling in soccer means something different than dribbling in basketball, but both are designed to advance the ball downfield. Tell this to the players.

2. Demonstrate the technique in slow motion with commentary, when appropriate, that again describes the action and its purpose. The visual impression reinforces the earlier description of the task, allowing players to relate and learn on two critical levels.

3. Have players to try the task themselves. This is crucial, because the players will need to be able perform this skill during scrimmages and games. Skills drills should be nonthreatening and supportive. This will be where players will measure their relative level of coordination and skill against your instructions.

   While players are practicing, look for overall trends that show whether they understand what they've been asked to do and whether they know how to do it. You should be able to tell quickly if your coaching has had the desired impact.

4. Review the process and demonstrate the technique again. By observing players, you will know which aspect of the skill needs to be stressed further. In the case of dribbling, perhaps ball control is an issue. Or maybe the balls are well under control, but the players aren't making any progress. Address these issues and repeat your demonstration of the proper way to perform the skill.

   The second demonstration may at first seem redundant. In reality, it may be even more valuable, especially for a novice player who now better understands what it feels like to perform the task and what his or her particular challenge may be in performing it well. The coach should be prepared to answer questions about the task.

Time Out

As your players train, remember to focus on incremental growth in skills mastery. Small steps are easier to take, especially for younger players. Incremental growth will do a better job of improving performance as well as maintaining spirit and enthusiasm for the game. One skill—or even one part of one skill—should be the focus of developmental practices.

5. Allow players to try the drill again. If they seem to be doing well, you may try firing commands at them during the execution of the drill. If they're still struggling, then you may have to repeat the process several more times over future practices, knowing this is an area where either the team or individual players need more work.

You may also want to make a certain skill a home practice assignment and suggest they work on the skill in their backyards, at the nearby park, or some other place outside of the formal practice. The better prepared they are when they come to practice and play, of course, the more valuable that practice and play will be. Stressing outside work—within reasonable expectations, of course—is one way to improve performance.

Learning the Skills

The balance of this chapter will focus on the five foundational skills of soccer: dribbling; passing and receiving; mastering ball control, also known as juggling; heading the ball; and shooting the goal. This skill set forms the foundation for most players on your team.

At this point we won't consider goalkeeping skills, which will get a chapter to themselves later on (see Chapter 15). For now, however, let's look at the skills that all players—including the goalkeeper—need to master for effective play.

Playing Tip

One way to start practice, especially for young players, is to have them assume the "ready to play" position. It's a stance similar to that used in many other sports—the feet are shoulder width apart, the legs slightly bent and the body leaning slightly forward, as if ready to leap.

The stance is no more than a centering technique, in which the players use their bodies to help clear their minds and make them ready for your direction and instruction. Experienced players tend to come by it naturally, but younger ones need to be told to do it. Just like your whistle, it will help them concentrate on the task at hand

Dribbling

If there's any skill that is a foundation move in soccer, the one around which all other action revolves, it's dribbling. Players unable to execute this skill really shouldn't be on the field because they likely won't be able to do anything else, either.

As we said earlier, dribbling means something different in basketball than its does in soccer, but it's used to do the same thing—move the ball downfield (or down court in basketball) toward the opponent's goal with the objective of setting up a shot to score.

Novice players think dribbling is generally about covering ground and will kick the ball far ahead of themselves, convinced they're dribbling. Covering ground is important, but controlling and keeping possession of the ball is more critical. Dribbling far downfield, only to lose possession of the ball and have it come right back toward your goal, is not an accomplishment. Dribbling slowly and confidently with an eye toward setting up a shot that will score a goal is really what good dribbling is about.

Playing Tip

In addition to moving toward the opponent's goal, a player uses the dribble to move the ball away from his or her own goal, making dribbling a defensive as well as offensive action.

Time Out

Young players just learning the sport will look down at their feet to make sure they're dribbling correctly. The sooner you get them comfortable enough so they look up and pay attention to where they're going while they dribble, the sooner they will perform more confidently and fluidly.

Two things need to be stressed when teaching dribbling:

◆ Ball control is accomplished primarily by foot position. Hitting the ball gently with the instep or top of the foot is a good way to move the ball forward and allows the player to exercise control because the ball moves in line with the body, forming a link between player and ball.

Some players use the insides of their feet, which may or may not be effective depending on the player's capability and sophistication. In that case, foot position becomes more critical and control more tenuous. Still, those able to manage control with the insides—and sometimes the outsides—of their feet have more options open to them when it comes to dribbling or passing.

◆ The dribbler's proximity to the ball also determines the relative amount of control. Novice players like to kick the ball hard, then run to catch up with it as if they're the only players on the field. The opposition will tune into this technique rather quickly and usually will have one of its own receivers waiting to take the ball away.

The ball should be about a yard away from the controller's kicking foot at all times. Such proximity makes it harder for the opposition to take the ball away, which is something they always will try to do. If the ball is too close, the dribbler can lose control by over-running the ball, leaving it open behind him or her or tangled up in the dribbler's feet. In both cases, this opens opportunities for the opposition to seize control of the ball and take it in the other direction.

The basic dribble: Players kick the ball ahead of them, being careful to keep the ball within their reach and control while moving as swiftly as possible behind it. Good dribblers are quick, agile, and always in control.

Take It Step by Step—Literally!

Dribbling is best taught incrementally, like any other skills, with increasingly advanced challenges and obstacles put in a players' way. For young players, learning how to dribble and maintain control is enough for the first few lessons. Obstacles can be added gradually as skills improve. But don't add them too gradually, otherwise that first game encounter will be enough to end their soccer career before it starts.

Having players dribble the ball downfield without opposition more than a few times is not a good way to teach the skill because it's not realistic. It also fails to teach the player that maintaining control while turning to avoid opposition is what real dribbling is about. Dribbling around stationary objects—pylons, cones, even other players—is a good way to practice control.

Playing Tip

Dribblers can become intimidated by having to face the entire field as they attempt to move toward the opposing goal. Conversely, they can become so fixed on their own small space that they may fail to see obstacles ahead of them. Encouraging your players to divide the field in quadrants, or at least thirds. Smaller sections of the field, just like smaller bites, will be easier for them to swallow. Moving the ball from one small section to another will be easier for them to accomplish.

As players get better at moving the ball while keeping it under control, those stationary objects will no longer offer enough opposition. Eventually, that stationary opposition can become active, thus better replicating player opposition from an actual game. Players able to master control and forward motion in the face of full-blown opposition will become effective dribblers during a game.

Follow the Curve

The challenge of dribbling is compounded by the fact that players rarely get to dribble in a straight line for very long. They will have to swerve to get away from encroaching opponents without losing the ball to the opposing team. That's why control is so very important and far exceeds distance coverage as dribbling's primary goal.

Much of this control has to do with turning the ball and changing direction. Control during forward trajectory is easy; it's when the dribbler comes up against opposition team members who want to take the ball away that the real skills come into play.

Youth players who can successfully turn the ball during a dribble can easily outplay their untrained counterparts.

Playing Tip

The best dribblers can use multiple surfaces of either foot to control, move, and shoot the ball. These players will be more successful in getting into position to shoot the ball. Teaching versatility in surface contact isn't easy. We tend to be right- or left-footed in the same way we tend to be right- or left-handed.

Dribblers turn the ball by literally running around it while dribbling. The dribbler must maintain control by striking the ball at different points around its outside, thereby changing its direction. Control and redirection, rather than speed, are the two most important elements during this maneuver.

Passing and Receiving

Players can also advance the ball down the field by passing it. Sometimes the ball advances much farther through a good pass than a long and protracted dribble. It's usually a combination of dribbling and passing that moves the ball downfield to put it into scoring position.

To pass the ball, players kick it with the inside or outside of the foot. If controlling the direction and trajectory of the ball was important in dribbling, it becomes even more important in passing. A misdirected pass can land at the feet of an opposing player or in some uncontrolled section of the field and at the mercy of whomever might be located there. At the very least, it may wind up out of bounds. That means it's given to the opposite team to be thrown in from the sidelines. None of those options should be considered acceptable.

Put Your Whole Body into the Kick

The player's entire body comes into play during a kick, and shoulders and hips should be as square to the ball as possible prior to the kick for maximum stability. This isn't always possible in the heat of a game, but as players advance in their skill development, this is an area all of them can work on.

At the very least, make sure the nonkicking foot is planted firmly on the ground to stabilize and support the kick. With rare exception, the kick should contain a follow through appropriate to the strength of the kick itself. Too little follow through and the ball will lack the force it needs to cover the desired distance. Too much follow through and the player may literally kick himself off his feet.

Just like dribbling, an effective pass requires that the ball be delivered to the right receiver at the right speed. Ideally, you want to pass the ball to where the receiver needs to be. Furthermore, you want the receiver to make it there uninhibited, and you don't want the pass to be intercepted in the process. At the very least, the pass needs to go where the receiver currently is so the play can continue.

Foot Positions Are Key

Passing is done with either the inside or outside of the foot. The toe needs to be up and the ankle locked. The passer's foot often is compared to the head of a golf club. The toe should be up because pointed toes are more likely to miss the pass and, worse still, drive into the ground and trip up the player. The ankle should be locked to provide a solid striking surface.

We advise a pre-pass touch, similar to a practice swing in golf, which sets up the ball to be passed. The pre-pass touch makes contact with the ball, perhaps pushing it into a little better position for the pass. When properly executed the pre-pass touch helps set the shot and allows the passer a split-second for planning and to visualize where the pass is going. The pass itself, then, is the second part of the move and really is little more than follow-through to the pattern already established in the passer's mind.

Passes may be best practiced initially from a stationary position until the foot configuration has been mastered. After that, all passes should be practiced on the run, first without opposition and later with it to replicate actual game situations. Tactical mastery always follows technical skills mastery, and effective passing requires both.

Receiving techniques usually are taught in conjunction with passing strategies because of the natural relationship between the two.

Receiving the Pass

Receivers are players on the other end of the pass, the ones to whom the ball is kicked. Once they take possession of the ball, receivers become dribblers or passers themselves, moving the ball down the field using either or both techniques.

Receivers must be able to capture the ball and immediately begin moving it downfield. The one-touch capture—capturing the ball with little change in speed or stride—and forward motion is important for not losing the pace. Players who require more time and touches to get the ball under control run the risk of merely setting it up for an opponent's kick. For receivers, speed and control may be even more important than for passers.

To receive a pass, players take control of the ball with a body part, usually the foot.

Once you've had the players practice receiving from a stationary position, pair players and have them run downfield, passing and receiving the ball. First have them do this without opposition, and then add obstacles or opponents to the mix.

Yellow Card _____

You can usually tell a team of novice soccer players by the fact that, like novice typists, their eyes are on what they're doing—in the case of soccer, that means they are usually looking at their feet. Players constantly having to watch their feet will be less likely to measure distance, take advantage of field position, or anticipate their opponents' moves. Players must learn skills well enough that they don't have to watch their feet and can keep their heads up throughout the game, thereby taking in the bigger picture and reacting appropriately.

Juggling the Ball

A large part of mastering the role of receiver comes in knowing how to juggle the ball. Any surface other than the hands and arms can be used, and master soccer players use as many of these surfaces as possible as effectively as possible to keep the ball under control and moving forward.

Juggling also is a good way for players to learn to keep their heads up. A receiver might actually do better receiving a pass and deflecting it downward off his or her chest to keep control, thereby trapping the ball at a higher level rather than running the risk of losing it to an opponent's foot. Juggling plays a critical part because of the added control it imparts, and care should be taken to master various aspects of it.

The best thing about juggling—also called ball control—is that it's something players can practice on their own during off hours and when team practice is not in session. If you ever see a kid bouncing a soccer ball up and down off his foot or knee over and over again, chances are that player is practicing juggling.

In fact, that's one of the ways to teach juggling. Arm each player with a ball and have them drop the ball, letting it bounce off the ground. Then have them regain control of the ball with their feet and begin to juggle it using various parts of the body other than the hands and arms. One touch for one bounce, of course, is the place where young players start, and they can mark progress with the number of contacts they make on the ball while still keeping it under their control. The more advanced they become, the more numerous and varied those contacts become.

Encourage your players to practice juggling the ball with their thighs.

Because they provide large juggling surfaces the thighs are good places to practice the technique. Start slow, with only two juggles off each thigh. The jugglers will look a little like they're part of a high-stepping marching band, but they'll be surprised by their level of control. Increase the number gradually and incorporate feet and other surfaces into play.

Juggling practice hones the players' control of the ball. And in soccer, control means success.

The ball is primarily juggled with the foot, bouncing it off the top of the foot, but other parts of the body—the thigh and the head—may be brought into play. Again, hands and arms may not touch the ball.

Playing Tip

Trapping, a term often linked with juggling, involves stopping the motion of the ball to bring it under control. In games where the ball is careening wildly around the field, trapping can be a good strategy to capture and redirect the flow. An airborne ball may be trapped by the chest or thigh, for example, then dropped down for control by the foot. You might also hear trapping referred to as air control or even just plain receiving. It's all the same thing.

When using the chest to receive a ball, the player must make sure his or her hands and arms are out of the way. Once the ball hits the chest, it can be deflected down to the player's thighs, feet, or the ground.

Heading the Ball

One of soccer's most unusual moves is the head. Players can use their head to strike the ball as part of a pass, trap, or even to score a goal. In a sport where use of hands is forbidden, every appendage counts, and the head sometimes can be the most effective one a player has.

Most youth players are afraid to head the ball. They don't want to look dumb, don't want to get a broken nose or black eye from doing it improperly. Their parents are afraid of neck and spinal column injuries. Although there may be the occasional bruise, it's very unlikely anything serious will happen, especially when the player learns to head the ball properly.

The forehead or front part of the crown is the most appropriate strike-point. Using the face, of course, is a bad idea and will only drive the ball to the ground and out of the player's control, while using the top or back of the head generally offers little or no control at all.

The ball should be met forcefully—like hands striking a volleyball. In addition, the heading player must keep his or her eyes open, mouth shut to avoid biting his cheeks or tongue on impact, and have a clear idea where the heading will put the ball. A player doesn't kick the ball without knowing where it should be going. The same goes for heading, even if it's done just to trap the ball and bring it under control for further play.

When heading a ball, the receiver hits the incoming ball with the upper part of the forehead in the direction he or she would like it to go. While this doesn't offer the best ball control, the head's hard surface can send the ball significant distance when it's most needed.

First, have players practice heading while standing in one place. Have them first touch and then bounce the ball lightly off each other heads. Sponges or foam rubber balls with little weight and a lot of give also are ideal for someone new to heading. Once players no longer fear the ball and are confident in their ability to head without injury, twosomes and groups can head the ball back and forth, first in stationary fashion and then on the run.

> **Time Out**
>
> Jumping isn't usually an effective part of heading. The power comes from the torso with the feet planted firmly on the ground to give the body stability. Sometimes players will jump higher than an opponent to head the ball in the direction he or she wants it to go. That can be an effective strategy if there is a receiver to take it forward.

Yellow Card

Train youth players to head carefully. Too many newbies run into the ball with their faces or try to head the ball with the crown of their head. The first mistake can results in bumps, bruises, and even breaks, while the second offers no control at all. Once again, player safety and ball control are the most critical elements of this drill.

Shooting the Goal

Ultimately, scoring is what soccer is about, but tremendous preparation goes into the process. Shooting is merely the final fulfillment of the set up.

The process of shooting—not to be confused with scoring—is relatively simple in concept, but devilishly difficult for some players to learn. Shots usually are tried when the player believes he or she has the chance to score. Those shots must be firm, direct, and swift.

Most young players want to kick the ball off the toes of their soccer shoes. That's a bad idea for a number of reasons: (a) control is compromised by the lack of additional covering on the strike point; (b) toes are not the strongest part of a foot and do not result in the best kick; and (c) toes can bend, bruise, and sometimes break when used for kicking. A broken toe rarely results in a goal.

> **Time Out**
>
> Advanced players sometimes manage to put a spin on the ball, arcing its trajectory around obstacles and into the net. As the coach of a youth soccer team, however, there isn't much likelihood that you'll have to worry about that technique too often.

Shooters should kick the ball with the part of the foot at just about the bottom of the laces on their soccer shoes. That's a hard surface, which results in a firmer strike and a farther bounce, and can be used to kick relatively hard without risk of injury to the player. Of course, it doesn't feel natural at first to young players and may take some time for them to get used to.

Have beginning players practice shots for goal from close to the goal.

The key to shooting is accuracy, more so even than power. Beginning kickers need to start close and work on aim. Once they get comfortable with that, they can begin shooting from a little further back until speed and power combine with accuracy.

Much like passing, shooting requires players to strengthen the striking surface by locking the ankle. Kickers should bend their knees, plant the stabilizing foot next to the ball, which helps guide the direction in which the shot must go. The kicker's shoulders should be positioned over the ball with an eye on the ball. The foot then should strike at about the middle of the ball.

Kicking should be practiced on the run, as opposed to kicking from a tee like they do in American football. First, there will never be a time in soccer when a tee is used, and secondly, part of the kicker's success will require the right foot position and approach. A kick with a foot and ankle that's firm will mean success. Anything less could lead to failure as well as injury.

Playing Tip

Shooting the goal successfully may provide soccer's highest high. But a lot of teamwork goes into bringing the ball to that point, and a good shooter never assumes he or she could accomplish the goal without his or her teammates. A goal is the result of the entire team's effort. As coach, make sure you teach that element, too.

Combination Drills

Combining exercises—shooting the goal while dribbling or as part of a pass-and-receive combination—allows the players to practice in a more realistic competitive situation.

In the next chapter we'll explain some drills and exercises you can use to help your players master these techniques.

The Least You Need to Know

- Skills development has intellectual, emotional, and sensual components, all of which the coach must address.

- Effective skills training includes description, example, and an opportunity to practice the skill.

- All players must master the five foundational skills: dribbling, passing and receiving, juggling the ball, heading, and shooting the goal.

- Dribbling the ball is the key skill around which the other skills turn, with control being the most important factor. Players who can't dribble should not be on the field.

- When shooting the goal, do so with a firm foot and strike the ball with the top of the foot.

Chapter 10

Skills and Drills

In This Chapter

◆ Warm-up exercises and drills

◆ Dribbling exercises

◆ Passing and receiving drills

◆ Juggling or mastering ball control

◆ Heading practice

◆ Shooting the goal

◆ Cool downs

In the last chapter, we discussed the five foundation skills all soccer players must have.

While all of this may have sounded very good, you probably wondered how to translate playing concepts to youth teams. In other words, how do you make sure kids newly interested in the game understand why you're asking them to do what they do when all they want to do is run and kick the ball?

Part of that will have to do with your effectiveness as coach in terms of communicating the principles in a way they can understand. Part of it also will have to do with their own interest in and commitment to the sport. You can create drills to help them understand and develop those skills at interest and ability levels suitable to their age groups.

That's the focus of this chapter. What follows are a set of drills and exercises designed to help younger soccer players understand and appreciate what you're asking them to do. These exercises emphasize simplicity and accessibility in the hopes that by capturing their interest and imagination, you'll be better able to keep them interested in the sport.

You'll note, too, that the drills can be combined, altered, expanded, and morphed into forms other than those we have here. Make the most of them, and don't be afraid to tailor them to your players' needs.

Warm-Up Exercises

As noted previously, warming up the players, even younger ones, is critical. By warming up, the kids stretch muscles and ligaments that may have been constrained all day by sitting in the classroom, thus reducing the likelihood of fatigue and injury. Warm-up drills also form part of the workout regimen, helping frame both practice and play. You may also use them to mirror upcoming training activities.

Yellow Card

There are more differences between coaching boys and girls' teams than meets the eye, not the least of which has to do with the way you might criticize their playing. Boys can be criticized as a team and not take it to heart. In fact, that's often the best way to bring problem areas to light. Criticize a girls' team as a team, however, and there will be a lot of hurt feelings. Constructive one-on-one suggestions are the better way here.

Playing Tip

Count the drills out in different languages—*uno, dos, tres* in Spanish for example—as a way to keep kids entertained and teach them something new.

For young kids especially, it helps if the warm-up exercises are fun. They can be used to get players in the mood and ready for the practice. A little light aerobics to start out—running in place, jumping jacks or the like—will get the blood flowing and the heart pumping. Then you may want to do some legitimate stretches to limber up joints, muscles, and hamstrings. Consider the following stretches.

Hurdler's Stretch

Have players sit on the ground and position legs in a runner's stride, with one leg in front and the other in back. Have the player tuck the heel of the rear leg under the buttocks and lean gently forward toward the toe of the leg extended in front. Have the player hold the pose for 5 to 10 seconds, sit back up, then repeat several times. Then switch leg positions and perform the stretch with the other leg extended.

The exercise stretches a variety of muscles in the legs and lower back. Makes sure that the stretch is performed gently and with no bouncing that might traumatize the muscle.

For the hurdler's stretch, players should sit on the ground, one leg extended and one tucked back with the heel under their buttocks, and lean forward toward the extended leg.

Tripod Stretch

The player stands with legs about one and a half shoulder width apart. Using both hands, the player bends and stretches first to the left ankle, then to the middle, then to the right ankle. The process is repeated 5 to 10 times.

This exercise stretches the inner thigh muscle, once again promoting flexibility and strength. The same exercise may be performed sitting down with legs spread in front.

With legs apart, the player should reach over and touch his or her toes. The spread legs will not apply undue pressure on cord and tendons while still loosening players up for play.

Toe Touch

Players sit in an L-shape, with knees together and legs extended in front of them. Players then lean slowly forward until they either touch their toes or grab their ankles. That position is held and, as muscles and ligaments stretch, they are encouraged to *carefully* lean farther forward. Players should not attempt to extend beyond what their body tells them is comfortable and safe to do.

During the toe touch, players should keep their feet together and legs extended and reach forward as far as possible to touch their toes.

You may even want to alternate these stretches with a minute or two of dribbling in between for variety and to keep their heart rate up. The more fun you are able to make routine exercises, the more likely your players will be to do them well.

Playing Tip

Don't forget to demonstrate everything you're asking your players to do. Your participation shows them that it's important. Plus, seeing the stretch or drill performed is the best way for them to learn the correct way to do it.

Keep in mind that young bodies tend to be supple and loose, which means (a) players will pay little attention to safety factors during these stretches, doing things that aren't safe or stretching beyond their boundaries, or (b) they will stretch only as far as everyone else, even though they may be able to stretch farther, and thus gain no benefit from the exercise. Take time to explain the purpose of the stretch and work with each of them in turn. Emphasize that stretching is a serious part of training and will reduce fatigue and injury.

Keeping Warm Ups Fun

Stretching can seem very dull to young kids ready to run, so take the time to do it right, but keep stretching to a minimum. There are lots of other, more enjoyable ways to warm up, which we'll explain in the following sections.

Relay Tag

Divide the team into four lines spread out down the length of the field. At the sound of the whistle, the first player in each line carefully dribbles the ball to the next player in line, then takes his or her spot after passing the ball off and tagging his or her hand. The second player does the same to third player, and so on until the ball reaches the end of the field. At that point, the same players perform the same drill in reverse until the players end up back at their own original spots and the ball is back at the start. The ball may not be kicked the distance to the next player. Should the ball pass the next player before it's handed off, the passer will have to get the ball and bring it back to the receiver, who may not move from his or her spot until in possession of the ball and the receiver tags his or her hand.

The purpose of relay tag is to be the first squad to complete the exercise. Players not running the relay should do light aerobic exercise to stay warmed up and to keep themselves active while other players are running (these are called working/recovery rest intervals). Besides serving as a warm up, this exercise practices ball handling techniques and teamwork.

Stoplight

This warm up operates similarly to Relay Tag for more advanced players, but with one important difference. A member of the coaching staff stands at the far end of the field with a card, on one side of which is a green circle, the other side a red circle. The game begins when the coach turns the red circle over to the green circle at the sound of the whistle. The drill ends when the "stoplight" card is turned at the coach's discretion *without* the sound of the whistle. The squad failing to stop for a red light has to go back to the start.

This exercise promotes the same physical and skills benefits as Relay Tag. It's also promotes "heads up" play by forcing players to keep their eyes focused on the field rather than the ball.

> **Time Out**
>
> Stoplight also can be played without cards by holding up right hands for red and left hands for green. Whatever you use, the importance of this drill is for players to keep their eyes downfield rather than staring at their feet.

Rotation

Each player is given a ball, which he or she dribbles onto the field. At the sound of the whistle, the players abandon their balls and take over someone else's ball and keep dribbling. As the exercise continues, the whistle is blown faster and the players are

Yellow Card

Care must be taken not to penalize young players who try and don't always succeed. There will always be natural athletes who seem to accomplish what you ask successfully and effortlessly. It's the other ones who need your help. Remember that there are many ways to succeed, and look for developmental methods to make all players winners, both in practice and in play.

required to respond faster. The goal is to always have a player matched to a ball, even if he or she has to head across field to find one.

In a variation called Musical Rotation, an assistant coach removes a ball each time the whistle is blown. The player unable to secure a ball is forced to leave the field. Players who leave the field should do stretches or some other exercise. In the end, the last two players remaining are declared winners.

This is another aerobic/anaerobic training exercise, this time working on speed, dexterity, and strategic thinking as well. The players who do well are the ones who know which ball they will go after even before the whistle is blown. That training prepares them for match play.

Dribbling Drills

Warm-up exercises, by their nature, include running and aerobic training, which is a large part of effective dribbling. In the wake of such warm ups, concentrate dribbling training on ball control and increased dexterity. Here are a couple of drills to start you off:

Zigzag

Several lines of cones are set up and players dribble the ball around each and back again. This exercise fosters greater control and speed.

Zigzag: After the coach has lined up four to five cones, players should then dribble the ball around the cones in a zig-zag fashion both out and back.

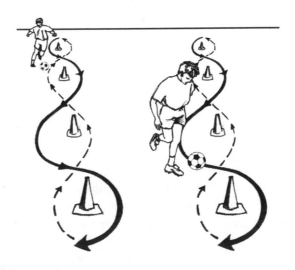

Once the skill part begins to take hold, coaches can then time each player's progress and keep a record of it. This allows the players to compete against their own times to get a sense of whether and how much they are improving. When players know they're not competing against other better players, progress comes rather swiftly.

Zigzag Tag

Similar to Zigzag, this exercise runs much the same way, but uses other players rather than cones. The stationary players act as if their right legs are rooted to the spot, but they can reach out with their left legs and attempt to steal the ball from the dribbler. This, of course, is a more realistic exercise and promotes increased dexterity and the necessity to maintain control in the face of opposition. In advanced Zigzag Tag, use a stopwatch to time players' progress against his or her own performance.

Crablegs

Most dribbling takes place as forward motion, but evasive tactics also are important to master. In Crablegs, the dribbler faces forward, but kicks the ball sideways, moving laterally across the field. The emphasis here is control first and speed second. The same timed drill can be applied to advanced Crablegs.

Care should be taken not to turn this exercise into a forward drill across a shorter expanse. True sideways motion will be challenging enough.

Foxes and Rabbits

All but one player are given a ball and lined up between two cones, with another two cones set up 15 to 20 yards downfield. The remaining player is designated the fox and stands alone downfield. The object is for all players to dribble the ball through the far set of cones without meeting the fox, whose object is to kick the ball off the field. Players who lose their balls join the ranks of foxes until all players eventually become foxes.

Dribbling the ball becomes more difficult as the number of foxes increases, requiring increased skills and abilities on the part of the remaining dribblers. This is a very good exercise for players of all ages.

Playing Tip

All exercises should promote ball control first and speed second. Speed will come more naturally once ball control has been mastered. If you emphasize speed first, then ball control might never follow. And then it won't matter how fast a player runs because he won't have the ball!

Passing and Receiving

Once again, the best passing and receiving exercises are done on the run, since that's how they will occur within the framework of the game. Initially, however, the idea of being able to kick the ball toward someone with relative accuracy among younger players may be challenge enough. The following exercises combine the two types of drills.

Basic Catch

In soccer parlance, playing catch has nothing to do with the hands. Catch means a pair of passer/receivers kicking the ball back and forth between each other. It's the most basic drill of this type and a good place for new players to start. One player kicks the ball to another, who traps it. The second player then kicks the ball back to the first.

Basic catch between a passer and receiver is one of the easiest and most important skills you can have your players practice. Start this exercise out with players in a stationary position, and have them kick the ball back and forth, trapping it each time. Eventually turn the drill into a running exercise in which the pair passes and receive as they run up and down the field.

Advanced catch is played on the run, with both players moving up and down the field. For really advanced catch, the coach will time the progress. However, accuracy and control should be stressed first. The players will acquire speed later.

Triple Play

Triple play operates much the same as basic catch, but involves three players, who take turns moving the ball amongst themselves. This can be done from a stationary position, with the players forming a triangle. One of three can be designated "Control" and can alternate the delivery pattern of the ball among the three.

Like basic catch, triple play is a good way to practice passing and receiving skills. Adding a third person to the mix allows for some diagonal passing as well as learning how to receive from players of varying styles and abilities. Again, start this as a stationary exercise and move to a running exercise. The players' standard triangulated position will change with the run, better replicating situations found in actual play.

In advanced Triple Play players move up field, either in triangulated position or stretched across the field. As many combinations of this play should be practiced as possible because, in addition to developing skills, it will also develop field strategy.

Round Robin

Similar to Triple Play, in Round Robin the team stands in a circle and passes the ball amongst the players. The circle can initially start out by simply sending the ball around in an orderly fashion. When the coach shouts "free style," then the players can kick the ball to whomever they want in the circle, meaning all players should be prepared at all times.

If the team is too large or the practice space too small, try having several games of Round Robin going on simultaneously.

Juggling or Mastering Ball Control

Juggling is the only exercise that can be practiced effectively alone and, in fact, should be done so if at all possible. Good ball control increases possession time, which, of course, enables the team to score more goals. This is one training area no team can afford to neglect. Try the following exercises.

Up the Ladder

This is a solo exercise that begins with a drop bounce. Once the ball is bounced the player attempts to keep it from hitting the ground by bouncing it off his or her foot, thigh, head, or other body surface other than the hands or the arms. The "rungs" of the ladder that the player is able to climb are determined by the number of times the player can bounce the ball without touching it with the hands or letting it hit the ground. More rungs, of course, mean greater progress.

> **Time Out**
>
> Double Ladders (or Triple Ladders) brings a new dimension of inter-dependency to training, a more strategic element that adds to the value of the exercise.

Double Ladders

This version of Up the Ladder is played with two people who must work together to keep the ball from hitting the ground. They can take turns hitting the ball or hit it as much as they can themselves before the other player jumps in to save them.

Heading

Few things are more frightening to novice soccer players than learning how to head the ball. The human instinct rarely includes running one's head into an inanimate object, especially one hurdling at you at what could be high speeds. It's the very antithesis of what we are taught, how we are subconsciously programmed to duck and cover when objects come our way. That means heading takes a lot of practice. Players first have to get comfortable with the idea of striking the ball with their heads.

Basic Headball

Basic Headball let's kids get comfortable with heading the ball. Gently toss the ball at the player, and have them head it back. The players should be confident, aggressive, and use the right surface of the head.

Once players have mastered Basic Headball and are comfortable and confident, then all manner of variations can be played, including the following:

- ◆ **Headball Tennis**   Two players head the ball back and forth to each other until it hits the ground. Two cones can be used to mark the "net."

- ◆ **Bull in the Ring**   The ball is tossed into a group of players, one of whom the coach names as the ball is tossed. If the person can leap higher than the rest of the players and head the ball back to the coach, a point is scored.

◆ **Headbanger**   The player bounces the ball off his or her head against a backboard or just up in the air until it hits the ground. This is a variation of the Ladders exercise mentioned earlier.

◆ **Headshots**   This really belongs in the next section, but we've put it here because of the emphasis on heading. In Headshots, players try to head the ball and hit the goal or some other target. Headshots can be done from a stationary position. There is also advanced Headshots, which is done on the fly.

> **Time Out**
>
> In addition to the head, mastery of other areas, such as the chest and thigh, can be developed to create trapping skills. In the same way Headball can be practiced, so can Chestball, Thighball, or whatever you feel your team can do. Many of the aforementioned training strategies apply.

In Basic Headball, one player tosses the ball and the other heads the ball, returning it to the tosser. Learning to strike the ball with the upper part of the forehead is the first and most important skill to master.

Shooting the Goal

Players always like to practice shots on goal, those point-scorers all soccer players and coaches live for. In all cases, these skills and approaches should be practiced from a stationary position until the players have a sense of the size and scope of the goal. Once they're comfortable shooting from a standing position, have players practice shooting on the run, at first without a goalkeeper present and then with one. Try the following exercises:

♦ **Straight Shooter**   As the name implies, this is a straight shot at the goal from the penalty box line, both unobstructed and obstructed, both stationary and on the fly. The purpose of straight shooter is for the players to develop strength and accuracy with their shots. The best players will master shots with both legs so they can take advantage of the best moment for the shot.

♦ **Long Legger**   This operates exactly the same as straight shooter, but from midfield. Not everyone will be able to do this, and they shouldn't be discouraged if they can't. More than anything else, Long Legger trains the shooting leg and promotes strength and accuracy. If a player can kick a good, strong Long Legger, imagine what he or she can do from the penalty box line!

♦ **Set and Shoot**   In this exercise, another player brings the ball up and sets up the shot, sometimes called a layoff for the shot. A second player comes and makes the shot. As players' abilities advance, those set ups can occur at odd angles or long distances from the goal. The setter will determine what the shooter has to do.

♦ **Jackknife**   As a variation on Set and Shoot, Jackknife involves a two-part set-up in which the ball is set up, then passed to another player who kicks it into the goal. The pattern that often emerges is that of a V-shape or an open-faced L, much like a jackknife partially opened. Different variations on Jackknife involving more players also can be developed. It all depends on how capable the team becomes at executing the basic skill sets.

♦ **Pockets**   As players become more advanced, they can train for shooting at certain parts of the goal net, or pockets. All the different configurations from Jackknife come into play. The only difference is that a specific area of the net, rather than the net itself, becomes the target.

Cool-Down Exercises

Like any physical activity, each practice should have a limited number of cool-down activities to signal the end of practice and to loosen up muscles and joints. Try the following simple exercises:

♦ **Long Field Lope**   Players can do one lap around the perimeter of the field at a pace comfortable to them. To keep them from acting like they're competing in a race, you may have them do the team chant or sing the team song as they run. This builds team spirit and reaffirms their identity as a team member.

- **Cone Races**   Presumably you have your practice field measured off by a number of brightly colored cones. The team can be divided into two squads and players can run relays up each side of the field to retrieve the cones, starting with the cones that are closest and working toward those that are farthest away. The winning team may qualify for extra treats. (You've probably noticed that this also saves you have from having to gather the cones after practice.)

Use your imagination and come up with other cool-down activities. They shouldn't be overly strenuous and, above all, they should be fun. But that's what your practice should have been all along.

The Least You Need to Know

- Coaches must create the appropriate skills drills aimed at the age groups they coach that promote continued interest in the sport.

- Stress ball control first and then speed second in all drills. Once the ball is under control, speed will come naturally.

- Players shouldn't be penalized if they are not able to perform all drills. Look for other ways to help them succeed and feel like part of the team.

- Practice should be bracketed with warm ups and cool downs. Warm ups help players' muscles and joints prepare for practice. Cool downs bring closure to the activity.

- Of all the skills, heading the ball is the most intimidating to the most members. Pay special attention to how well and how often players head the ball and work on it with players who might be afraid of the concept.

Athlete Health, Conditioning, and Safety

In This Chapter

- ◆ Pre-season physicals
- ◆ Understanding athletic stress
- ◆ Promoting healthy lifestyle
- ◆ Nutrition and youth athletes
- ◆ A recommended pre-game diet

When kids play, they sometimes get hurt. Every parent knows that. When kids play organized sports, every effort is made to have them play safely. Still, kids sometimes get hurt. Every coach knows that.

It's the coach's responsibility to make sure kids are practicing and playing safely. In the event that injury occurs—and it will—it's also the coach's responsibility to act quickly to minimize further trauma and get the injured player the proper help. Sometimes that may mean going beyond the supplies in the first aid kit we advised you to pack in Chapter 1. A little preparation and knowledge about what to do in crisis situations can go a long way toward keeping a bad situation from becoming worse.

There's an entire science of sports medicine that we can't expect you to grasp here. Nor should you. You're not a physician and shouldn't act like you are. But as coach, there are things you should know about your players, potential injuries, and the basics of good athlete health to keep players safe and maximize the performance potential of your team.

Even though you're not dealing with professional athletes, you'll want them to prosper and grow as soccer players. Safe practices, good nutrition, and healthy habits will help make this possible.

Get a Physical Before Getting Physical

In sports the best defense is always a good offense, and the same holds true for monitoring athletes' health and fitness. That means all your young players should have some form of pre-season health check-up.

Unlike high school, college, and pro teams, pre-season physicals aren't always mandatory for youth soccer. You may not be able to make it mandatory, but you should stress to parents and guardians that not knowing a child's relative fitness level prior to sports participation is dangerous because there may be pre-existing conditions that could escalate with exertion. A seemingly healthy child may suddenly collapse mid-game, suffering from acute asthma that developed in response to exertion, a heart condition that heretofore had gone undetected, or some other serious malady. Such things rarely happen, but when they do, it can result in a potentially life-threatening situation.

Yellow Card _____

We've said this before, and we'll say it again: One of the foundations to safe play is good conditioning. That means stretching and warm-up exercises before each practice and game. Injuries occur more readily when muscles are not prepared for what sports ask of them. While kids' muscles and joints certainly are more supple than those of adults, they also are less mature, meaning care has to be taken not to push them too hard. Conditioning can help them ease into play and protect them from more serious injuries.

To screen players for health problems, stress the importance of pre-season physicals and, if at all possible, make them mandatory. It may be the only routine physical some kids get, and their health and safety depend on it.

The American Academy of Pediatrics (AAP) suggests kids get a complete sports physical at least once every two years and six weeks prior to the start of the season. That allows the family physician to work with any problems or conditions they diagnose before the practice season begins. We suggest that you require forms from physicians saying the exam has been conducted and the child is cleared for sports participation before letting him or her play. This will not only help ensure your players are healthy, it will be proof that you took proper safety precautions in case an injury or illness results in a lawsuit.

Health Problems You Should Know About

Some health conditions might prevent kids from participating effectively. Obesity, obvious musculoskeletal problems, or physical conditions that restrict movement are all relatively easy to detect. Other less obvious conditions that would show up in a routine physical also might raise red flags. Some of the more common and serious ones are as follows:

◆ All manner of cardiac conditions and heart disease are of concern. With everything from high blood pressure to heart valve problems to heart murmurs a possibility, the family physician must give the unqualified stamp of approval on the body's most critical organ before the player may participate. Some conditions are relatively benign, while others are not. Carditis, an inflammation of the heart, can lead to sudden death through exertion. Players with carditis must not participate.

◆ Diabetes mellitus can cause problems for players who fail to respond to the needs of the disease. With proper attention to diet, hydration, and insulin needs, there should be no problem with sports participation. Players who fail to follow doctor's orders, however, could wind up in a diabetic coma after routine exertion of practice or play. Untreated, that can lead to serious health problems or even death.

◆ Asthma can be aggravated through sports exertion. As long as the player is on proper medication, there should be no problems.

◆ Kids with a history of heat illnesses pose a special problem for soccer teams and other sports that require constant running, which raises the body temperature. Those conditions should be carefully reviewed by the family physician before allowing the player on the field.

Playing Tip

Kids suffer from all kinds of maladies. It's part of growing up. But Rule Number 1 should be that kids can't play when they're sick. Seemingly minor symptoms may indicate something a great deal more serious, or conditions may be exacerbated by the stress caused by sports participation. In any event, sick kids belong home in bed, not running the length of a playing field. They may want to play and may be willing to play hard, but as coach you must learn to say no. It's for everyone's own good.

It's Gotta Be Pain Free

The AAP lists soccer as a "contact/collision sport" along with football, wrestling, boxing, and martial arts. That means special attention should be paid to musculoskeletal problems, including previous injuries players have suffered, and to players' range of motion for arms, legs, backs, and other joints. Players should be able to play the sport without pain. Players who can't execute the necessary moves without pain, swelling, or more than a 15 percent loss of strength should not be playing.

Yellow Card

The medical community has debated the relative safety of the heading maneuver in soccer, especially for kids who may inadvertently head each other as well as the ball. The end result can be a concussion, which is a bruising and swelling of the brain after impact. According to the Centers for Disease Control, sports lead to more than 300,000 traumatic brain injuries every year, ranging from mild to severe. As if that number weren't frightening enough, realize, too, that subsequent concussions only increase in the severity of the damage they do to brain tissues.

The day may come when kids will wear helmets for soccer, the same way they do when riding bikes. In the meantime kids suffering from suspected concussions should see a physician immediately. The player may not return to the field without clearance from that

Understanding Athletic Stress

As a rule, participating in sports is one of the great stress relievers of life. People of all ages, cooped up in a classroom or office all day, yearn for the freedom to run and play. It's the best way to burn off repressed energy and frustration caused by demanding teachers or bosses and other demands of life.

But there is a flip side to the situation. Sports can exert its own form of stress on players who feel they're not capable, talented, or good enough in the eyes of their peers, their coaches, or their friends and families. This can result in low self-esteem and withdrawal from the sport. It also may lead to reduced self-esteem in other areas, such as personal relations and academic studies.

To keep sports as stress-free as possible, coaches, parents, and sports administration organizations need to take an active approach to sports stress management by doing one or more of the following:

- ◆ Stress participation and growth as the ultimate value in sports. Not everyone can excel but all can participate, and that needs to be positioned as the most important.

◆ Keep winning in its proper perspective. It's the striving for victory and the personal and team values that come from that striving that are the real rewards. Coming out on top in a match is a byproduct of that success.

◆ Make sure players and teams are matched as closely as possible so that players at approximately the same achievement levels can play and learn from each other without being intimidated or feeling inferior to the other team or its players.

◆ Consider not scoring games or keeping individual performance statistics. If effort and participation are enough, then numeric assessment may only undermine them.

◆ Adjust the length of the games, the size of the field, and other relative factors to ensure greater success for younger athletes.

◆ Adjust your coaching style to include self-esteem and relationship coaching as well as skills training.

◆ As much as possible, make sure parents are supportive of their young players without being pushy or obnoxious. Too many sports parents attempt to live through their young athletes and the end result is bad behavior and the eventual withdrawal of the player from the team. Poor player performance should never be a family catastrophe.

Make sure that that parents know that disruptive or negative behavior can seriously affect the mental well-being of their kids. Ask parents to abide by the following rules during games and practices:

a. Don't yell instructions, comments, or criticism at the child while he or she is on the field.

b. Never make derogatory comments to the opposing team, its coach, referees, or other personnel.

c. Remain seated and orderly and *never* interfere with the child's coach.

> **Time Out**
>
> One of the keys to preventing sports injuries and illnesses is to make sure players have the proper gear. Minimally, youth soccer players should have cleated shoes and shinguards. Players without those shouldn't be allowed on field for their own good. Furthermore, teams that look more professional usually play better, a message your team's corporate sponsor needs to hear loud and clear.

Promoting Healthy Lifestyles

In today's fast-food instant-gratification society, physical growth and development is one of the few remaining areas of life where progress takes work and work takes time. Most kids can get good at sports and some can achieve greatness. But they won't get there without work. There's nothing on the Internet to short-cut training efforts. To be a top-notch soccer player, young athletes are going to have to stretch, run, kick, and train again and again and again. That's just the way it is.

Kids need to maintain a minimum level of health and fitness to train for and play soccer. It's not unreasonable for a coach to expect and perhaps even demand the following good health habits to be exercised by his or her players:

Playing Tip

Hold kids' sports heroes up as role models—encourage them to follow their favorite players' lead by living a healthy lifestyle.

- No smoking or using tobacco products of any kind. The dangers of tobacco are well known and their impact on general health and aerobic ability has long been understood. Players should not use them for any reason. With luck that may be a lesson they take with them long after they've left the team.

- No alcohol consumption of any kind. Chances are none of the kids you coach will be of legal drinking age, so the point should be moot. Too often, however, it isn't. And kids need to know that at certain levels alcohol becomes toxic to the body. It adds weight, impairs judgment, and affects a person's general health, especially if that person is in training for an athletic team. Just like smoking, alcohol consumption shouldn't be tolerated.

- No drugs. First, they're illegal. If that's not enough, they can be highly addictive, damaging, and ultimately lead to ruin that goes well beyond a youth soccer career. Need we say more?

- Good nutrition is a must. We'll cover that in more detail shortly. Right now it's enough to say that players who exist on a candy bar/corn chips/soft drink diet are destined to have a very short soccer career.

- Use the physical activity in sports to balance other aspects of your life. Players who don't give training and conditioning the proper emphasis won't be very good athletes. Conversely, players who do nothing but sports won't be very good people. As in everything else, success is achieved by maintaining balance.

- Keep the right perspective about your sports achievements. Some young athletes are criticized—and rightly so—for becoming arrogant and obnoxious as their playing and reputations in the sport improve. These athletes fail to realize that they have been given a gift in terms of their abilities and those are abilities best shared with other, less capable athletes.

Yellow Card _____

Too many young athletes attempt to balance schoolwork, sports participation, jobs, family obligations, and other requirements, usually at the expense of a good night's sleep. Growing kids need eight to nine hours of uninterrupted sleep every night. Players who start sacrificing sleep to other obligations won't be as sharp, nor will they have the necessary stamina. Lack of sleep will affect sports performance as much or more than it will everything else. The right amount needs to be factored into your training cycle.

Young Players Are What They Eat

When Mother told us to eat our vegetables, she apparently knew what she was talking about. Studies show that athletic performance improves by eating a healthy balanced diet. It also increases energy and improves performance.

And by "balanced diet," we do *not* mean that you need both Big Macs *and* Whoppers. In fact, you probably would be better off without either. The world at large may love its high-fat high-calorie foods, but in terms of providing balanced nutritional elements, there are more efficient and effective ways to get there from here.

In the following sections, we'll pass along what the AAP recommends for athletes in training. It's not bad advice for coaches, either.

Balance Your Diet Effectively and Completely

AAP guidelines state that young athletes should balance their diet so between 55 and 75 percent of calories come from complex carbohydrates, including fruit, vegetables, and starch; 25 to 30 percent should come from fat; and 15 to 20 percent from protein. That intake should be between 1,500 and 3,000 calories per day for athletes in training. Those on strictly vegetarian diets should augment their consumption so they get a sufficient supply of nutrients.

Carbohydrates include the familiar breads, cereals, and grains as well as fruit and vegetables. Fat sources generally are butter, and oils, which are often found in many protein-rich foods. Protein sources, of course, are meats, fish, poultry, as well as dairy products, eggs, tofu, legumes, and nuts.

The guidelines allow some flexibility but athletes should operate within the limits mentioned in order to gain extra energy and strength they need. A good balance can satisfy hunger and appetite cravings while building an energy level critical to performance success.

Note the balance ratios. Carbohydrates provide the energy we burn, which means it's a central fuel. Distance runners often fuel up on spaghetti the night before a big race to supply the energy they'll need the next day. When it comes to carbohydrates, however, more is only better if you plan to use the calories in physical activities. Excess carbs, like anything else, turn to fat. And remember to vary those carbs—including fruits and vegetables that offer other nutritional elements—for maximum effect.

> **Time Out**
>
> When it comes to complex carbs, many health care professionals will advise kids to "eat a rainbow." In other words, make sure the fruits and vegetables cover the color spectrum for maximum intake of vitamins and minerals. And a rainbow of red tomatoes, yellow beans, lettuce, oranges, blueberries, and grapes not only is colorful, but also flavorful and very appealing.

At one time there was a belief that protein, especially large quantities of meat, helped build muscle mass. That's not the case, which is why protein sits at the bottom of the list in terms of percentage. A certain amount is necessary in a balanced diet, of course. But the body stores excess protein as fat, and the kidney has a hard time processing protein. Too much protein will slow you down and make you sluggish, just the opposite effect of what you might expect.

Stay Hydrated

One of the biggest problems athletes of all ages face is dehydration. The body loses water rapidly during sports, and even more rapidly if it's hot outside. Dehydration can lead to fatigue, irritability, and sudden drops in performance. Athletes should drink between 4 and 8 ounces for every 15 to 20 minutes of athletic activity.

No matter what, plain ol' water is always best. Sports drinks also can be good, but never use carbonated or caffeinated beverages because of the negative effects they have on the body and its functions. And the athletes should never wait until they're thirsty to consume fluids. Dehydration can occur quickly, and thirst isn't always a reliable guide.

Be Wary of Nutritional Supplements

Too many athletes rely on nutritional supplements as a way to keep excess weight off while still satisfying the body's needs. Some supplements do provide value, but a steady diet of mostly supplements is a quick way to ill health and reduced performance, especially for young athletes.

The process of "burning" calories is just that, and the body needs an adequate supply much like a fire needs an adequate supply of wood and oxygen to burn brightly. If your caloric intake falls below what your body needs to perform, your ability—like the flames of a fire—will be dampened because you haven't provided enough fuel. Provide too much fuel and those calories get shoved to the side and become fat. Supplements can augment diet, but you still need the right balance of actual calories to perform and excel. Don't cheat your inner fires.

Pre-Game Meals

When you consume those balanced calories often is as important as which calories you consume. The right mix consumed at game time still may make you sluggish on the field as your body labors to digest what you consumed. Time that consumption so your body is dealing with the caloric energy the food has brought to you and you'll be much better off.

The American Academy of Pediatrics suggests the following possible foods and when to consume them:

Three or More Hours Before Exercise or Game

If you're stoking up the furnace for a game or practice and you have enough time to digest your food, you can consider going a little heavier in your consumption, including:

◆ **Carbohydrates** fresh fruit, fruit or vegetable juice, pasta with tomato sauce, breads, bagels, crackers, or English muffins.

◆ **Proteins** peanut butter, yogurt, lean meat, low-fat cheese, cereal with low-fat milk.

Two to Three Hours Before Activity

You have less digestion time, so lighten the load and drop the proteins. They take too long to digest. Try fresh fruit, fruit or vegetable juice, breads, bagels, crackers, or English muffins.

One to Two Hours Before Activity

You have no time to digest anything substantial, limiting your choice to juice or fruit. That's all.

Of course, water is good any time and, in fact, should be consumed throughout the practice or game. If you keep everything in balance, water intake will displace fluid loss and you should weigh exactly the same after the activity as you did before.

The Least You Need to Know

♦ If possible, insist on a pre-season physical to uncover any underlying health problems that could affect player performance. The greatest dangers lie not in what you see but what you can't see.

♦ Sports participation can relieve stress but also causes its own stress. Create the right environment so everyone can benefit and have fun.

♦ A healthy sports lifestyle includes no smoking, no drinking, and no drugs. Make that mandatory for your team.

♦ Athletes need a balanced diet with more carbohydrates than protein. Carbs form the fuel that athletes burn, while proteins, although necessary, are harder to digest.

♦ Eating heavily right before a game can make players sluggish and slow. Balance what you eat with when you eat it for maximum performance.

Part 3

Playing the Game

Youthful athletes can only practice so long and then it's time to take the field against opponents. Games shouldn't be considered life or death struggles, but an extension of the enjoyment they have had thus far during practice. Assuming all things are going well, your young players should be looking forward to testing their new skills.

As a coach, you're ready for the next phase of action, too—that of translating skills and drills into strategic initiatives. Even at the youngest levels, there is a method to the madness, and you may be surprised at how well the team responds to strategic and tactical direction.

This section increases the odds a little bit, ramping up the action and getting more specific about the needs and goals of the players and the team. We're going to build on areas we've already discussed, giving you a new set of tools with which to continue honing the skills of your team.

Chapter 12

Understanding and Applying Strategies

In This Chapter

- Understanding the field
- Knowing your player positions
- Organizing players on the field
- Your youth soccer strategy

A team by any other name is still a body of athletes—defensive as well as offensive, shooters as well as defenders—aimed at one specific objective, that of scoring goals and winning the game. That takes effort, energy, training, and talent. Above all, it takes an effective strategy on the part of the coach, and that's something you can't afford to ignore.

Victory is usually the result of a sound strategy effectively executed. Strategy is the plan by which your team expects to overcome obstacles and score goals. Whether it helps to think of it as a battle plan or a business plan, the effect is still the same. Strategy is an organized method by which you will best use the 90 minutes of play—less if you're coaching very young players—and make the most out the opportunities as they present themselves. You can be sure that the coach for the opposing team is thinking along those same lines.

Got Plans?

For coaches of advanced players, this strategy—or game plan—is critical. The players pound away at the opponent's goal much like an attacking army pounds away at a strategic defensive position. For some, it's war. If that analogy helps you, then by all means cry "Havoc!" And let slip the dogs of war.

Waxing too philosophical or struggling too hard intellectually with how to go about overcoming obstacles for youth team strategies may seem like so much wheelspinning. We're dealing with kids, after all, who really are there to have fun and do some running around and kicking before going home to supper, homework, video games, and a host of other activities. Your players are fully engaged for the moment, to be sure. After that, they have other things to think about.

Chances are, as a volunteer coach, you feel much the same way. You have only so much time to give, after which lying awake nights thinking, about plays might be something you don't have the hours, energy, and inclination for. Still, there are ways to approach even the most rudimentary match that will give your team a good enough strategic advantage so its members can enjoy the experience of winning as well as that of playing the game.

That's our goal—to add to your coach's tool kit with some more ideas, concepts, and a slightly deeper level of understanding you can use to enhance your team's ability and soccer experience. Use what's here to develop your own strategic base on which to build plans unique to your team. Spread out and expand your offense; compact and concentrate your defense. Then watch the victories mount up.

Time Out

A *strategy* is a system of play, a game design, a plan by which goals might be scored. *Tactics* are the methods by which that strategy is accomplished. A matter of semantics? Not quite. It's the difference between planning and execution. A team needs an overall strategy, or plan, to follow and methods, or tactics, by which to accomplish that plan. Mistake one for the other and you might find you have only part of the understanding you need to win.

Getting to Know the Field

To this point we talked about the field only in terms of size and length and whether or not it's appropriate to the age and sophistication of young athletes. Sometimes it is, while other times it will be too much for them to handle. In conjunction with your league officials you'll determine what works best for the age group you coach and then adjust accordingly.

What we haven't touched on are the different sectors of the field and what they mean. That comes into play because we'll be looking at systems of play in this chapter. To understand player positions and strategies, you need to be familiar with the parts of the field.

Soccer fields of any length, breadth, and depth have the following parts:

♦ **The Goal** is the net the opposing team shoots for in hopes of getting the ball past the goalkeeper. The goalkeeper works inside the 18-yard by 44-yard penalty box (also called a penalty area).

♦ **The Defensive Area** is that area immediately in front of the goal. It's occupied by defenders whose job it is to protect the penalty box so the goalkeeper has little more to do than protect the net. It often works better in theory than in practice.

♦ **The Midfield** comprises roughly half the total field and is divided by the halfway line, also called the midline, which separates the teams' halves of the field. The halfway line bisects the center circle, where the starting kick occurs. Games often turn based on who has the ball in the midfield and which direction that ball is headed.

♦ **The Forward Area** is the defensive area for the opposing team. It's the place where forwards from one team attempt to penetrate the defenses of the opposition and score goals.

♦ **The Four Corner Arcs** indicate where corner kicks take place.

Time Out
Players should be positioned where their talents can be put to the best use. But teamwork demands that players' skills be complementary, too. As coach, you need to know who works well together and who doesn't. Part of your training should be to build as many complementary relationships as possible, maximizing the potential combinations among team members. Understanding and complementing other players' skills and strengths—both during practice and play—will make the most out of your team's assets.

Players aren't locked to their spots on the field by anything other than the coach's strategy. However, the goalkeeper that strays from his of her net without *very* good reason is taking a chance the other team will score. Forwards, midfielders, and defenders who leave their zones and cluster in some area of the field open the rest of that field up for unobstructed advances by the other team. There are reasons players are assigned either to other players or certain areas of the field. Violating that positioning strategy without reason can contribute to goals for the other side.

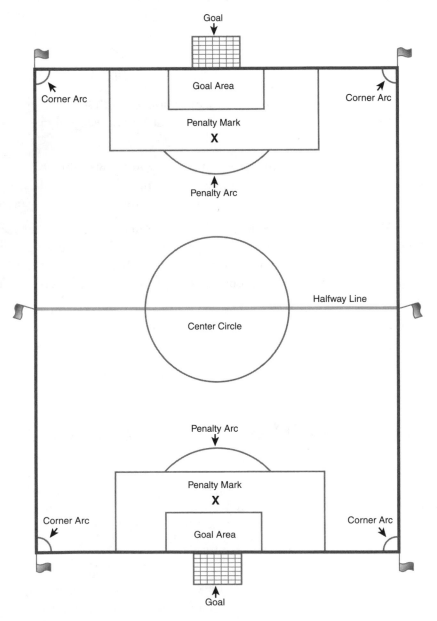

A soccer field.

Understanding the field has more to do with understanding how the various teams will use its various sectors. There can only be one goalkeeper in place for each team at a time, of course, but how you distribute the rest of your players will determine your strategy. These distributions are called *systems of play* and rely on some fairly common configurations that we'll talk about shortly (you'll also hear people call systems of play *formations*).

Know Your Players

Before we delve into the various systems of play, however, let's review what each of the 11 players do during a game:

- **The Goalkeeper** defends the goal and controls the penalty area. Once the ball enters the penalty area, he or she may pick it up or boot it out. Once the goalkeeper picks up the ball, playing ceases and all players are required to move out of the penalty area. Future play will be determined by how the goalkeeper distributes the ball.

- **Defenders** cover the penalty area and protect the goal and goalkeeper from as much excessive engagement as possible. They should strive to get the ball back to midfield and out of the defensive area as quickly as possible, but always with an idea about where it will go from there.

- **Midfielders** play a mixed defensive/offensive game, depending on which way the ball is traveling and who is in control. They occupy that great middle expanse of the field, supporting the forwards and shooting at the goal when appropriate.

- **Forwards** play close to the opposition's penalty area, and it's their job to score goals or, at the very least, keep the ball in the forward area until goal-scoring opportunities present themselves.

Playing Tip _____

Earlier we suggested that you allow every player to play every position so they gain an appreciation for the challenges their teammates face. There's also a practical consideration to our recommendation. On occasion, forwards might find themselves defending, while defenders may suddenly find themselves in scoring position. The flow of play is so fluid that it's anyone's guess from one moment to the next as to what they may be called on to do. Players should be comfortable moving from one position to another.

Each player has a specific job as determined by his or her position on the field. (We'll talk at greater lengths about each position in subsequent chapters.) Systems of play arrange these players on the field like pieces on a chessboard. The effectiveness of those systems is a result of the skill-level of the players in each position and the strategy employed.

Systems of Play

Despite some criticism as to their effectiveness, the foundations of most team's strategies are determined by their systems of play. Systems are the way teams line up for play in the different sections of the field. How those players are distributed will tell the opposition rather quickly if the team is playing a defensive or an offensive game. Each approach has its merits and uses, of course, and the system you choose for your team at any given time will be determined by the basic strategy you adopt.

Conservative strategies tend to favor a strong defensive position. A more aggressive strategy will take a more offensive approach, which means more forwards and fewer defenders. It all depends on what you know about your team's capabilities, what you're expecting from the opposition, and how you plan to play the gap between your team's capabilities and what you expect from the opposite team.

There is no single right system of play. The one that's right for you is the one that helps you win. In the following sections, we explain some of the more common configurations. The strategies are conceptually simple enough to use even with young players. In fact, the structure may help them better understand the identities of the positions you've asked them to play. Don't expect too much grasp on the strategic nature of the positions, however. Having them do their best to maintain the positions will be challenge enough.

The 4-4-2

We always count from the goal but never include the goalkeeper. That means the 4-4-2 is the most conservative of all the popular configurations. The 4-4-2 describes four defenders protecting the goal, four midfielders, and two forwards. The idea is that by concentrating most players toward the mid- and backfields, your team will bottle up the opposition, making it difficult to move the ball beyond midfield.

This configuration puts a lot of pressure on the two forwards to score, so they'd better be the top shooters on your team. Midfielders also should be looking for opportunities to set up shots for the forwards, since the forwards themselves have to concentrate on shooting and recovering missed shots.

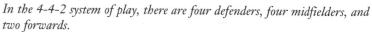

GK Goalkeeper   M Midfielder

D Defender   F Forward

In the 4-4-2 system of play, there are four defenders, four midfielders, and two forwards.

Despite what seems to be an imbalance, this strategy is common and can be very effective because of the way it helps concentrate play at midfield and in the opposition's defensive zone by making it more difficult to move the action past your defenders. With a little practice, this can become a very successful strategy.

The 4-3-3

This strategy of play stretches out the player lineup so it's a little more evenly balanced on the field. The numbers refer to four defenders, three midfielders, and three forwards.

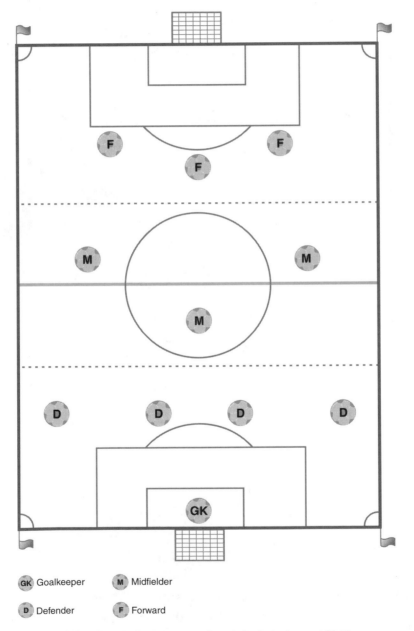

In the 4-3-3 system of play, there are four defenders, three midfielders, and three forwards.

Some schools of thought consider this an attacking formation, one that throws an extra forward into the mix to help pound the goal and penetrate defenses. While it's not the most aggressive formation, the extra forward can make a world of difference, especially to an opposing team used to the standard 4-4-2. Play that extra forward as a wild card or sweep position and you might effectively be able to take an upper hand over more conservative defensive formations.

Of course, moving that extra player forward weakens the defense in the middle, something that will have to be accounted for when the opposition has the ball. If your bottom-end defenders (the ones closest to the goal) can deal with that and the team as a whole is comfortable with the ball popping into their defensive area frequently, then this could be a good compromise between a highly aggressive strategy and a more conservative formation.

> **Time Out**
>
> Sweep is the name given to wild card positions. They have a flexibility to move wherever their help is most needed.

The 4-2-4

The 4-2-4 is the most aggressive pattern of play, requiring some highly talented team members who know exactly what they're doing.

The line up, of course, is four defenders in the backfield, two midfielders and four forwards hammering the opposition's defensive area. It may appear that all efforts are placed on offensive play, but there also is a strong defensive element to this configuration. The four forwards and two midfielders need to be capable of tying up the ball at the front end and keeping it there for as long as possible.

The 4-2-4 is a gutsy strategy that can work surprisingly well when properly executed. However, the challenge comes in recognizing and accommodating its defensive shortfalls. It's a strategy often best used by more advanced players who can compensate for the lack of midfield defenders. If you can do that, then you'll be that much better off.

 Yellow Card

With so little support at midfield in the 4-2-4, the defenders are under tremendous pressure every time the opposition has the ball. Those times need to be kept to a minimum.

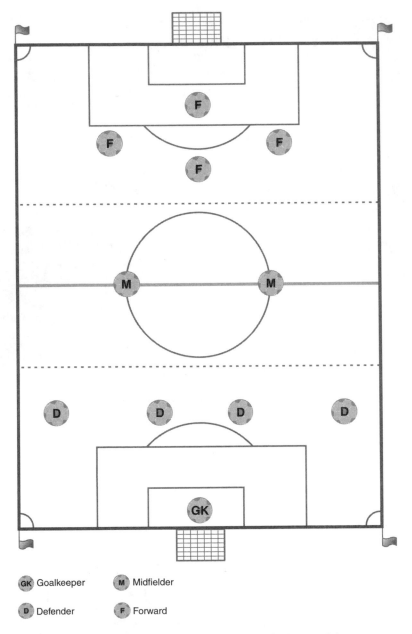

GK Goalkeeper   M Midfielder

D Defender   F Forward

The 4-2-4 system of play: four defenders, two midfielders, and four forwards

The 3-5-2

For teams whose skills aren't quite up to par, the 3-5-2 system of play is a good way to centrally concentrate players at a point where limited skills may be put to the greatest use. This configuration is built with only three defenders and two forwards, but its turnip shape allows for five midfielders who can operate toward either end as the play demands. Needless to say the opposition gets heavily bottled up in the middle trying to move the ball past this wall of defenders.

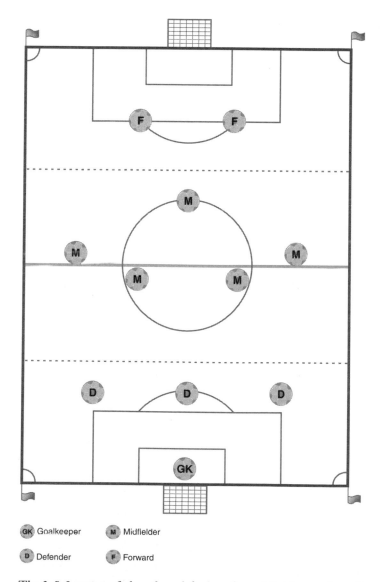

The 3-5-2 system of play: three defenders, five midfielders, and two forwards.

The drawbacks to this configuration are obvious. The defensive squad is a little lighter, while the forwards may be spread a little too thin to score too often. The 3-5-2 is a strategy that can be used effectively, however, and has been both by novices and pros.

The 3-6-1

If you found the 3-5-2 overly conservative, the 3-6-1 probably strikes terror in your heart. And it should, because teams using the 3-6-1 are playing a dangerous and overly defensive game.

Three defenders make the backfield seem a little light, but that's not totally out of line. Where things go wrong is in the midfield. While this is a heavily defensive position that the opposition will have difficulty penetrating, the midfielders by nature have to play a tougher offensive position, working to set up shots for the single forward on the field. The single forward must be a brilliant player, or this will be a low-scoring game for them.

Yellow Card

A lot of emphasis is placed on soccer's systems of play, but the plain truth is this: No system works if the players are unable or unwilling to support each other. No matter where the players happen to be standing, they have to be trained to interact effectively. Otherwise you can play 4-4-2, 3-5-2, or any combination in between to no effect whatsoever.

Some teams can use the strategy effectively while for most the imbalance becomes horribly constricting, resulting in few if any goals. Whereas the 3-5-2 can be a way to offset lower performing team, the 3-6-1 is almost too extreme, with the potential of making bad situations infinitely worse. Unless you have a specific reason to try this configuration, we suggest you steer clear of it.

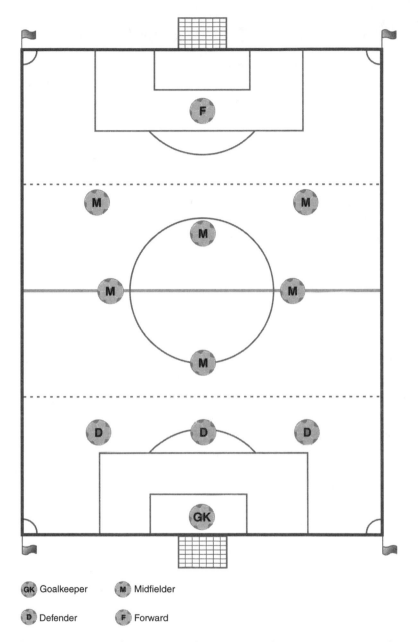

GK Goalkeeper   M Midfielder

D Defender   F Forward

The 3-6-1 system of play: three defenders, six midfielders, and one forward.

Defining Your Youth Soccer Strategy

The systems of play we just discussed are the result of generations of professional playing experience, not to mention cultural and geographic preferences on the part of players from different countries. As we mentioned in Chapter 1, no matter where you go in the world, there usually is a soccer—or *futbol*—game going on, and any one of dozens of strategic variations may be at work.

Time Out

Soccer is the world's most popular game for a reason. There's a beauty in its simplicity, an egalitarian appeal in the fundamental elements of its skills. Because just about anyone in relatively good health can play soccer is exactly why so many do.

So here you are, looking out over a band of pre-teens intent on playing the game, but without the ability to add 4 + 4 + 2, let alone understand the strategic implications of what the 4-4-2 means in soccer parlance. Is it realistic to expect the team to develop and execute the right soccer strategy to ensure victory?

The answer is "yes," as long as several things are kept in perspective:

◆ Strategies are relative to the level of sophistication and needs of those who design and execute them. The business strategy at Microsoft likely is just a little more sophisticated than that of Family Grocery, the mom-and-pop shop just down the street. That doesn't mean Family Grocery doesn't have a business strategy and that it doesn't serve its owners very well. It just means the corner store's strategy is a little less complex than that of the software giant, if for no other reason than because it can be while still functioning effectively. The same goes for your youth soccer team as compared to the pros. The right strategy for your team will not be the same as the right strategy for a professional team, a college team, or even the local high school team.

◆ There will be few youth league participants who have a strategy that is any more sophisticated than that of any other youth league participant. If there is a difference between your strategy and that of others in your league at all, it's that you may have one, while the opposing team probably doesn't.

◆ Any kid who understands that he has to participate in soccer practice before he gets the after-practice cider and cookies, that he has to do his homework before he tunes into the Cartoon Network or MTV, or that he has to behave in school Monday through Friday if he doesn't want to spend Saturday in detention, understands the concept of strategy.

Remember what we said earlier: A strategy is no more than a plan. Tactics are the means by which that strategy is executed. A strategy can fail because it is inappropriate to the situation, poorly conceived, or because the wrong tactics were used to attempt to execute it. As a youth soccer coach, you run a certain level of risk from all of these.

In defining the appropriate youth soccer strategy, you need to answer the following questions:

- **What is the team's purpose and why are the players practicing and playing on a regular basis?** If the team is made up of young kids, the purpose may be to develop an appreciation for the sport and an interest that will last a lifetime for its members. Older teams may be interested in developing skills and preparing to play at advanced educational levels. Obviously, the goals of the two different sets of players are very different and strategies should be drafted to reflect those goals.

- **What is the skill and sophistication level of the players on the team?** The younger the players are, the less sophisticated they are. Any corresponding strategies should reflect that level of sophistication. Nothing damages team morale faster than asking players to do things far beyond their capacity. The same holds true for advanced teams who lack the level of coaching sophistication necessary to help them meet their level of needs. Strategies have to meet or beat the abilities of the players. When you can give them that little extra pull that successfully stretches their reach beyond their grasp, then you're ahead of the game.

- **What is my level of sophistication and how far can I expect my coaching abilities to stretch?** You may be the perfect coach for 10-year-old newbies who have never even seen a soccer ball, but you may be way out of your league with 15-year-olds who have been around the game for half their lives. In the same way you shouldn't try to coach beyond your ability, don't attempt to design and execute strategies you can't manage. It's not fair to you, to the players, or the league.

- **What relative sophistication can I expect from other teams in the league?** Teams are seeded based on experience and ability, and nothing throws things off faster than a team whose abilities and strategies aren't suited for the league they're in. If you're too far behind the curve in either, your team will suffer big losses and players will be quick to drop out or look for other teams in less advanced leagues. If you're too far ahead of the curve, there will be no opposition, your players will not be tested in their playing, and roughly the same thing will occur.

In defining strategies, keep the answers to these questions in mind. Only you will know which approach you need to take, how you can maximize systems of play to your teams advantage, and how you can make your team effective competitors in their respective league while still providing players with an enjoyable learning activity.

Playing Tip

Simple strategies are sometimes more difficult than they look, but they also can be effective if they tie into a player's skill level successfully. A simple strategy for young players may be no more than concentrating on a zigzag field advance with the goal of reaching one player down field, whose job will be to set up the ball for another player to take the shot. It's a strategy that's easy for kids to understand and practice and can be challenging for the opposition to cover. It also can be very successful.

Consider the following additional factors when defining your team's playbook and set of strategies:

◆ Use strategies that can be understood and executed by your players. For really young kids, keep things simple. For older kids, make sure there's enough challenge so they can grow their skills and increase their abilities.

◆ Know your players' level of sophistication and abilities and develop strategies that maximize those abilities. Stretch their abilities if possible so they get the most benefit from the experience.

◆ Understand the true purpose behind why you're playing. If your coaching philosophy is to stress enjoyment and education for your players, your strategy may be to rotate all your players through all the positions as often as possible so they have the full soccer experience.

Conversely, if you're attempting to prepare older players for slots in advanced teams, train them for specific positions, work them hard in those positions, and call on them to understand complex strategic concepts and execute difficult plays. In both cases, it's the experience more than the victories that matter. Define your strategies to accomplish whatever goal is most important.

◆ Use strategies that teach teamwork and sportsmanship. Both these attributes lay at the heart of team sports and are central to the accomplishment of any goal, especially winning. Your strategy should enhance those characteristics because of the value they bring, both to the game and to life.

Soccer is a simple game that's sometimes very difficult to execute. Strategy will help in that execution, but only if it's the right strategy. Once you know your team, your league, and yourself a little better, you'll know what strategy to pursue. And only then will you be successful.

The Least You Need to Know

- Despite soccer's apparent randomness, victory is usually the result of a sound strategy effectively executed.

- Effective coaches employ a strategy that's appropriate to the team and its goals.

- The different sectors of the field—the defensive area, midfield, and forward area—and their use play an important role in the execution of any strategy.

- Systems of play—the way team members are positioned on the field—can communicate whether a team is playing a defensive or offensive game.

- Know your team, its ability level, and those of other teams in the league before determining the sophistication of your strategy.

- Make sure the strategy you define is one you as the coach can execute effectively.

13

The Characteristics of Defense

In This Chapter

- ◆ Defensive positions and play
- ◆ Mounting a good defense
- ◆ How to take control of the ball
- ◆ The many ways to tackle
- ◆ The evolution of defense

With the possible exception of goalkeepers—unique players who get their own chapter later in the book—all players are created equal. However, all positions are not. Each has its own task to perform and obligation to fulfill. No position is more critical to the safety and internal strength of a team than the defensive players.

Anywhere from two to four defenders occupy the defensive zone and flank the goal box, helping the goalkeeper stop the other team from scoring. Defenders do what their name implies—defend the goal—and, as such, form the strong foundation of the team.

Defenders may not be flashy scorers like forwards, or as seemingly energetic as midfielders, or as colorful as goalkeepers. But they need to be strong, committed players who can hold up against constant assaults.

It's Time to Get Defensive!

All players need to play defensively whenever the opposition has the ball. This is especially true of midfielders, who may share defensive as well as offensive responsibilities almost equally. In our overview of defense those players, too, will be included.

Before we broaden the scope to discuss defensive skills, let's take a look at defense as a position and the players who occupy it.

Time Out

The number of defenders usually determines the type of game being played. In the classic 4-4-2 configuration, the team has four players in the backfield, which signals a defensive strategy. Some coaches opt for three defenders, meaning there is one more on offense and the approach is a more aggressive strategy. Watch the opposition's defense placement and you'll know what you're up against.

Defensive Positions and Play

More so than offensive players, who may find themselves flying solo as they zero in on the opponent's goal, defensive players have to have a strong team orientation that gains its advantage from numbers, interaction, and formation. Offenders attack; defenders block. And the more defenders a team has, the better a job of blocking they should be able to do. Defenders are also regarded as the best tacklers on the team.

They are fearless, tenacious, and willing to commit themselves physically to the game.

Although revered as the foundation of any team, defenders can play a solid game throughout, only to be booed when they let their guards down for that split second and allow the opposition to score. In the eyes of many, they are as responsible as the goalkeeper for letting a stinger slip by and have to be willing to take their share of the lumps. By and large, however, such scorn is rare and defenders are appreciated for what they bring to the team.

Time Out

Tackling in soccer is similar to tackling in American football except that it is a player-to-player confrontation. No one is taken to the ground (at least not intentionally). You tackle an opponent by disarming that person of the ball, rather than by intercepting the ball in flight.

There are two types of defenders on any given soccer team:

- **Outside Fullbacks,** also known as wings or wingbacks, cover the team's left and right flanks. They become anchors in their respective spots on the field. Their efforts go a long way in protecting the goal and foiling efforts to set up side shots, also known as crosses, that come down the edge of the field.

  A wingback's role is to stop opponents and then to support the team's attack on the opponent's goal. They may need to step out of position to pressure the ball, or shift into the middle to help support central defenders or provide balance. Wingbacks should do a lot of shifting and sliding—both forward and backward and side-to-side.

- **Central Defenders** watch the front of the goal box and operate in various pairings and positions to stop the ball. The position closest to the net itself is sometimes called the sweeper and is the last line of defense before the goal.

  In front of the sweeper there sometimes will be a stopper who covers the center forward position—in this case really a defensive position played forward toward midfield—and adds another defensive dimension to the backfield. Central defenders also may function side by side as extensions of the wing, almost forming a cowling that covers the goal box. Central defenders' distribution depends on the team's overall strategy.

The stopper also may be known as the hammer. The stopper's job is to stop attacks, cover loose balls, and do a lot of midfield tackling, which is a very dangerous area for the opponent to have the ball. If these loose balls are not tackled or challenged by this player, opponents will gain time and space to attack on goal. That's something a defense should never let the opponent do.

> ### Time Out
>
> The sweeper is the organizer and communicator and cleans up all of the loose play behind the other defenders. Sweepers usually start a lot of attacks, thus should be calm, cool, and collected, as well as aggressive enough to attack the ball if anyone breaks through the line of defense.

As we said earlier, all players need to be prepared to take the defensive position, sometimes frequently during a game, in the same way that defenders may find themselves in an offensive stance (this is sometimes called overlapping).

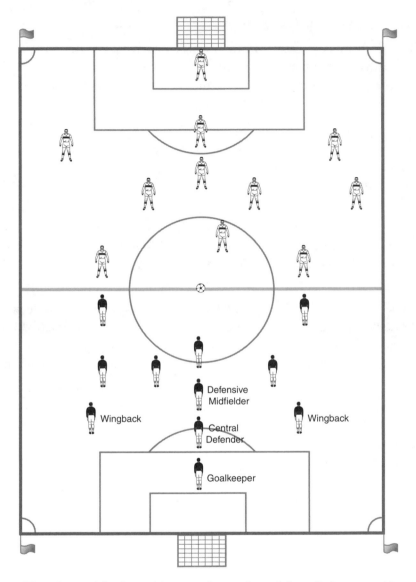

The primary defensive positions stay close to the goal, but all players provide defensive support when the opposition has the ball. This 3-4-3 strategy shows three defenders and one midfielder assigned to defense. The other three midfielders work with the forwards to advance the ball toward the goal.

From a full-team perspective, there's one more category of defender we should mention:

♦ **Defensive Midfielders,** sometimes referred to as stay-at-home midfielders, do just that. They hang back and support the defense position, stationing themselves a little farther forward on the field but with the same basic duty as formal defenders.

The big advantage to this position is that from the midfield vantage point these upfront defenders can do a better job of picking off passes and moves gone awry, powering the ball farther into the opposition's defensive territory, thus saving a little wear and tear on the backfield defenders.

Playing Tip

The number of defensive midfielders usually is limited to one or two players. Most defenders and goalkeepers would like to see a whole lot more.

Zone vs. Player-to-Player Defense

In addition to there being two different types of defenders, there are also two different types of defense:

- **A Zone Defense** is in play when the defenders are responsible for a specific area, covering whichever players enter that area. Also called Zonal Marking, this defensive style allows area coverage without the pressure of having to play man-to-man. But there can be confusion among zone defenders as to who covers which area of the zone, something the opposition can use to its advantage.

- **Player-to-Player Defense** requires the defender to shadow his or her chosen target throughout the entire game, covering his or her movement and, with any luck, more effectively preventing any shots on goal. In player-to-player, there is no confusion about how the opposition should be covered or who should do what. Making sure all players are covering counterparts of like ability, however, may cause some problems if the team is mismatched. This can be especially problematic with youth teams.

Playing Tip

Rotating your defenders through forward positions may be one of the best ways to hone their aggressive edges. They may find, in fact, that while there are differences between the tasks, there also are some intrinsic similarities, many of which may be put to better use by the defender whose eyes have been at last opened to possibilities.

Whichever strategy you use with your team, it should be consistent throughout the game and practiced as aggressively as the offense. Too many novices feel that the defenders' role is to sit back, wait for the action to come to them, and then react. Not so.

Good defenders follow the strategy and take an active stance in meeting incoming forwards head-on in an attempt to drive them back. First-time coaches sometimes are surprised at how successful an aggressive strategy can be. The players usually are not.

Factors in Defense

Effective defenders do more than merely try to form a human wall between the other team's offense and the goal. In fact, there are four distinct tactical maneuvers to mounting a good defense:

- Pressuring the offense
- Providing defensive support
- Tracking your opponent
- Attacking the ball

Each of these, in turn, goes a long way to helping protect the goal from the opposition. Taken together they create a formidable and effective defensive opposition. Let's consider each in turn.

Pressuring the Offense

In pressuring the offense, defenders make every effort to decrease the time and space the attacking player has to pass or dribble. By compromising opposing players' abilities to execute basic tasks, defenders effectively upset the players' rhythms of play and reduce the likelihood of them shooting or setting up for another player to make a shot.

Time Out
"Immediate chase" is a term that means to pressure the ball once the opponent has taken the ball away from you or dribbled past a defender. The aim is to swarm the ball and get players behind the ball.

To effectively pressure the opposition, defenders have to position themselves between the opposition and the goal at a distance of about 2 yards. Stand too far out and there won't be enough presence to make a difference; too close and the opposing player may easily elude defenders' advances. The right distance and constant attention will make it difficult for the attacker to execute a forward pass. That restricts the opposition's progress, which is exactly what defense is supposed to do.

When the ball is in the opposition's possession, everybody pressures because everyone becomes a defender. Pressuring is the primary defensive move that all players must exercise in order to effectively defend the goal. The real purpose of pressuring, of course, is to seize control of the ball. Once the ball is back in your team's possession, then everyone goes on offense. Then it's the other team's turn to pressure you!

Providing Defensive Support or Cover

Players who pressure the opponent with the ball need support to prevent the ball handler from getting past him. That's where the defensive support, also known as cover, comes into play. Think of pressure and cover as tag teams designed to completely box the opposition in and allow no effective advance toward the goal.

Just as the pressuring player stays within two yards of his or her opponent, the defensive supporter should stray no more than four to six yards from the player with the ball. That way, if the ball handler manages to elude the pressuring player, the defensive support player is right there to pick up coverage and immediately apply the necessary pressure.

To that end, the role of defensive supporters comes down to three tasks:

   ◆ The defensive supporter must be aware of where other defensive players are on the field. The team can't afford to have everyone clustering around a single player and leave the rest of the field wide open.

   ◆ The defensive supporter must be aware of how the opposing ball handler likes to play. If he or she likes long kicks, playing a little farther back might be a better strategy.

   ◆ The defensive supporter must have a sense of the area of the field and how the attacking player might play that area.

Defensive supporters also are in position to do a little pressuring of their own. From a broader vantage point, they can see player activity patterns the pressuring player might miss. The defensive supporter's ability to point his or her teammate in particular directions or positions may prove very valuable to the overall direction and outcome of play. That's all part of the teamwork in action that you've been teaching your players all along.

Time Out

When coaching players on how to pressure opponents, have them imagine a 2-foot length of rope between them and the opposition. Their job is to always keep the imagined length taut—never letting it get shorter or longer than 2 feet. This will help them maintain position.

Good observation skills by all players at all time is all it takes. After a while, even younger kids may begin to see patterns and know what to expect.

Tracking Your Opponent

Whether playing zone defense or player-to-player defense, all defenders know how critical it is to stick with their attackers. The important thing is to stay between the opposition and the goal, of course, but players shouldn't be content merely to occupy similar space—they should always be anticipating their opponent's next move.

Tracking also involves keeping an eye not only on the ball but on the player who possesses it. Remember our drill for "heads up" soccer (see Chapter 10)? This is where it comes more completely into play. Players concentrating too hard only on where the ball is may have trouble judging where that ball will be going. Being able to anticipate that is an important part of tracking.

Attacking the Ball

The majority of goals are scored in soccer because the defense has failed to clear the ball from the defensive area before the opposition has had time to set up for a successful shot on goal. Sometimes, of course, this is inevitable. At other times, however, a goal could have been prevented by just a little more effective defensive play. More than anything else, that means attacking the ball.

There's an aggressive side to defense that can mean big saves for most teams, but the defenders have to take the initiative and not merely wait until the ball comes to them. Here are some things that defenders can do:

Be first to arrive at the ball.

When the ball is kicked, even if it's between two players of the same team, it is, for the moment, a free ball and available to anyone who can reach it first. In the case of a kick on goal or even just in the defensive area, the defender must be first to the ball in order to take control. It doesn't matter how strong, how agile, or how talented the player is. If he or she isn't first to the ball, then none of that talent matters.

Go for height on the kick.

Defensive areas, by their nature, are crowded, and ground kicks, no matter how accurate or strong, rarely travel far without running into some kind of obstacle, such as the leg or foot of another player. Depending how they react to that contact, the ball may be catapulted back into the line of fire or even directly into the goal itself.

Once the defender reaches the ball first, he or she should go for a high kick, even if it's straight up in the air. That's done by digging the foot deep under the ball and letting go with a strong top of the foot strike designed to move the ball far from the area. It's critical to get the ball past the nearby opposition, then to get the ball out of the defensive area as quickly as possible. High kicks do that better than anything else.

Shoot for distance.

Height is very important, but so is distance. The two have to work in tandem, however, otherwise distance becomes force which, in a crowded area, could easily backfire. Players who combine height and distance effectively send the ball up and out of the way of the goal quickly and cleanly. And that's exactly what they want.

Play the ball wide.

Much like height and distance, playing the ball wide and sending it into relatively unpopulated areas of the field buys time and distance in protecting the goal. There are even times when it's better to play it so wide that it sails out of bounds. The first goal is to get the ball out of the defensive area and as far away as possible. If the best strategy proves to be kicking it out of bounds—far enough away, of course, so that the opposition doesn't simply bring it back into the defensive area—then that becomes a sound strategy to pursue.

As all these suggestions demonstrate, the best strategy is an aggressive one designed to turn the course of action by deflecting or regaining possession of the ball. At the very least, your defensive strategy should be to get the ball as far away from your defensive area as possible.

> **Time Out**
>
> In any game involving running and kicking, there is an inevitable third element: falling. Players should be encouraged to get up and back into play as quickly as possible. Time spent on the ground is time not helping the team work toward scoring a goal. Those few seconds could interrupt momentum to allow the other team to score a goal.

Taking Control of the Ball

Defenders must not only protect the goal but also, if possible, intercept the ball and change the rules of possession. This happens frequently in soccer, sometimes due to errors on the part of the team with the ball and other times by tactical design. We can't affect the former, but in terms of the latter, there are ways that defenders can gain possession more often. It all depends on the approach.

Interception and its related tactics require speed, skill, and a full awareness of the situation's implications. But doing so effectively may turn the tide of the game:

Playing Tip _____

Players should remain as flexible as possible, and need to be able to change directions and turn quickly. Speed is important, as is staying with the other team's players they have been assigned to.

◆ The art of **interception,** of course, is merely making the right moves to take the ball away from the handler while the ball is in between passes or in mid-dribble. The best approach often is from the side and at a slight angle. Head-on approaches are too easily outmaneuvered and you can rarely disarm a player in motion by trying to catch up with him from behind. An angular approach as early in the player's run as possible is the best method for success.

◆ **Tackling** involves disarming that person of the ball, instead of waiting until the person passes the ball to intercept it. When you tackle the ball, you take the ball from the opposing team.

◆ **Forcing the player out of bounds** while tracking him on the run is a legitimate strategy, resulting in a stoppage of the opposing team's forward momentum and forcing them to sacrifice possession to you. Sometimes you may not have to force the attacking players out. Forcing players close to the line may cause them to stop. Either way, the ball no longer is moving toward your goal.

◆ Attacking players also may be **forced inside,** meaning their forward motion down the line is cut off by a wingback or other defensive player, forcing them to stop and change direction. That slows action, impedes progress, and does all those other things good defenders do.

A Closer Look at Tackling

If dribbling is an offensive move—and whenever you have the ball and are taking it to the goal, you're on the offense—then tackling is the antithesis of that move. Tackling is designed to take the ball away from the opposition. Experienced players rarely let you intercept the ball, especially during dribbles. You will have to tackle them, pure and simple.

Effective tackling in soccer, as in any sport involving confrontation, involves more than an explosion of energy and a flurry of feet. There needs to be a strategy based on opportunity that allows you to secure possession of the ball. Here are some techniques you can use to successfully tackle your opponent.

Toe Pokes

It's one of the simpler tackles and one of the most effective, but it requires assistance from the player with the ball. That player must expose the ball to you long enough that you can reach in with your foot and poke the ball out into the open, and hopefully to one of your teammates who can take control. Once again the ankle of the leg used to poke is locked to offer maximum strength. In this case, timing is everything.

One way to disarm an opponent who has the ball is to execute a toe poke through his or her legs. The offensive player advances from behind and pokes his or her toe through, kicking the ball out of reach of the player who had it and to a teammate, who can now reverse the direction of play.

Funnelings

You might also call these two-against-one take-aways. Two players approach the player with the ball and compromise his field and playing position. With legs bent and taking short steps, the players close in to block the opponent's advantage, perhaps with one using a toe poke to disarm the player and pass the ball to the other.

Block Tackles

This is a more aggressive tackle and one where the player leans into the attacker, overstepping the ball and making it nearly impossible for the player to do anything with the ball. Often, the block tackler straddles the leg of the attacker as it extends with the ball. The attacker knows that he can't move forward, nor can he withdraw his leg without sacrificing possession of the ball. When executed correctly, the block tackle can be very effective.

An able blocker will seize control of the ball and either move it forward or kick it to a teammate.

Sliding Tackles

Slide tackles are the showcase tackles of soccer, the ones that get the most replay time on the 11 o'clock news because they are the most visually evident to the fans. When most people think of tackles, in fact, sliding tackles come to mind.

In a slide tackle, the defensive player meets the carrier from the side or at an angle and literally slides into the ball to drive it out of the carrier's control.

In the case of both the conventional sliding tackle and the hook sliding tackle, the approach is taken from the side. The tackler literally slides in front of the oncoming player to disarm that player of the ball with his or her outstretched leg. The conventional slide comes across the front of the player, whereas the hook slide brings a leg around to propel the ball to the rear of its former possessor. When executed properly, both can be effective tackles.

Yellow Card _____

When executing slide tackles, care has to be taken not to foul the opposing player or intentionally trip him up. That may happen anyway, but it must be clear to referees that the tackler's intent simply was to disarm the ball carrier.

Practice tackles with your team and concentrate on simple skills for teams that are younger. Save the slides for older, more advanced players.

Yellow Card _____

Although it may seem necessary at times, it's never a good idea to try and tackle from behind. If you find yourself in that position, it means your player-to-player coverage has gone bad in the first place. If you attempt a from-behind tackle, chances are you'll get the player rather than the ball, which results in a serious penalty and perhaps even ejection from the game. It's better not to even attempt such a move.

Defense Comes Into Its Own

Until recently, soccer was played with a much greater emphasis on offense than defense. Soccer was an attacking player's game with the majority of the players upfield hammering away at the goal. There may have been one or two players assigned to defense, but by and large everyone was on the offensive line.

In the past few decades, soccer has become more strategic in its thinking and tactical in its approach. What that means is a more balanced team with a greater emphasis on defense and a surprisingly heavy presence at midfield. A lot of teams believe the game is either won or lost at midfield, and often that proves to be the case.

Midfield is a decisive area. The ball can shift hands—or, if you will, feet—while still being played in a neutral area. This allows the balance of power, both in terms of the offense/defense balance and the balance between the two teams to be on a more even keel.

Time Out

Some might argue that, compared to historical precedents at least, today's defense operates much more like an offensive mechanism than those of the past. This is probably true, but these days players have no other choice.

But whether in midfield or elsewhere on the field, an active defense, one that strikes as well as defends, is critical to success of the team.

For the sake of your team, cultivating a solid and sound defense is vital to your success this season and for player success in future seasons. Young players, especially, should be taught how to defend aggressively and with special emphasis on learning and cultivating technique. Your scores and standing in your league will be your measure of success.

The Least You Need to Know

- Throughout the match all players will at times play a defensive game and they should be prepared to do so.

- A good defense is aggressive, not passive, and engages the opponent before waiting to be engaged.

- There are three types of defenders: central defenders, wings, and midfield defenders.

- There are two defensive strategies: player-to-player defense and zone defense.

- Defenders can intercept the ball, tackle the opponents, or otherwise wrest the ball away from the other side. And they should do so frequently.

- Mastering the five types of tackling will make good defenders even more effective.

Chapter 14

A Good Offense

In This Chapter

- ◆ What forwards do
- ◆ Key offensive tools
- ◆ Shooting the goal

Do we really need to say it? Doesn't everyone already know that the best defense is a good offense? Since we're following so closely on the heels of our defense discussion, it's probably the time and place to point that out. It's a lesson that, once learned, will lead to success.

Offense, of course, is when your team has the ball and is moving down-field toward your opponent's goal. The moment you lose the ball—and you will fairly often—your offense switches to defense and the opponents' defense becomes offense. When you're on offense, you not only protect your goal but usually have more opportunities for more shots on goal. That's how and why a good offense is considered a good defense.

You already know that player configurations on the field—the 4-4-2 system, for example—indicate whether a team is playing a defensive or offensive game. Good teams play a balanced game; great teams somehow manage to take advantage of the natural strengths of their team members, find the edge over their competition, and win consistently.

How to use your offensive players will be the secret to your success.

Assuming the Forward Position

Because positions operate so fluidly on the field, moving from defense to offense and back again, our discussion of offensive plays and strategies refers to any player in the offensive mode, no matter their position. However there are players whose primary duty is offense. Let's take a closer look at each of them.

Playing Tip

Roles change rapidly on the soccer field. Just as forwards must become defensive players when the opposition has the ball, so must defenders take an offensive position when your team has the ball. That doesn't mean they change positions or titles. It simply means that defensive players attempt to execute offensive plays until they're called upon once again to fulfill their primary duties.

Time Out

In the pro leagues strikers are the highest paid players because they're the ones who most consistently charge the goals and the ones who most often score. That's not to say, however, that a great striker is a goal-kicking machine. One score per game is an exceptional average, with one score every other game being a more likely, yet fully acceptable, performance.

The Forwards

Every player has the opportunity to score, but those charged specifically with scoring goals are called forwards. They are the aggressive chargers who play deep into "enemy" territory and whose job it is to set up and score goals. Many of soccer's most famous players earned their reputation because of their scoring abilities. Scoring, after all, is how a team wins. Forwards also get the most criticism when scores are low or nonexistent.

There are two basic types of forwards:

- **Strikers,** also called center forwards, are the glamour boys and girls of the game. A good striker operates effectively in tight quarters and is very aggressive in pursuit and capture of loose balls. The striker needs to be durable—willing and able to take physical punishment without flagging his or her effort. Energy and strength are a must.

- **Wings or "wingers"** flank the strikers and play the sides of the field, much like wings on defense. It's the offensive wings' job to set up the shot for the striker, capturing balls that come their way and kicking them to center of the field so the striker can kick the ball into the net. Wingers need to be fast so they can get by the opposition and make the necessary headway in an attempt to score.

This primary duty doesn't stop the wing from taking advantage of any scoring opportunity that may come his or her way, but shooting at the goal isn't the position's primary strength. The best wings bring the ball to the point where a talented striker can score. If the wing has done that much, then he or she has done the job exceptionally well.

> **Time Out**
>
> Forwards also are called "targets," a name that refers to the fact that, as the ball moves upfield, the forwards become the targets for offensive passes designed to be set up for a shot on goal.

The Midfielders

The offense also can count on support from midfield:

- **Offensive midfielders,** often called attacking midfielders, offset and often out-number their defensive midfielder counterparts. The attacking midfielder has good opportunity to pass the ball, helping the wings set up the shot for the striker. A good offensive midfielder who excels at passing, for example, is invaluable to getting shots into play and ready for the striker. Combination plays that utilize offensive midfielders working with the forwards can be surprisingly effective.

A good offensive midfielder begins the drive to the goal before the midline if possible and makes sure the momentum has been ratcheted up to the highest level possible when he or she passes the ball that sets up the shot for the goal. If they have strong legs, the midfielder can shoot the goal, but the better strategy is to have the mid-fielder place the ball and have the striker score the goal.

Systems of Play = Offensive Strategies

Remember those combinations of numbers (4-4-2, 4-3-3, 3-5-2, and so on) from Chapter 12? At the time, we called them systems of play, and pointed out the various advantages and disadvantages to each of them. The system of play you choose determines your offensive strategy. Because the system of play you choose directly influences how many goals your team will score, let's review them here:

- A stronger backfield, such as a 4-4-2 or a 4-3-3, means that you're playing a more defensive game. The more players you have assigned to guard the goal, the safer that goal will be. However, the offense will have to be twice as capable to make up for the loss of support.

♦ If you adopt a 4-2-4, you've assigned more players as forwards and attacking midfielders, and you've set a more aggressive scoring agenda. Those left to play defense will come under greater pressure when the opposition gains control of the ball. Some might see this more offensive strategy as a bigger gamble, but they fail to realize that not having enough offensive players runs its own risk in increased pressure on existing scorers.

To determine the appropriate strategy for your team, measure the team strengths and judge the opposition based on what you already know about them as well as the system of play they employ. Those factors should help determine just how you will proceed over the next 90 minutes.

And don't be afraid to make changes at half time. If your team is down a goal, for example, you can shift to a more offensive system of play. Some coaches try to emphasize to the team that while they have the ball and are attacking their team is in a 3-4-3, but while defending they should shift into a 4-4-2. This could be a little too high-level for certain ages, however, so only employ it if your team has mastered their primary strategy of play.

A successful compromise might be a more extensive midfield cluster with the proper number of players designated defensive and offensive. Remember the school of thought that holds that games are won and lost at midfield? It's based on experience, and perhaps a 3-5-2 approach might be the best fallback position in an uncertain situation. The 3-5-2 could be a successful strategy for younger players of limited ability as well as teams struggling with performance problems.

Playing Tip _____

Systems of play can be adjusted to fit the needs of play. Based on its success, you may want to change the system of play during the game to offset unanticipated strengths on the part of the opposition, weaknesses among your own players, or simply to rebalance the equation now that you know what the other team is about.

Playing Tip _____

Your team's forwards will be followed by markers—the defensive players from the other team assigned to the forwards or to the space you occupy (depending on whether they are playing zone or man-to-man defense). The trick is to teach your forwards to shake their marker or to catch them off position just prior to a shot. Speed and ability are essential, but often markers will still match players move for move. The secret is to understand the nature and moves of the markers and outwit them. Just like a boxer waiting for an opponent to telegraph a punch, you need to teach your forwards to learn markers' habits and operate counter to them. That's done through practice, skills mastery, and keen observation of their opponents' moves and habits. Obviously, this is easier for older, more developed players.

Team strategies play a greater role than might first appear—even for youth soccer teams. A superior offensive player can work with the existing strategy, adapting tactics to the situation and taking advantage of unexpected opportunities that come up. Certainly, this is an important skill for all players but for forwards and attacking midfielders it is critical.

Tools of the Offense

The most important tool for any player on the offense is understanding and following the strategy developed by the coach because it's designed first and foremost to help the offense accomplish its goal, which is to score.

Forwards and attacking midfielders who don't follow the pre-arranged strategy had better have a very good explanation—backed up by the appropriate number of goals—to prove why their idea was better. And while you can't be as demanding of younger players, you can make sure you scale your strategy to the skill of the team and let them know you expect them to follow the strategy.

In the rest of this section we'll review other important offensive tools.

Moving the ball toward the goal is an important part of the offense, making dribbling skills crucial.

For a longer discussion of dribbling, refer to Chapter 9. Dribbling is important to all players but perhaps most important to midfielders and forwards moving toward the opposition's goal.

Once again, control is the most important factor, followed by enough speed and agility to be able to snake that ball around the opposition and put it into position for a scoring kick. All the directives about distance from the ball and support from other players apply here, but in spades.

Playing Tip _____

Dribblers many times draw a defensive crowd, thereby freeing up other offensive players. Those dribblers can then pass to open teammates to create a scoring opportunity.

Good passing and receiving skills will mean greater success.

It's all about controlling the ball and moving it forward. Dribbling will do that in most cases. What dribbling may not be able to do is move the ball as quickly as it needs to be moved, and it rarely can be used effectively to set up for a goal shot because the maneuver becomes far too obvious and the shot easy to anticipate, thus block.

Effective passing and receiving can move the ball quickly downfield while the rest of the players are still upfield, thereby setting up the forward for a relatively unobstructed shot on goal.

Styles may vary, but there are three basic types of passes:

◆ The **forward pass** is an aggressive maneuver and can be risky because it's kicked toward the opposition's goal and, presumably, the opposition's defenders. Unless executed by a skilled player who can place the shot with precision, the opposing team will likely intercept the ball. When it comes to forward passes, it often pays to be bold but not foolish. Bold passes are based on clear opportunity combined with good passing and receiving skills. Foolish passes are aggressive passes taken without the right opportunity or appropriate skills.

Yellow Card _____

A poorly conceived and executed backward pass can be even more dangerous than a foolhardy forward pass. A backward pass is kicked in the direction of your own goal—the direction your opponents want to see the ball go—and you may find the receiver to be one of their forwards who will then carry the ball on to a goal against you.

◆ Conversely, the **backward pass** sends the ball in the direction of your own goal and is used to get out of tight situations when forward motion— either by dribbling or passing—is not an option. Some coaches feel passes should *never* be sent in the direction of your own goal because of the possibility of having them be intercepted by the other team and taken in to score. Players should use them sparingly, carefully, and with only enough force to get themselves out of a jam. No matter what the philosophy, players will inevitably use them, so it pays to practice and do them right.

◆ Some coaches stress the **square pass**—a pass that is made laterally with no forward motion—as being the safest pass to execute. We say no! Square passes rarely if ever achieve forward motion, which means they're stagnant at best. More often than not, they serve to set up an interception by the opposition, who welcomes the fact that you have made it so easy for them. There will be times when a square pass may get a player out of a jam, but we recommend it only as a last resort … if that!

Despite the hazards, forward passes are the only ones that consistently move the player forward. Players should execute them wisely and with care, but they should strive to shoot forward rather than in any other direction.

In addition to the direction of the pass, the type of pass itself could mean the difference between success and failure.

Soccer players have mastered several types of passes, and we'll explain a few of the key types here.

The most important thing to remember in all cases is that the ankle remains locked and foot and ankle act as one unit. A solid kick is made even more solid when the kicking surface of the body is firm. That firmness aids in strength, propulsion, and bounce of the ball toward its intended target. A limp ankle affects speed, control, and direction, not to mention the fact that a player may hurt him or herself in the process.

Playing Tip

When kicking, the position of the nonkicking foot, also called the stabilizing foot, is just as important as the kicking foot. Ideally, it should be immediately adjacent to the ball, although the exact position varies since games are played on the run. No matter its position, the stabilizing foot should *always* be planted before the kick is made. Players who don't plant their nonkicking foot may find they have kicked themselves right off their feet!

Basic Passing Shots

With ankle locked and foot aimed, your team should learn the following passes.

The Push Pass

The push pass, sometimes referred to as the instep pass, is forward motion over short or medium distances, at the goal or at another player. The ankle is locked and the ball is struck with the inside of the foot in order to control the ball's trajectory.

The basic pass, known as a push or instep pass, is executed with a kick on the inside of the foot. After a brief toe touch to set up the pass, the player literally pushes the ball as he or she kicks, which gives the kicker more control over the shot.

For the greatest accuracy, the kicking foot should remain parallel to the target—close or open the span of the foot too much and the ball will miss its mark. Novice and youth players should attempt to align their bodies with the target to better control the position of the foot, but more experienced players who have the necessary control need not do this.

The Heel Pass

The heel pass can be used to execute a backward pass. Players in tight situations can redirect the ball by stepping in front of it and striking it with the heel of the foot. A wild heel pass can result in a dangerous advantage for the opposing team. Heel passes are designed for very short distances and always with adequate forethought as to the effect of the maneuver.

For the heel pass, the player steps in front of the ball and kicks it behind him with the heel. Because heel passes should be used to cover short distances, there should be very little follow through on the kick.

The Outside Foot Pass

The outside foot pass uses a less controllable surface—the outside of the foot—to move the ball downfield. That makes it a good alternative for infrequent situations with passing needs of 10 yards or less. The advantage is that you may be able to pass beyond or around an opposing player more easily, who may be expecting a regular push pass. Players attempting this pass should make sure to strike the ball closer to the top so it remains low to the ground. The ankle, as always, should be locked for maximum distance and control.

Putting the Ball in the Air: The Chip Shot

To cover long distances or vault obstacles, players often use the chip shot. The player strikes the ball with the top of the foot, much like an American football punter. The stabilizing foot is placed next to the ball before the kick is made. The strike tends to raise the ball so it arcs down the field, often covering long distances. Done with accuracy, a good chip shot can deliver the ball to a forward downfield, who then may be able to set it up for a shot on goal.

The chip shot also can be used to lob the ball over the head of the goalkeeper and into the net. This can be done if the goalkeeper is a little too far away from the net or in some other way compromised.

Yellow Card _____

Chip shots are used infrequently because they often arc over the net as well, but they can be effective under the right circumstances.

The chip shot is executed by getting underneath the ball and using the top of the foot to elevate the ball over an obstacle. In this case, the obstacle is likely the goalkeeper, who may have strayed a little too far from the net.

There is no follow-through on the kick because the player wants arc, not distance, to drive the ball to its target. The best chip shots lob the ball *and* give it backspin to limit the distance the ball travels.

Time Out
Successful kicks always are the result of a stable support foot that has been solidly planted in appropriate relationship to the ball before the kicking foot is engaged. Sometimes that foot is planted next to the ball, other times slightly behind it. Without the stabilizer, there's a good chance the kick will go awry and result either in a missed opportunity or a ball lost to the other team.

Teach Passes According to Skill Level

Kicking is the heart of the game. Simple, straightforward kicks are best for younger players. As they get older they will be able to increase their repertoire. The more styles they can master, the more effective a player they will become.

For more advanced players, remember to vary the types and styles of passes throughout the game and among passers. If the team embraces a certain type of pass or a certain player becomes known for always doing the same thing, those passes become easy to anticipate, thus intercept. Stress this point in practice as well as during games.

Shooting the Goal

The purpose of executing any offensive strategies in soccer is to get in position to take a shot at the goal and, with any luck, score a point.

Shooting the goal is the most difficult task to accomplish for the following reasons:

◆ The opposition will do whatever it can within the rules of the game to prevent those shots.

◆ Except for penalty kicks, shots on goal are almost always done under extreme pressure and always on the run.

◆ In the heat of battle, the rudiments of the proper setups often are forgotten.

◆ Force, rather than accuracy, becomes too many players' mantra, meaning they overshoot conditions and miss the goal.

◆ A lot of opportunities to make successful shots are missed by forwards merely trying to stay on their feet and keep from being tackled or having the ball intercepted.

Shooting for a goal is the ultimate offensive action, and we have an entire chapter devoted to scoring techniques later in this volume (see Chapter 15). At this point, it's enough to say that shots on goal require practice, practice, and more practice under as adverse a set of conditions as possible. Remember the following points when teaching shots on goal to your players:

- Stress accuracy over speed or force and learn to master it under all conditions.

- Make field observations a part of the training and make sure forwards practice with their heads up and an awareness of what's going on around them.

- Teach goal shooting as a strategy as well as a skill.

- Emphasize that, as much or more than anything else, shots on goal are the result of planning and full team involvement, not the luck of a single hot dog player.

- Have forwards look for opportunities to shoot and create them if they're not there.

Remember that the goalkeeper isn't going to get out of the way. He or she will only move to block the ball. If you can give the goalkeeper reason to move one way and then shoot the other, you may be able to put a point on the board. And that point might be enough to bring your team to victory

The Least You Need to Know

- Strong defense is important, but a good offensive strategy is the only way your team will score points and win the game.

- Everyone plays offense when the opposition has the ball, but forwards and attacking midfielders are the ones specifically charged with setting up the shots and scoring the goals.

- Passing and receiving is the fastest way to send a ball upfield and in position for a goal kick. Depending on the type of pass and skill of the passer, it also can be the most dangerous.

- When executing any kick, the ankle of the kicking foot should be locked, forming a solid kicking surface. The other foot should stabilize the player so the player isn't knocked off-balance.

- Stress accuracy rather than force in all passing shots and look for opportunities to make as many good shots as possible.

The Care and Feeding of Goalkeepers

In This Chapter

- ◆ Goalkeeping basics
- ◆ Catches and saves
- ◆ Positioning, positioning, positioning
- ◆ Supporting the defense
- ◆ Giving the ball a boot!

To this point we've looked carefully at defense and offense, strategies and tactics, plans, and executions. We've discussed at length the roles played by 10 of the players on your team, delving into their performance psyches, motivations, and needs.

But that was only practice. Now we come to the goalkeeper, and it's clear from the start that we're entering uncharted territory. As the lynchpin of any soccer team, an effective goalkeeper can make or break a match. If a forward misses a pass or a defender loses the ball, there are other offensive and defensive players to pick up the slack.

But there is only one goalkeeper. No matter how well that player does throughout the majority of the game, one missed pass could lead to a point for the opposing team. And that one point may cause you to lose the game. Goalkeepers are heroes and villains, saviors and failures—often within the context of the same game. It takes someone special to be a goalkeeper (and there are those who believe that a little craziness also never hurts success in that position).

Even younger goalkeepers soon realize and understand the importance of their role, and a surprising number rise to the occasion.

What Sets Goalkeepers Apart

Differences between goalkeepers and regular players abound:

♦ While they can range far afield, goalkeepers tend to stay within the confines of the penalty box.

♦ Goalkeepers are the only players allowed to touch the ball with their hands. They can catch the ball and throw it back into play, pick up the ball and kick it downfield, or bat the ball away with their hands. Chances are they will do each a dozen or more times during the typical 90-minute game.

♦ Goalkeepers dress differently than their teammates as a way to differentiate themselves in the penalty box in the heat of action.

> **Time Out**
>
> The best goalkeepers become very passionate and vocal about keeping their penalty box clean of the opposition. They do a lot of vocal encouraging and demanding from their teammates. This shows that they are in charge.

♦ While there is no size requirement for soccer, goalkeepers tend to be a little larger and taller so they have more reach, thus are better able to keep the ball from entering the net.

♦ Fast footwork is the secret to any goalkeeper's success. By the time the ball reaches the penalty box, the margin for error is gone and the keeper will have to respond rapidly, precisely, and with strength to make the save.

♦ Goalkeepers may be a little older than the rest of the team with more experience and be better able to anticipate incoming shots on goal and prevent them.

♦ Goalkeepers have a different understanding of the game—many have gone on to become coaches because of the way they see things.

♦ Younger goalkeepers may lack the sophistication of older players, but they learn quickly that they have a different role than their teammates. They can use their hands, which sets them apart from the crowd.

Although team ability is built on the strength of both coach and players, the cornerstone to the success of the team just may be the effectiveness of its goalkeeper. It's that player who executes the ultimate defensive position. And for the goalkeeper, there's no margin for error.

In the end, goalkeepers must have a special presence on the field. They're the backbone of the team. They must have command of their penalty box. They must lead and organize their teammates.

Time Out
Every sport has its own nomenclature, and when it comes to soccer, the person who stands by the net to keep the opposing team from scoring is called a goalkeeper, or keeper for short. That person is not called a "goalie" or "goaltender." Those are names of different positions in different sports. Misidentifying a goalkeeper with those names or any other names will identify you as a rookie. And that's never a good position for a coach to be in.

Catches and Saves

You can discover who on your team is the most likely candidate for the position of goalkeeper by rotating players through the position. All different types make up the goalkeeping world, but among teams of younger players, it's often those who appear a little more mature and capable of standing and waiting—because that's a lot of what goalkeepers do—and can anticipate the action and position themselves accordingly

Goalkeepers train by blocking goals. Period. An endless array of different shooters coming from different angles is the best way to condition goalkeepers, who need to be prepared to block a shot from any given direction. Even the best one can't be in more than one place at one time, yet it sometimes appears that they have to be. They must learn to read the field and position themselves accordingly.

The proper goalkeeper is always on alert, hands poised to intercept any kicks that enter the penalty box. Action happens fast so the goalkeeper has to be ready to meet the ball before it comes to him or her and respond accordingly. Like any good defense player, the goalkeeper takes an aggressive stance and engages the ball and player before it's too late. The goalkeeper has no backup and good ones know the fate of the game—at least when the ball is that far downfield—rests on them.

 Playing Tip

Size and maturity are sometimes as important as skills and flexibility when it comes to young goalkeepers.

Catch Me If You Can

But the goalkeeper has an advantage other players don't. He or she can do whatever it takes to capture the incoming ball and redistribute it to confederates downfield. There are no limitations on which limbs can be used, and the ability to make a good catch is essential.

Some of the more common catches goalkeepers employ to stop the ball's forward progression include the following.

The Chest Catch

The chest catch is executed when the ball is shot right at the goalkeeper, who is able to catch it with both arms against the chest. It's important to keep the body between the ball and net; that way, if the trap fails, the goalkeeper's body has still blocked the ball from scoring a goal.

Goalkeepers perform the chest catch by using both hands and drawing the kicked ball to their chest as they catch it. Because they have their body positioned behind the ball, it is usually consider the safest and most secure type of catch.

The Collapse Dive

The collapse dive might also be called a falling chest catch because it once again places the body of the goalkeeper between the ball and net. The collapse dive is most effective when the ball is on the ground no more than a few steps either to the right or left of the goalkeeper, who drops to the ground in front of the ball—not on top of it—placing his or her body between the ball and net and catching it between arms and chest.

In a collapse dive, the goalkeeper reaches as far possible in the direction of the oncoming ball, collapsing to the ground and using his or her body as a full-length block to stop the ball from entering the net.

Yellow Card

The proper way to land is on one's side. Landing on one's side will prevent goals *and* injury. Novice goalkeepers will land on their stomachs, elbows, or backs, positions that are more likely to cause injury and let the ball slip through. Have goaltenders practice the diving collapse while kneeling. Then practice the dive from a crouched position; finally, from a standing position.

The Diamond Catch

The diamond catch is a two-handed overhead catch executed *from a standing position.* The "diamond," or W catch, refers to the way the thumbs and forefinger of the catcher's hands are positioned on the back of the ball. It's important for the goalkeeper to keep as much of the hands as possible between the ball and the net in the event that the ball pops loose. Once caught, the ball is then brought down to chest level, much like a chest catch.

In a diamond catch, the hands are open to provide the maximum amount of stopping surface, with the thumbs and forefingers forming a diamond-shaped pattern.

The Overhead Catch

Overhead catches involve catching a high ball, usually one that's been headed toward the goal, while it's still in the air. The goalkeeper leaps into the air and executes a two-handed diamond catch—before dropping down and cradling the ball to his or her chest.

The Full-Extension Dive

The full-extension dive is similar to the collapse dive, but requires a full extension of the body to catch, or at least block, the ball from the net. This usually happens when an opponent shoots toward one of the goal's far corners. The goalkeeper should take the largest first stride possible and stretch his or her body out as far as possible.

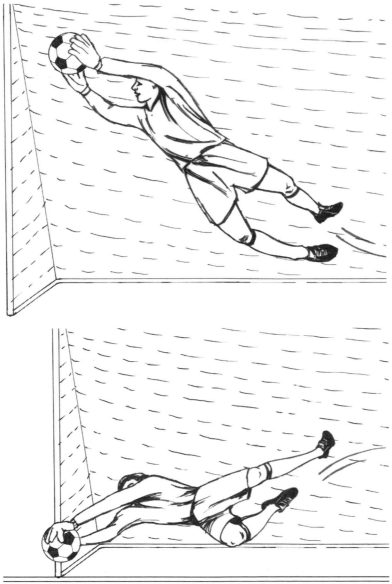

In a full-extension dive, the goalkeeper leaps, extending his or her body its entire length with hands out. Whereas the collapse dive is done from a stationary position, in this dive the goalkeeper extends his or her reach by first striding toward the ball.

Playing Tip

Another and sometimes more successful variation of the full-extension dive involves taking one or two small shuffle steps before the lunge. Some players find it offers them more control before executing the extension, as well as giving them a little extra distance.

The One-on-One Catch

The one-on-one catch is just that: The goalkeeper challenges an oncoming player, staying upright until the last minute and then diving to take the ball away from the opponent. This can be very effective, but it also may be dangerous to the goalkeeper, who puts both face and body at risk of being kicked. Be careful if and how you teach it to youth players. We don't recommend it for very young players.

The Scoop Catch

The scoop catch is used for low shots or those rolling along the ground. The goalkeeper creates a scoop with his hands and shovels the ball up into his or her chest and to safety.

In the scoop catch, the goalkeeper reaches down with both hands and "scoops" the ball up from the playing field. The goalkeeper positions his or her body behind the ball to provide maximum stability for the catch and an additional block in case he or she fumbles the catch.

Catches are something the goalkeeper can do that other players can't. They also provide the opportunity to hold and keep the ball and interrupt the opponents' momentum. Once the goalkeeper takes possession of a ball, players are required to return to the field, away from the goal, so the goalkeeper can deliver the ball back into play. The goalkeeper throws or kicks the ball to his or her own teammates so they can move the ball toward the other team's goal.

Other Ways to Make a Save

Whenever possible, the ball should be caught with the hands and held. If that's not possible, there are other ways to keep the ball away from the net:

◆ Goalkeepers can **deflect the ball,** knocking it aside and, with any luck, to one of their own players.

◆ They can **parry the ball,** a two-handed move made with fists closed much like you would if you were playing volleyball. Unlike deflection, this is something that can be done with greater direction and skill.

◆ Goalkeepers can **punch the ball,** a more aggressive move designed more for distance than accuracy. A punch is designed to take a hard surface (the fist) to the ball and drive it down field, or even just up in the air and out of harm's way.

◆ They can **kick the ball,** either while it's moving in the direction of the goal or punter style, again with the idea of moving it away from the goal and downfield.

The most important thing, of course, is for the goalkeeper to get the ball away from the goal. If possible the ball should be delivered to an offensive player on the goal-keeper's team. But that often depends on the nature of the situation and the skills of the players involved. As with any play in soccer, control and accuracy must be stressed over speed and force, but only as long as it doesn't cost the team a goal. Because of proximity to the goal, the goalkeeper is playing a little higher-stakes soccer. Both you and the goalkeeper need to keep that in mind.

Don't Just Stand There!

Goalkeepers often appear to be lonely characters stationed at the net while the defense and offense run the ball upfield and battle it out in the opponent's defensive zone. In the best of all soccer worlds, the goalkeeper has little to do, and you want to keep it that way!

Of course, that's not going to happen. The goalkeeper will be put to the test repeatedly, sometimes severely, and that's when the real skills come into play.

Over time mature goalkeepers develop enough soccer sense to know how to position themselves in relation to the net, to the oncoming players, and to the play in progress. It's a skill that seems to develop out of a sixth sense, an intuition about when and how an attempted shot will occur and where the goalkeeper needs to be to block that shot. Some experienced goalkeepers make it look so easy, in fact, that you wonder whether or not they're able to read the opponent's mind.

Goalkeeper Positioning

In some cases, they are. It's not reading his or her mind exactly, but understanding that the player approaching from a particular direction is likely to execute a certain kind of kick and that positioning him- or herself at such a point is the best way to block it. There are general guidelines that help the goalkeeper establish the proper distance from and relation to the position of the ball on the field:

- When the ball is downfield and away from the goal, the goalkeeper should come to the edge of the penalty area, being as far forward in his or her zone of defense as possible to anticipate and plan for any sudden counterattacks and staying connected to the rest of the team as the last line of defense.

- When the ball is close to the penalty box, the goalkeeper should play close to the net in anticipation of the inevitable shots on goal.

- When the ball is approaching from the left side of the field, the goalkeeper should follow, moving to his or her right. If the ball is to the right of the goal, the goalkeeper should move to the left, always positioning him or herself between the opposition and the net.

- It's important that the goalkeeper also consider his or her position in relation to his or her own teammates. Goalkeepers who fail to understand their field position in relation to key defenders run the risk of doing the wrong thing at the wrong time and losing the point.

Playing Tip

It helps when the shooter can be intimidated, thus forced to shoot high and/or wide by compromising the angle of the shot. A lunge or advance by the goalkeeper may do that, disrupting the set up of the player and compromising the shot.

There are no flawless goalkeeping strategies, of course, and the position requires a lot of judgment on the part of the goalkeepers. The net is always much larger than goalkeepers themselves, which means sticking tight to it opens wide avenues that the goalkeeper probably won't be able to defend and standing too far away allows an offensive player to lob a chip shot over the head and into the net.

The Near Post Save

The cardinal rule for goalkeepers is always to make the near post—the goal post that's closest to the advancing forward—save. If an opponent is going to score, make sure it's done into the far corner of the net. This strategy also helps the goalkeeper to communicate to teammates to force opposition to the near post areas when guarding so that the goalkeeper can anticipate a near post shot, and make the near post save.

Most importantly, teach your goalkeeper never to assume that when the ball is downfield, the goal is safe—in other words, they should never let their guard down. Scores have been made from midfield or farther. But when the goalkeeper is paying attention and anticipating the action, he or she can usually fend off a midfield attack.

Time Out
Can a goalkeeper score? It's happened, but never without an assist from a forward. The goalkeeper gives the ball a long boot to the forward, who then sets up the ball and scores. That may make good sense with your existing strategy, or you may want a more localized pass from the goalkeeper to another player. But the long boot for setup will at least get the ball out of the zone, which is what the goalkeeper should be doing.

Supporting the Defense

The positions on the field are layered so that if one person is bypassed another is there to take his or her place and meet the oncoming opponents. The goalkeeper is the last line of defense and needs to be protected at all costs. But that goalkeeper also should act in support of fellow teammates, providing one final layer so that if the ball does get by them, the goalkeeper is there to stop the ball.

Supporting the defense involves a twofold strategy:

♦ The goalkeeper must position him- or herself at an angle that supports the defensive players should the ball get by them.

♦ The goalkeeper should stand between the closest defender and goal. The goalkeeper should never stand beside the defenders because that sacrifices the advantage that layering offers.

Once again, the strategy here is about depth and positioning. The deeper the defensive web, the more likely it is the ball will be trapped and not hit its target. If the defenders know the goalkeeper is an active part of that defense, they'll be in much better position to protect the goal. And they will be working more closely together. That coordinated effort is the strength of any team.

Playing Tip

One of the greatest skills a goalkeeper can have is the ability to concentrate on the game. Good concentration allows for better play anticipation, which is the only way the goalkeeper will be able to anticipate when and where to be when he or she needs to stop the ball.

Giving It the Boot!

Besides using their hands to throw the ball back onto the field, goalkeepers can also kick it back into play. Sometimes a good downfield kick is better than a throw.

Capable goalkeepers can employ the following kicking methods:

♦ The **midfield boot** is probably how most keepers use their kicks during the heat of play. One of the goals, as we have said, is to get the ball far away from the penalty box and well on toward the opponent's goal. An accurate kick that allows a fellow team member to head the ball toward the opponents' goal can be very effective. At the very least, it will allow the team to control the kick and keep possession of the ball.

♦ Kicking a **short pass** to a defender who can capably dribble or pass it downfield is a way to more accurately position the ball for future shots against the opponent's goal without running the risk of the ball falling into enemy hands—or feet—quite so rapidly. The pass should be strategic, sent to a defender ready to receive and then do something constructive with the ball.

Playing Tip _____

One rule of thumb might be to distribute the ball to the opposite and open side of the field.

♦ The goalkeeper also can **dribble** the ball a certain distance, usually in preparation for a pass to another player. This can be a little dangerous for all but the most expert dribblers as opponents can tackle the dribbler and seize the ball. To dribble, the goalkeeper must be fast, accurate, and have a specific purpose in mind.

Any move the goalkeeper makes to put the ball onto the field must not be random, but based on a prearranged strategy and be directed toward a specific teammate.

The Least You Need to Know

♦ Goalkeepers are unique individuals usually chosen for size and strength and for intelligence and maturity. In addition to skills, theirs is a judgment game.

♦ The goalkeeper position is distinguished by the ability to catch the ball and otherwise use their hands during play.

♦ The goalkeeper's most important duty is to get the ball away from the goal.

♦ Mature goalkeepers develop enough soccer sense to know how to position themselves in relation to the net, to the oncoming players, and to the play in progress

♦ Goalkeepers have an obligation to support their defensive players and add depth to the defensive zone.

♦ Goalkeepers can kick as well as use their hands and should do so when it fits the play strategy.

Restarts

In This Chapter

- ◆ Turning restarts into opportunities
- ◆ Offensive and defensive restart strategies
- ◆ Corner kick plays
- ◆ Free kick plays
- ◆ Throw-in plays

Soccer is a game of speed, skill, and nonstop action. That has a lot to do with its international popularity. There are no long, slow innings like there are in baseball. There's no time out for commercial breaks and referee reviews of past plays like there is in American football. When a soccer game starts, there is very little to stop the action once the whistle blows. Except, of course, when the ball goes out of bounds.

When the Ball Goes Out of Bounds

In the same way American football players might run out of bounds to stop the clock during the last minutes of play, soccer players also tend to kick the ball out of bounds or simply let it roll out of bounds in certain situations. Unlike American football, however, whoever kicks or touches the ball last before it goes out of bounds loses it to the other team.

Yellow Card

Is kicking the ball out of bounds a mistake in play? Given the penalty, it often is an error, and if it happens close to the goal you're trying to defend, it may be a grievous one. But it also can be a strategic opportunity for either side prepared to take advantage of the restart.

This rule discourages players from dribbling the ball close to the sidelines or endlines unless they can bounce it, either purposefully or inadvertently, off the shins of a player from the opposite team before sending it out of bounds. No matter what the case, loss of the ball out of bounds brings the action to a grinding halt, resulting in a restart of play.

This chapter takes a close look at restarts and how to manage them strategically, both from an offensive and defensive position. Your players may make a mistake by sending the ball out of bounds, but played right they may be able to turn it around and save the day. Let's consider some of the ways that such a thing might happen.

Identifying Restart Opportunities

What is a restart? By definition, it's the chance to start something over, in this case a soccer game. Sometimes it's called a set-up play because it occurs after the regular motion of play has stopped and begins again from a prescribed setup, such as a penalty kick or throw-in. And restarts in soccer mean just that—the chance to start play all over again, this time in a different direction and with the other team in possession of the ball.

Specifically, there are four restart opportunities in soccer: the corner kick, the free kick, goal kicks, and throw ins. Each comes to bear, not at the discretion of either team, but based on the foul that occurs or the way the ball leaves the field of play.

Because of restarts' penalty nature, all kicks and throw-ins are unobstructed. In most cases, players can't get closer than 30 feet to the player with the ball. This provides an enormous advantage for the team with the ball.

Let's look at each restart play in turn.

Corner Kicks

Often a defender, attempting to block an incoming offensive play, will inadvertently be the last one to touch the ball as it nears the goal. If it goes over the goal line and into the net ... well, that's a goal for the other side, and few things make young players feel worse. More often, however, the ball crosses the endline outside the net, which does not result in a goal.

When the ball crosses the endline, the opposition gets to make a corner kick.

A corner kick also can be awarded when the goalkeeper tips a high shot over the net and the goal line. Either way, the opposing team is given the opportunity for a free kick from one of the two corners closest to the goal. And, given the proximity of the kicker to the goal, that's never a good thing, because it allows the possibility of a setup that could result in a goal.

There are three types of corner kicks, each designed to accomplish a different objective:

♦ In executing an **inswinger,** the kicker drives the ball in the air toward the near post—that's the goal post that's nearest to the corner from which the ball is being kicked—to a team member particularly good at heading, or who is at least tall. It's a setup shot designed to allow the on-field player to score a goal.

In addition, the inswinger many times can be "flicked," or redirected, near the goal, which may handcuff the defense and allow for a tap in goal, a rebound goal, or even a goal by a defender who inadvertently redirects the ball into their own goal.

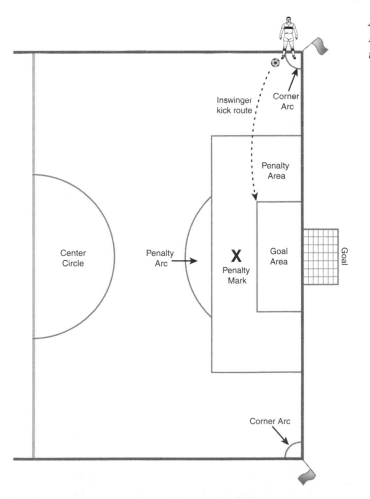

An inswinger corner kick. Notice that the kicker directs the ball to the near post.

♦ An **outswinger** is aimed to the outside edge of the penalty box, to a confederate capable of a good, long-legged kick to drive the ball into the goal from that distance.

An outswinger corner kick. In this restart the kicker directs the ball to the outside edge of the penalty box.

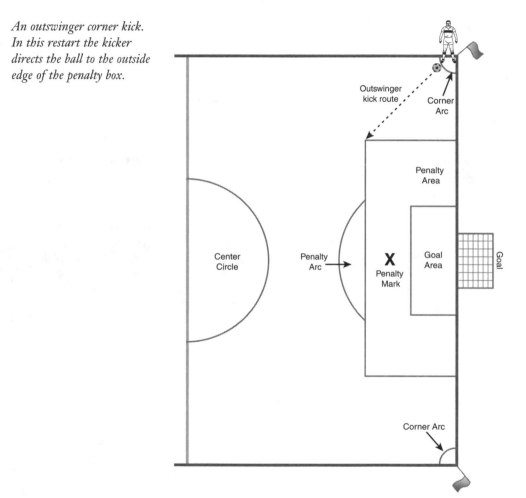

♦ The **short pass** is just that—a quick kick to a confederate in good position and able to dribble the ball in or pass it on to yet another player for a score. This can be a good strategic move because it can really catch the opposition off guard.

The choice of kick will depend on the situation, the position of the opposition, and the skill of the kicker. No matter what kind of kick, the on-field teammates need to be ready to kick it in.

Playing Tip

Both inswinging and outswinging kicks can also be placed approximately 8 to 12 yards from goal, which is one of the best areas to score from since the goalkeeper doesn't want to come out too far away from the net. Attackers should position themselves 8 to 12 yards from the ball when receiving a corner kick.

Free Kicks

When the opposition gets a free kick, that means your team did something wrong. One of your players tripped or otherwise fouled another player, causing the referee to award the other team a free kick at your goal. Free kicks generate the greatest opportunity for the opposing team to score.

There are two types of free kicks, awarded by the referee depending on the nature of the foul:

◆ **Direct kicks,** or kicks directly at the goal, are awarded when a player from the defending team has direct and undesirable physical contact with the ball carrier. This includes such things as kicking, striking, tripping, or violently charging the player. This could also result from restraining the player with his or her hands and/or intentionally touching the ball.

A direct kick is directed at the goal. The opposition must stand at least 10 yards from the kicker.

◆ **Indirect kicks,** directed to another teammate, are awarded when a player behaves in a way that may be dangerous to opponents, but doesn't actually cause injury or harm. Such actions may include obstructing opponents or blocking the goalkeeper from distributing the ball.

The indirect kick differs as it cannot be made directly on goal, but must be kicked to another player as a set-up shot. It will be up to the other player to shoot for a goal.

In either case, the kick is taken from the spot of the foul, with the opposition standing at least 10 yards from the player with the ball. Players obstructing the kick may get a yellow card, two of which result in ejection from the game.

Direct kicks can be awarded anywhere on the field. The ones that pose the greatest danger are those kicked close to the goal because a strong forward or midfielder may be able to make that goal.

Strategies for direct kicks include the following:

◆ The **power kick** is usually a single shot by the strongest or at least most accurate player fired directly at the goal. Direct shots are sometimes easiest to block, but if it's a strong, well-positioned kick, then it may result in a quick and clean goal for the other side. Because the ball is kicked with such force, it's likely that the goalkeeper will be unable to trap the ball, and it might rebound back into the field, giving the offense another chance to score a goal. All players should be ready for this situation.

- The **long kick,** from as far away as midfield, may take the opposing goalkeeper by surprise, especially if it's a move your team hasn't done before. Used strategically, it could be very effective.

- Some teams execute a **combination kick,** something unnecessary on a direct kick, in which several players position the ball for a shot on goal. Depending on your strategy, this may be an effective maneuver.

- There also are **distraction plays,** a sort of soccer "sleight of foot" in which steps are taken to make the opposition think you're planning to do one thing, when you're really planning to do another. Fakes, diversionary passes, and false disagreements between members of your team may trick the opposition into letting its guard down, which is your opportunity to fire at the goal. Quick takes, in which the restart is done faster than might be expected, also might catch the opposition off guard and give you a better chance to score.

When it comes to indirect kicks, many of the same strategies apply. The only difference is that another player from your team must touch it after the kicker has touched it before it can be shot on goal. That eliminates direct power kicks and perhaps the long field kick, but just about any other kicking strategies can be effective.

Yellow Card _____

You may hear the term "banana kick." That's when a very skillful player seems to be able to bend the arc of his kick so the ball seems to go around obstacles like goalkeepers and into the net. This, of course, has to do with the way the ball is kicked and the spin the kick puts on the ball's trajectory. It's not something many players can do successfully, but with the proper encouragement young players can learn some of the rudiments. Just don't expect too much too soon.

Goal Kicks

A goal kick is awarded when a player is fouled in the penalty area. That includes tripping, hitting or any other aggressive action the referee considers deliberate or unnecessarily rough. Goal kicks can be the most frightening because they are executed in the penalty area. It's one offensive player—and it doesn't have to be the person who was fouled—and the goalkeeper, in a one-on-one duel.

Goal kicks can be almost as chilling for the kicker as for the goalkeeper because so much rides on the kicker. There are no diversionary tactics, no other obstacles to get in the way.

The best strategy may be to pick a spot in the net—perhaps a corner, either high or low—and shoot for that spot. The kicker who is fast and accurate may be able to elude the goalkeeper's reach and score. Once the shot has been made, other players may re-enter the field of play, something they should do with all due haste.

Goal kicks can be stressful for players of all ages. They are meant as punishment, and the fear of defending against them is part of that punishment. All you can ask is for the goalkeeper to do his or her best.

Playing Tip

All teams practice kicking, but not enough of them spend time practicing specific restart skills. Make them an important part of practice.

Yellow Card

The ball is not out until the whole ball crosses the line. This is true for a goal as well, which often leads to controversy about whether the ball actually crossed the line or not. A good rule to teach your players is that the ball is not out until they hear the whistle from the referee.

Throw-ins

The one time when ordinary players may use their hands is during the throw-in. A throw-in is awarded when a team kicks the ball over the sidelines and out of bounds. A long or particularly accurate throw can be as dangerous to your team as a kick, particularly when it's part of a set-up. Never take throw-ins lightly. They cause as much trouble as any other restart.

Offensive and Defensive Strategies

For each of the moves just described, you can develop specific offensive and defensive strategies designed to take advantage of the opportunity. Remember that it won't be enough to execute the kick correctly because the opposition will no doubt be talented enough to block the kick effectively. If you're on the offense, you'll need to have a specific strategy in mind before the player's foot strikes the ball and propels it into play.

Playing Tip

The closer the thrower is to the opponents' goal when he or she executes a throw-in, free kick, or other restart, the more aggressive the opponents will be. However, unless they're extremely well coached, they will also be sloppier and less likely to have a distinct strategy. Teach your players to watch for breaks in defense and to be prepared to take advantage of situations that arise.

The same holds true when you're playing defense. The opposition is in control, which means that your team will need to react to the opposition's strategy. They'll also need to be prepared to disarm them of the ball and take control. That, too, requires a strategy, and one that your players should be ready to execute.

Given that your dealing with youth players, you can't expect them to execute anything that requires highly mature playing abilities or physical skills. But even having a few tricks up your sleeve may be enough to give you the edge during play.

The following six plays are designed to give you some foundation strategies. Over time you'll want to adapt these to fit the needs of your age group or even develop your own. None of these plays are very difficult except, though younger athletes may find them challenging.

Executing a Corner Kick: The Flood

One of the greatest advantages a team can have is to be able to restart from corner kick position as the result of a penalty by the defending team. In addition to reversing possession of the ball, corner kick stops the momentum of play and allows the team now in possession of the ball to use the opportunity to their strategic advantage.

The corner kick is especially dangerous to the defending team because it takes place at the corner nearest to the goal. Even thought the angle isn't the most convenient for scoring, a play can easily be set up that enables the offensive team to score. If your team has the ball, a well considered strategy can give you tremendous advantage.

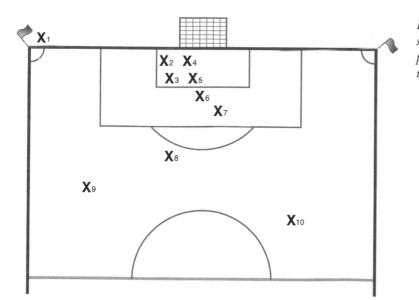

In "The Flood" play, offensive players flood the near post to create an opportunity to score.

The main idea behind the "Flood" offensive play is to flood the near post—that's the goal post that is closest to the side of the field where the corner kick is being executed. Forwards situate themselves close to the net to gain both physical and psychological advantage over the goalkeeper. This also allows the midfielders playing farther out to find one or more likely kickers to shoot the ball in hopes of scoring a goal.

As the diagram indicates, X1 kicks an inswinger—a kick direct at the near. X2 receives and controls the balls while X3 supports his offensive position by playing close to X2 and the net. X4 blocks the goalkeeper.

X5 and X6 run a criss-cross pattern as a diversionary tactic, while X7 runs to the far post—the goal post farthest away from the original kicker—to maintain team control of the ball if it comes his way.

X8 performs a similar function at center field, while X9 and X10 stay closer to mid-field in a defensive posture in case the ball comes their way.

Whiles all this is going on, X1 through X4 should be in position for a shot on goal. If all goes well they will be able to make that shot quickly and score the goal.

Defending a Corner Kick: Zone in the Goal

In "Zone in the Goal," players also flood the penalty zone, in a manner of speaking, and play a defensive game set in a triangular pattern. In this case, it's almost as if the defenders have formed a large web to protect the goal from a corner kick or even a throw in. Done right, this could be an impenetrable position.

In the "Zone in the Goal" strategy, players create a defense web to fend off a corner kick.

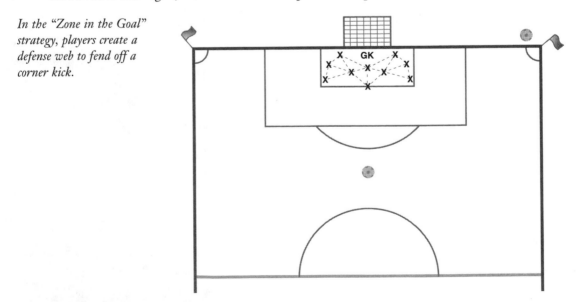

The "Zone in the Goal" play is unique in two ways:

♦ The players position themselves in small units of three, creating a triangular structure that provides both depth and breadth of coverage.

♦ The players use this positioning to play a zone defense, covering any forward or other offensive player who enters their particular zone.

Player density in the goal box can make this a very effective defensive strategy that can do an excellent job protecting the goal no matter what offensive strategy the other team may try. Providing youth players understand the concept—and it's not a very difficult one—even the youngest athletes may find this an easy play to master.

Executing a Direct Free Kick: The Peel Out

A direct free kick can be the most dangerous play for any team because it allows the team with the ball direct access to the goal. The defending team can and does create a wall of players to stop forward motion, but that wall can be overcome with a little planning. "Peel Out" is designed to do just that.

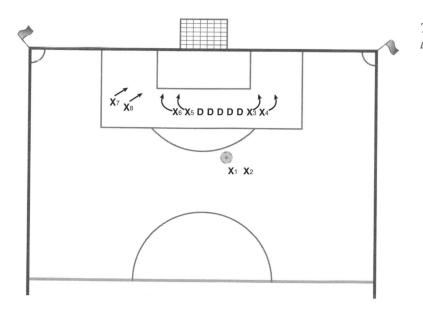

The "Peel Out": Overcoming the defensive wall.

In "Peel Out" X1 and X2 are both in kicking position, but decide before the start of play who will actually kick the ball. This is a diversionary tactic designed to confuse the defenders, who shouldn't know who the kicker is until he or she kicks the ball.

X5 and X6—positioned to the left of the defenders—and X3 and X4—on the right—"peel out" at the start of the play, running toward the goal to be in position to assist in making the goal. X7 and X8 come from the left, adding strength to that side and forcing the goalkeeper's attention in that direction.

Depending on the nature of the kick and the response of the defenders, this allows the kicker to play to the mass of players on the left—where the goalkeeper's attention is most likely directed—or play to the two on the right—which gives the team a little less firepower but, more likely, a more open goal. The strategy differs depending on which side the ball is kicked to, but success can come from either direction.

Executing an Indirect Free Kick: The Castle

In the case of an indirect free kick, the ball must be touched by a teammate of the kicker before it can be launched into the goal. That may make it a little daunting to the team defending the goal but if done properly, can make the kick even more effective.

The Castle: Play behind your opponents' wall!

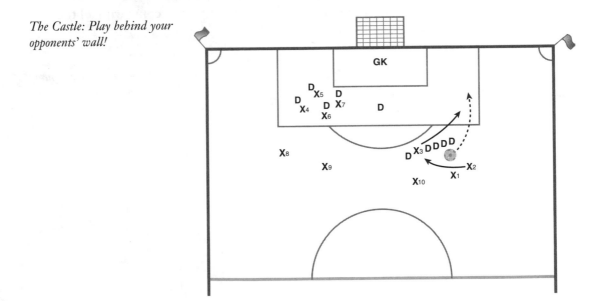

This play is called "The Castle" because the offensive players will attempt to "scale" the wall erected by the defensive team, indicated by the Ds in the diagram, and score a goal.

X1 and X3 take off in the same direction to the right of the goal. X1 will pass to X3 to satisfy the kick's "indirect" requirement. X2 takes off in the opposite direction toward the center of the goal in an attempt to confuse the opposing team into thinking that he or she will be the recipient of the pass.

X4 through X7 congregate at the far end of the penalty box, ready to receive the kick if the ball carrier sees an opening. If done with relative speed, this can put potential receivers at the near, middle, and far end of the goal, ready to take advantage and score the point.

Throw-ins: Isolation and Triangle

A lot of soccer strategy is designed to confuse the opposing team into thinking you're going to do one thing when, in reality, you're going to do something quite different. "Isolation" is a good example of how that concept works in practice.

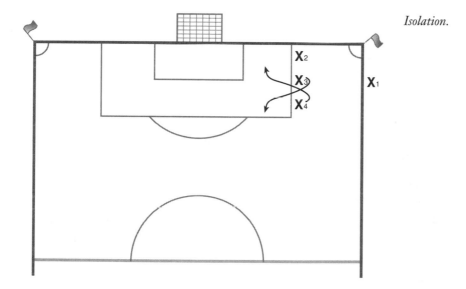

Isolation.

X1 will throw the ball in from out of bounds. At the start of play, X3 and X4 will take off, running a criss-cross pattern toward the center of the goal designed to confuse the other team. Their position closer to center of the field will make the defenders think they will be the likely receivers and should draw defenders' attention.

Assuming this works, that will leave X2 isolated in the corner of the field. Generally X2 will be one of the stronger players, one capable of receiving the ball and driving it home for a goal. If that doesn't work—in other words, if X2 receives heavy coverage by defenders—then X4 becomes the back up receiver and attempts to score after he/she receives the ball

"The Triangle" is another throw-in play that's intended to confuse the opposing team and gain competitive advantage. Once again, timing, speed, and accuracy of the throw will make or break this effort. It seems confusing at first, but conceptually it's not too tough. It just requires some practice.

The Triangle.

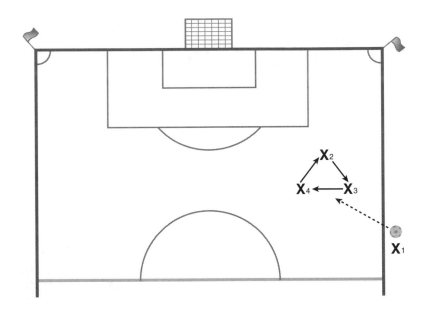

X1 is the thrower. X2, X3 and X4 are roughly positioned in a triangular shape. Chances are their position won't be immediately obvious to the opposition, but it should govern how the three potential receivers perform.

Once the play gets under way, the three receivers essentially change positions as shown on the diagram. X2, now in X3's former position, receives the ball and gets it under control. Both X4 and X2 continue their runs along the arms of the triangle, prepared to receive the ball from X2. Whichever player is open—and that includes anyone else on the field not shown in the diagram, may receive the ball and, with any luck, score a goal.

Practice Makes Perfect!

Try these plays during practice with your young team and see which ones click. Create your own once you understand the concepts behind the play. The idea is always to make the opponents think that you're executing a maneuver other than the one you're really doing. If you can do that, the play doesn't have to be complicated or even spectacular. All it has to do is score a goal. No matter how awkward or ordinary a play may be, scoring a point will be the real measure of success.

The Least You Need to Know

◆ Restarts occur when a player is fouled or the ball goes out of bounds. Depending on who's at fault, it could be an effective strategy to interrupt momentum and change the direction of the game.

◆ There are four types of restarts: corner kicks, free kicks, goal or penalty kicks, and throw-ins.

◆ A kickoff is considered a type of restart, but it's different because it starts play rather than occurring mid-game.

◆ Free kicks can either be direct or indirect. In direct kicks, the player kicking the ball in may shoot directly for the goal. In indirect kicks, that ball must be touched by another team member before it can be kicked in for a score.

◆ Kicks can be short or long, involve a single player or a combination of team members. It all depends on the strategy of play.

◆ Throw-ins are the one time ordinary players can touch the ball with their hands.

Understanding Match Analysis

In This Chapter

- ◆ Systems of play
- ◆ Analyzing the field options
- ◆ Scouting the opposition
- ◆ Teaching change

As a youth soccer coach, you may find yourself at a distinct disadvantage when it comes to strategy. Depending on the age and sophistication of your team, it may be enough of a challenge to keep the defensive, midfield, and offensive players in their assigned areas and prevent them from bunching around the ball every time it's put into play. Exercising strategies any more sophisticated than that may be, for your team, whistling into a very harsh wind.

But there also may be ways that you as coach can have a more profound impact on mounting strategic play and achieving tactical outcomes than you might think. Remember that most offensive strategies within soccer are based on systems of play, those 4-4-2 and 3-4-3 combinations that we talked about in Chapters 12 and 14. Whether playing defense or offense, all teams have them. It's part of the worldwide soccer culture and allows for some significant successes overall.

The system of play in use by a team at any given time is based on the strength of the team and its players, as well as the perceived strength of the opposition and *its* players. Like any coach in any sport, knowing what you're up against helps determine what your ultimate strategy will be.

Knowing how your strategy adjusts to that of the opposition is called *match analysis.* It simply means that you are analyzing the opposition's field position and play methodologies—which represents their strategy—and attempting to measure the match of your strategy against theirs with an eye to adjusting if necessary.

Sound simple? In concept, it is. But anytime you try to apply concepts to real-life situations, you have to adjust for the many variables—a reality that causes most coaches to go gray. And just when you think you've got those adjustments made, your star forward turns an ankle and is out for the rest of the game, causing you to have to start from scratch. But then those are the kinds of adjustments you would be getting paid for if you were indeed getting paid in the first place.

Analyzing the Field Options

A quick analysis of the systems of play outlined in Chapter 12 makes it clear that there are three basic options for field position:

- **A strong defensive strategy** positions more players in your own defensive zone as a way to support the goalkeeper and block goals. The popular 4-4-2 system is considered defensive, as is the less common 5-3-2 configuration.

- **Strong offensive strategies** have been used in tournament play and other situations where a team feels it may be fighting an uphill battle against a more powerful opposition. A 4-2-4 play system is considered an aggressive strategy.

- The final variation is **a balanced strategy** characterized by strong midfield positioning, with swing duties as either a strong offense or defense, depending on who has the ball. With the increased emphasis on strengthening the midfield, a system of 3-5-2 often makes the most sense for young players. By clustering more players in the middle, your team can form a wall that is less penetrable, while at the same time putting your team in a better position to score.

Time Out

One of the simplest match analyses is determining whether your opposition is playing zone defense or player-to-player defense. In zone defense, the team sticks to specific areas of the field, covering any of your players who happen to wander into that "zone." Player-to-player defense matches one of their fielders to one of yours throughout the period of play. Adjust your strategy to meet theirs.

No matter what strategy you choose, it's important to be aware that even the most evenly balanced teams embracing the same strategy will not play the same game.

Earlier we referred to the massive number of variables that affect your ability to match and beat your opponent's analysis. Those variables include the players' skill level, your abilities as coach, and even such details as the weather and the time of day.

While there's little you can do about most of these factors on game day, you can decide what strategy, or system of play, your team will employ. To that end, it becomes a valuable tool that will contribute to your success.

> **CAUTION**
>
> **Yellow Card** _____
>
> Systems of play are critical to success, but match analysis gives you greater flexibility to adjust to changing needs. If your team plays its best games in the 4-4-2 configuration, that's obviously your strong card to play. But don't assume it will work every time—be prepared to adjust if necessary. Without flexibility your strategies may be useless.

Scouting the Opposition

Good match analysis requires knowing what your team is up against. That means scouting the opposition to determine what their apparent strategy is. Are they playing a defensive or offensive game? Are most of the players clustered at midfield? What is their apparent approach?

Unlike, say, American football, where the lineup changes with every play, soccer strategies are more evident right from the start because of the systems of play the sport employs. However, that strategy can change throughout the game, so keeping a close eye on it will tell you how they think your team is performing, and you can adjust accordingly.

Checking Out Their Defense

In the following sections, we'll provide some questions you should ask about the opposing team's defense.

Are they using zone or player-to-player defense?

Adjusting your assault tactics as you pass from your defensive zone through midfield and into their striking area may be the single most effective thing you can do. Whether the opposing team is playing zone or player-to-player defense, you may be able to cluster your players to one side of the field, opening the other side wide in preparation for a fairly effective shot on goal that might meet with little opposition.

What's the shape of the defensive team on field and what does it communicate?

Some form a defensive arc, others position themselves to create a weblike defensive depth, still others appear almost random in distribution. For a good team, however, it all signals a certain strategy. Playing against that shaping strategy, rather than merely running into the fray, will result in a more effective offense.

How does the defense respond to your penetration efforts?

Once you determine their shaping strategy, note next how they respond at various points of penetration. If there is a weak spot known to them but not to you, you can quickly find it out by probing the defense. If you break through easily or suddenly find a lopsided, less-organized, and more frenzied attempt to repel your advances, then you've uncovered a weak spot—or perhaps several weak players. That's where you should focus on subsequent attempts to score goals.

What's the sweeper situation?

First of all, is there a sweeper (that's the wild card player coming from behind to fill in the gaps)? The presence or lack thereof may indicate their relative confidence in their defensive position or your perceived lack of offensive ability. Sweepers locked into center may be stabilizers for a more fluid defense, while a fluid sweeper may signal a more solid goalkeeper and stronger reliance on an effective offense. You can adjust your attacks on goal accordingly.

Playing Tip _____

As you study your team's impact on the opposition, also consider the opposition's impact on your team. If you have succeeded, what have you done? If you miss an opportunity, how could you have made a better attempt? You can learn more about yourselves from missed opportunities than you can from successes, but it all provides you with the information you need to win.

How effective are your setup shots and what repelling strategies do they employ?

You have your own offensive setup strategies that you use. How do they respond to these attacks? Do they have one source of strength or skill that they always seem to employ, or are they varied in their approaches? Unless your players have no skills whatsoever, less flexible defenses usually are easier to get around. A more varied defensive skill set could be more difficult to circumvent, unless those skills are used randomly or their execution is forced, thus not as effective. Watching not only strategy but execution will give you a better idea how best to respond.

Finally, when you score, how is it done?

Success is the most telling variable, and how you score once will likely be how you score a second time. Scoring can be a matter of circumstance, or it can signal a tear in the defensive strategy that can be successfully exploited. Watch closely all the particulars of any score you make and look for ways to replicate that success. That could be the single most important outcome of your match analysis efforts.

Looking Over Their Offense

In measuring the opposition's offensive strategies, keep an eye on the following situations and characteristics:

First and foremost, how do they attack?

What is their style and strategy for coming at your goal? A more mature team might spend an entire upfield run setting up for the shot on goal, while a younger team might have all they can do to dribble that far and not have the ball taken away. Watch for patterns in the assault. If they exist, those are the patterns to be overcome.

Is the opposition's approach direct or indirect?

A direct approach is more obvious, thus sometimes easier to intercept and head off or tackle and commandeer the ball. This isn't always the case, but direct attacks that come fast and furious often can be contained if your players are skilful enough to do so. You already know where they ultimately are headed and can brace for and respond to a full-frontal assault.

Indirect attacks move the ball around in many different ways, usually with short passes and plenty of opposition players around the ball. These indirect attacks may make up to 15 to 20 passes prior to shooting on goal. (The direct method may utilize one to four passes.)

Sometimes there's no way to tell where the strategy will place the setup and strike. In this case, attempting to understand the strategy behind the play can be more challenging, but there's a good chance it's there and will become more evident through observation and analysis.

Do they drive down the center of the field, in a zigzag passing pattern, or up the sidelines?

The pattern often is an indication of how they see their strengths and what can be done to countermand their approach. Teams that go up the center know they have a broad field to play on, veering to one side or the other as needed to avoid your defensive efforts. Those that advance will require broader, more diffused coverage.

Those teams that progress by passing in a zigzag fashion may have more control, but they tend to be more predictable. If the last pass has been to the far right side and the passes have generally been the same length every time, you already know there will be a hard left pass at any moment, most likely at a diagonal to take care of forward progression as well. Your pass interceptors can be waiting and reading to take command of the ball.

Teams that tend to run up the sidelines know they have to defend from assaults to only one side, but they have precious little room to maneuver. Good blocking makes tackling easier against teams using this strategy than any other.

The important thing, of course, is to be flexible and adjust to their moves, no matter what they are. That's the quickest way to gain control of the ball and the game.

How functional are their forwards?

It's usually the forwards who score, although anyone in any zone of the field can kick the ball into the net. From an offensive standpoint knowing how the opposition's forwards are going to act is one of the single most important factors.

No forward will operate in a vacuum, but some appear more independent than others, capable of taking the ball in without an elaborate setup. Others operate at the top of the pyramid, executing the final punch that puts the ball into the net. Knowing what kind of forwards your team is facing and how they play against you will enable you to better block them and handle their opposition.

Yellow Card

Rather than bemoan the goals scored against you, study them closely. Note who made them, how they were made, and what part of the field they came from. Did they hit the net high or low? Were they seemingly lucky breaks, or the result of a hard-fought drive? Were they long kicks or short punches?

Time Out

During games, keep a coach's playbook to record observations and note revisions in strategy. Making note of those areas that need improvement both offensively and defensively will help you draft strategies for future practices and plays.

Finally, when they score, how do they do it?

Even though the team may have two or three hot-shot forwards, you may find that goals have been kicked from midfield or even appear to be flukes. That may be part of the strategy the other team is employing—creating a plausible diversion while the real hitters go to work.

The most important question to ask, of course, is what hole in the defensive line did they exploit to score the goal? As you will see in Chapter 19, all goals by the opposition are the result of failures in your defensive efforts. We don't say that to be nasty. Rather, acknowledging this and finding out where these holes are will help you plug them up, thus avoiding similar goals in the future.

The goal of all this is to make the necessary corrections midstream and adjust the match analysis so your team is more likely to win. It often is a real test of a coach's ability to make this happen, especially with younger players. But even one step toward this goal can make a significant difference, because chances are your opposition isn't even trying.

Such analysis information and knowledge gives the coach something to share with players both on and off the field. In addition, studying the game helps keep coaches from getting too emotional—by analyzing the game, they are more likely to stay calm and levelheaded.

Teaching Change

Change is never easy, and expecting your players to adjust to an ever-changing field environment, especially if they've just mastered the skills necessary to play the game, is more than some players—and some coaches, for that matter—can handle. To teach change successfully, you're going to have operate at the height of your skills, whatever they may be.

Call this ultimate coaching, if you will, but if you expect change, especially change made on the fly, you're going to have to go about teaching it the right way. Here's how.

Demand Concentration

This can be difficult for young players, but they have to do it if they're going to improve. The mind has to be on the game or practice, not on what happened in social studies class or the birthday party they attended yesterday. Concentration takes effort, but it needs to be cultivated as a core skill. It's also a skill that will help them in school and throughout life, so it's worth making the effort to teach it.

Practice Hard and Well

Practices should be far from haphazard opportunities for socialization. You'll need to impose as much discipline and structure as there is for a game to generate successful results. True, you can't act like a boot camp drill instructor, but you can stress the importance of practice and respecting one another and you.

Set Goals

Your practices, like your games, should have a goal. This becomes very important when that goal is improving skills, because it requires more work and adjustment by your players. Practices that fail to achieve their goals fail, period. Practices that occur without goals in mind probably shouldn't be held. The one exception might be the occasional free-game practice. But a full-blown scrimmage is like a dress rehearsal for a play, and that's a goal in itself.

Conserve and Direct Energy

This is as important for the coach as it is for the players. No matter how dedicated you may be, there is only so much you have to give to soccer, mentally and emotionally as well as physically. Good discipline helps conserve energy critical to performance, and that's almost as important in practice as it is in play. The trick is to make all efforts— or as many as possible—constructive to the accomplishment of the goal. And that goal? Winning the game, of course.

Stay in the Day

We said it before and we'll say it again. The players are there either to practice or play. They can't afford to dwell on other things because that saps concentration and gives them fewer resources with which to work. Players who concentrate on the moment tend to turn in much better performances than those who don't.

As for coaches … well, all the above advice works just as well for you as it does for your players. And when it comes to steering your team in a new strategic direction in the heat of the game, you're going to need all the personal resources you can muster.

The Least You Need to Know

- ◆ Match analysis involves understanding the opposition's strategy and adjusting your strategy to counter their strategy.

- ◆ Strategies can be defensive, offensive, or balanced based on the needs and abilities of the team and its players.

- ◆ Without the flexibility, strategies are less effective.

- ◆ Studying offensive and defensive behavior will give you a better understanding of the opposing side and its strategies.

- ◆ Studying how the opposition scores may be the single most important defensive lesson you can teach.

- ◆ Players have to be at the top of their form to embrace change, and coaches have to be at the top of their form to teach it.

Chapter 18

Team Tactics: Attack and Defense

In This Chapter

- ◆ The importance of team tactics
- ◆ Mounting a team offense
- ◆ Developing team defense

We talked earlier about teamwork and why it's critical to player success. We stressed the elements of teamwork throughout, noting the difficulty you may have in convincing some your younger players—and perhaps older ones, too— that they're part of a larger effort. For those who haven't experienced it before, sometimes the most difficult concept in the world is showing them that putting the goals of the team before their own personal goals is the best way to achieve success.

That may seem like pretty heady stuff for a soccer book, but it really all boils down to this: The team that learns to function most effectively as a team will be the one that wins the game, the tournament, and the championship.

This chapter talks a little more about team tactics, specifically as they relate to mounting an offense and defending a goal. There may be days when getting all your young players to face in the same direction is challenging enough. But once you get them to operate as a single offensive or defensive unit, your team will have reached a new level of maturity.

Mounting a Team Offense

We've all seen games in which the player makes the heroic run down the field with the ball, eluding all opponents and mounting all obstacles, a one-person wonder who makes the goal with relative ease to the roar of an enthusiastic crowd. This is especially true in televised coverage of American football, which specializes on the close-ups of the run that vaults the player across the line and into the goal. Touchdown!

Time Out

Despite soccer's seeming non-stop action, studies have shown that the average soccer player maintains possession of the ball for less than 5 minutes per game. That leaves 85 minutes when your players could see themselves as having nothing to do! That's why teamwork support is so critical to success in the sport.

What that television coverage fails to show is the strategy that led to that player being in a winning position in the first place or the heroic efforts of all teammates—who made the blocks that made the touchdown possible.

Occasionally players do get a lucky break, are in the right place at the right time, and single-handedly run the ball and score the goal that wins the game. Most of the time, however, that happens in Hollywood. In reality, the vast majority of goals are the result of a hard-fought effort fronting a well-defined and executed strategy. And that strategy always involves the entire team.

Offensive Teamwork

Teamwork is especially important when your team is on the offensive, because the ball carrier needs maximum support to score a goal. That player will not make his or her downfield run without significant opposition. It's up to the team members who don't have the ball to make themselves available and create the right opportunities for passing, setup, and scoring.

What this means, first and foremost, is that players on the field always should be in motion. Strategy may limit them to their relative positions—defenders should never be at the edge of the opposition's penalty box, for example—but the strategic "shape" of the team should be such that it flows forward with the motion of the ball, providing both the breadth and depth of support necessary to aid the ball carrier in his or her run.

That's called "creating space," a term that refers to your field configuration and its support of the player in possession of the ball. Players in constant motion should be taking steps with an end purpose in mind. For forwards and midfielders, that may be a move upfield and in specific relation to the ball carrier in the event he or she needs to pass that ball to gain yardage or avoid being tackled. For defenders, that may mean a general forward motion to move the line of defense forward and exert greater pressure on the opposition. Whatever the case, the player who merely stands at his or her post does the team little good

Diagonal runs usually are the most effective methods for forward motion for the ball carriers as well as support players. For support players, running in a diagonal ahead of the ball increases their chances of being in a good position to receive a pass from the ball carrier.

Dribbling the ball is in some ways the safest way to move the ball, since it doesn't open the ball up to the dangers of a pass, which can more easily be intercepted. Dribbling becomes more daring the closer to the opposition's goal the dribbler gets. The opposition will likely play harder when the other team is in their defensive zone, and will do everything they can to tackle and take control of the ball. That may make short passing a better strategy because of the opportunity to set up for a goal.

Playing Tip

Make your field choices based on overall team strategy. Coaches who segment their strategies to highlight star players may succeed in the short term but will compromise their team's overall effectiveness, which will cost them dearly as the season wears on.

Offensive Strategies and Field Positions

A lot of your offensive strategy will boil down to what's best for the team strategy. What follows is an overview of ball movement strategies relative to the particular third of the field the ball happens to be in while in your possession:

◆ In the defensive third—that's the area closest to your goal—minimize all risk in terms of ball handling or passing. The purpose is to get the ball out of the area so opponents don't take control and score a goal against you. Team members should be positioned to support the ball carrier's dribbling efforts and accept short, safe passes. You're a long way from scoring at this point, so stepping out too far and wide in your offensive efforts is inappropriate and unsafe.

◆ At midfield things loosen a bit as you get farther from your own scoring area. The ball carrier can afford to take a few more chances by attempting to outrun the competition with the dribble or making longer, more aggressive passes.

Again, the support players know what the strategy is. If the ball carrier is running along the right sideline, pass recipients should be positioning themselves at various points forward on the field so the carrier can kick the ball into setup position when the time and opportunity are right.

◆ In the attacking third of the field—that's the other team's defensive zone—the opposition will play its hardest to defend its goal. It's at this point that dribblers and passers take the greatest risks, but also stand to reap the greatest rewards. Good team offense is perhaps most critical at this point because of the high level of opposition you will experience.

Playing Tip

The best offensive team setup is usually the triangle, allowing the ball carrier to pass the ball to a teammate, who then sets it up for a third teammate to kick into the goal. In volleyball, it's called a hit-set-spike and operates much the same way, except that in soccer, you want the ball to go into the net rather than over it.

No matter where you find the ball on the field, however, good team tactical support is critical for success. That means every player should be moving forward within the confines of their position as the ball moves forward—almost as if they have the ball, in fact—so that the depth of support is there when the ball carrier is ready to make his or her move.

Developing Team Defense

Good defenders, as already mentioned, don't wait passively for the ball to come their way. They are proactive in their defense and aggressively anticipate the ball before it ever enters their area or zone. The best defenders manage to play as if they were the last line of defense, but also operate as part of the team's defensive fabric, making sure they are in position to support their teammates' defensive efforts as well. In the military, that's called covering your buddies' backs—okay, so they use a term that refers to an area a little farther down—and it's much the same thing.

That means good defenders are strong, energetic, and unafraid of conflict. Defenders don't set out to score a goal; they set out to stop another player, and that requires a slightly different attitude. There are distinct ways to do this to maximize effectiveness. You'll find a few ideas in the following sections.

Attack Aggressively and Unremittingly

You team will be at its most vulnerable the first few moments following loss of possession. The transition from offense to defense requires reorientation, which opens a window, however slight, for team members now playing offense to gain ground and position. This means the defender closest to the ball must launch an immediate counter-attack to allow his or her teammates the opportunity to re-orient and regroup.

Care should be taken to make this counterattack as disciplined and strategic as possible, not merely a run at the player with the ball. The sacrificial flailing of feet is easily out-maneuvered, often putting the defending team in even worse position. If nothing more can be done than momentarily stalling forward progress by the ball carrying, that may be enough to allow the rest of your team the time it needs to regroup.

Funnel the Position to Protect the Goal

Your players should already know where the opposition is going to go once it takes possession of a ball: toward your goal. That means your first priority should be to contain that effort, followed by attempting to regain control of the ball. One of the most popular containment options in soccer involves a more advanced strategy called funneling. It's a technique designed to drive the oncoming player to the smallest space possible so the ball motion can be stopped and the ball ultimately taken away.

The funneling process is similar to what's done with fences when cattle are led to slaughter, an analogy we find especially appropriate. The cattle enter the pen as a group and are led down a chute that gets smaller and smaller, so that the cows eventually end up following each other nose to tail, making control and ultimate dispatch of hamburger on the hoof easy and quick.

In the funneling process, defenders form a chute with their bodies as a means to draw the ball carrier in a certain direction while keeping the other offensive players at bay. Once the ball carrier has been more or less contained, defenders can work to gain control of the ball.

If there's no opportunity to funnel, a line of defense similar to a battle line can be drawn to prevent penetration to the goal. But make sure there is enough depth of defense so that if the line is penetrated, there is someone in fallback before the goalkeeper to save the ball.

Protect the Space Goalside

When the ball is in play, defenders should automatically position themselves between the opposition and the goal. This speaks to the need for the depth of defense we raised in the previous section. In the same way good offensive team play requires other players to provide continued opportunities for players to pass and to protect the dribbler, good defensive play requires levels of protection so that if one defense is penetrated, another is there to protect the goal.

Yellow Card

Teach your players to defend against diagonal assaults—also called cross-field runs—and you'll be in better field position at all times. Teams that can't grasp the nature and effectiveness of diagonals, both as offensive and defensive strategies, will be less effective.

Keeping the ball in view and staying in motion as play progresses is the best way for players to stay between the ball and the goal.

Watch for Tackle and Passing Options

As opponents approach your goal, passing becomes a more dangerous threat because it allows the opposition to set up scoring opportunities.

There are two ways to successfully block passes:

♦ **Close player-to-player marking** will help prevent opportunities for the other team to set up the shot. If the ball carrier is tightly covered, any passes he or she makes will have to be longer ones. That means less control, less accuracy, and less likelihood that such a pass will be successful. We've stressed player-to-player coverage at several points throughout this book. Obviously, it's more than just an individual exercise and contributes to the overall success of the team strategy.

♦ Another way to block passing is **just to stay in the way of the passing lanes.** A passing lane exists between two teammates running up the field who can pass the ball back and forth between them. Running in the passing lane will interrupt the pass. A pass isn't good unless it's received. If your defenders are able to intercept, or at least block, the kick, they will have defeated the pass and perhaps even changed the possession of the ball.

> **Time Out**
>
> Few forwards will ever have the opportunity to dribble the ball into the goal (and if they do then you deserve to lose), which means that most teams score by passing the ball.

Force the Opposition into Predictable Patterns

By eliminating options, defenders can force the opposition into a predictable pattern of action. When that happens, then the defenders can anticipate the opposition's moves and perhaps seize control of the ball. Consider it a little bit like the intellectual equivalent of funneling. Once your team begins to drive the actions of the offense, you'll find they won't be the offense for very long.

The Value of Teamwork

No coach can put a price tag on effective teamwork, such is its value to the outcome of the game. Like anything that's difficult to learn, it will reap greater benefits for your players and undoubtedly lead to a more winning season. But with younger players, especially, getting them to understand what's meant by real teamwork is often difficult. But once you try it you quickly realize that the extra effort it takes will be some of the best that you expend throughout the season. Best of all, your players will gain benefits they'll carry with them both on field and off.

The Least You Need to Know

♦ Operating effectively as a team, both on offense and defense, likely will make the difference between winning and losing.

♦ All players on field should be in motion at all times regardless of whether they have the ball.

♦ Creating the right support environment for the ball carrier will mean better overall team performance.

♦ Good team play on defense is critical to keeping control of the game and its outcome.

♦ When you force the opposition to play in predictable ways, you have a better chance to take control of the game.

Chapter 19

Preventing Goals

In This Chapter

- ◆ The problem with goals
- ◆ Giving the ball away
- ◆ Pressuring the ball carrier
- ◆ Supporting the challenger
- ◆ Tracking your opposition
- ◆ The sorrow of set plays

The number one goal in soccer—after learning team play, sportsmanship and having fun—is to score goals. Whether your players are on offense, defense, or serving as goalkeepers, they all are concentrating on two things: scoring goals and preventing the opposition from doing the same.

It's a pretty simple equation, really, and is easily grasped by even the youngest players and the newest coaches. It is, in fact, what we have spent the bulk of this volume discussing. How then is it that teams still score goals? Very simple. All goals scored—either yours or theirs—are the result of errors in play.

Make No Mistake

A good defense is designed to prevent the other team from scoring goals. If and when that team does score, it must be the result of a hole in the fabric of that defense, a letdown either in player performance or coaching strategy that leaves an opening large enough through which the other team's forward can score.

> **Yellow Card** _____
>
> Young players may take the concept of goals being "mistakes" personally, fostering doubt in their abilities, which in turn could rapidly erode their interest in the game. A term like "filling the holes" or "plugging the leaks" may help them see remedial action as a positive step rather than a criticism.

But don't feel bad. That's the nature of the game. In the same way you've trained your defense to prevent goals, you've trained your offense to exploit the other team's weaknesses. And that's exactly what every coach does, which means they're putting the same pressures on you that you're applying to them.

But that also means that goals by the other team aren't something magic, they aren't part of the inevitable stream of life or in any way pre-ordained. Goals are the result of holes in the defense. And like holes in anything, once they're discovered there's a good chance at least some of them can be repaired. In this chapter you'll find out how.

The Problem with Goals

The soccer field is alive with energy as the team brings the ball down the field, alternately dribbling and then passing until it gets within range of the penalty box. There is give and take among the players as the ball is batted back and forth, even a change of possession or two, but the ball never quite leaves the defensive zone. The effort throughout the play has been intense.

The player-to-player defensive coverage has been flawless to this point, but suddenly a big rent in the fabric opens up. A forward sees the opportunity and seizes it, booting the ball into the net just ahead of the goalkeeper's valiant full extension dive. The weight of ball bulges the netting in the back. A cheer goes up from the crowd, and a point is added to the other team's score column on the board.

Sound familiar? No doubt you've been on both sides of that equation, feeling both elation and defeat. More astute coaches will worry less about the point and immediately question why it happened:

◆ The scoring coach will want to know how the goal occurred and what can be done to duplicate the effort.

- The losing coach will want to know what happened to the defense and how to prevent it from ever happening again.

Invariably, the answer lies somewhere in the breakdown in defensive performance or strategy or lack of maturity in its execution. In the latter situation, you've got to accept the fact that young teams without the physical strength and agility or maturity to think as effectively as they need to will always give up points. But, then again, so will their opponents, making for a pretty even match.

In the case of a breakdown in defensive strategy, they are usually due to one or more common errors. The most common of these errors involve the following situations:

- Your team member inadvertently gave the ball to the opposition.

- Your team wasn't putting enough pressure on the offensive player with the ball.

- The player challenging the ball handler didn't have adequate support from his teammates.

- The defenders weren't tracking the ball carrier as closely as they should have been, allowing him or her to get out of their range.

- A set-up play, such as a corner kick or throw-in, went wrong.

There may be other reasons, but these are the most common, which makes them the most dangerous as well. Let's consider each situation in turn and what might be done about it.

> **Time Out**
>
> Keep in mind the importance of good team "shape"—that is, keeping player on player and mirroring the opposition's structure. Also called "numbers around the ball," this helps maintain a strong defense and creates opportunities to take possession of the ball.

Giving the Ball Away

There is no surefire way to prevent the opposition from taking possession of the ball. To score, the ball carrier has to move upfield, which creates opportunities for the opposition to tackle and intercept the ball. Good ball handling and the sixth sense that some players seem to develop go a long way toward managing this potential ball-loss scenario. There are a few other things, too, that can help minimize the risk:

Design and stick to an offensive strategy.

A good coach will have both an offensive and defensive strategy in mind based on the strength of his or her team and the perceived weaknesses of the opposition. Deviation from either of those strategies, while often necessary, puts the ball at risk because players will have to make up variations on the fly, and not everyone will arrive at the same conclusion.

Deviation from strategy can leave the ball carrier unprotected when he or she might need that protection most. Moreover, lack of or deviation from strategy allows your players to fall more quickly into the strategic plans of the other side. The closer you can stick to your own strategy, the safer and more effective your play will be. And that means fewer giveaways to the opposition.

Think two or three steps ahead before taking advantage of unexpected opportunity.

That sudden hole that opens up in the defense may be by happenstance or it may be by design. Players may find that the clear avenue they think they have is really a blind alley with the opposition at the other end waiting to take control. If it looks too good to be true … well, you know the rest.

Legitimate opportunities do present themselves, but before the offensive strategy is altered the player with the ball had better be able to see far enough downfield—both physically and figuratively—to make sure he or she isn't kicking into a trap. Extensive forward motion means nothing if it doesn't result in a goal. It means even less when it results in the ball being taken away.

Time Out

Coaches should learn to "play the clock," and strategically maximize opportunities to score or minimize threats from the opposition. That includes stretching out plays—in effect stalling—so the clock runs out before the opposition can take the ball. You may not need another goal, but you may need to keep your opponents from scoring in order to win. Change the nature of your play accordingly.

Learn to recognize the characteristics of opportunity.

Experience teaches us there are patterns in everything, including soccer. We create some of those patterns, the opposition creates others, and still result from the chemistry of the two teams. The sooner you understand the basic patterns of the game and your team's method of play and how they react to certain situations, you'll be better able to fend off opponents, as well as be better prepared to take the ball from the other side.

Playing Tip

We spend a great deal of time applauding and honoring players who score. As coaches we need to spend more time honoring defensive players who prevent scores. Theirs is the tougher job because it lacks the glory of getting on the board, yet is just as instrumental—if not more so—to winning the game. The public rarely cheers a good save, so that means you should. Reward good defense during practice and play. Your efforts won't go unnoticed or unappreciated.

Pressuring the Ball Carrier

Whether your strategy is player-to-player defense or zone defense, someone has to put pressure on the opposition team member who has the ball in order to keep him or her from scoring. There's nothing more dangerous than a ball carrier unfettered by sufficient coverage.

Coverage is defined in many ways, but it all boils down to one thing: Adequate coverage is determined by on-field relationships. What do we mean by relationship? Consider the following:

Make sure the defender sticks close to the ball carrier.

The defender needs to operate within about 2 yards of the player he or she is covering. That gives the defender adequate room to move while still applying the necessary pressure to influence the outcome of play. If that relationship to the ball carrier isn't as tight as it needs to be, the ball carrier will have too much latitude for movement, creating an opportunity for the ball carrier to elude the defender and perhaps score a goal.

Make sure the defender is between the ball carrier and is in position to block shots on goal.

This bears repeating: At all times the defender should be operating between the ball carrier and the goal. Sometimes the ball carrier will slip through the defender's grasp, but when that happens the defense needs to work quickly to reestablish position.

Playing Tip

The right approach to coverage doesn't always mean head on. Defenders should look for ways to angle their trajectories in counterpoint to the direction being run by the opposition, effectively heading them off before they can pass. Just about any effort that results in a clean block of forward progression is an effort worth making.

Supporting the Challenger

As noted previously, the challenger's teammates must provide proper defensive support for the challenger so the challenger can stay within 2 yards of the ball carrier and compromise his or her ability to dribble, pass, or other wise get any closer to the goal. To be effective, the supporter needs to be 4 to 6 yards from—and very evident to—the ball carrier.

Both challenger and supporter also should be prepared to switch positions. In the event that the ball carrier slips past the challenger, the supporter will be right there to pick up the slack. The supporter then becomes the challenger, and the player who was the original challenger takes on the supporter role.

This simple idea of pressure and support is balanced by yet other teammates. The players behind this active area are called balancing players. All the balancing players—including the goalkeeper—should always be ready to become supporters or challengers themselves and should always be positioned between the ball and the goal. Balancing players often verbally encourage teammates to keep up the pressure on the ball and tackle.

Yellow Card _____

Too often supporting players fail to position themselves in such a way as to truly provide support. They need to be between the ball carrier and the goal, but at enough distance and angle to give the defense depth. When the support player operates as close as the challenger, he or she simply becomes another challenger, leaving no support. An adept forward might elude them both and go in to score. It's the positioning that makes the difference.

Tracking Your Opposition

Whether your team is assigned player or zone defense, chances are they are responsible for shadowing one or more specific players. They must keep close tabs on that player and work to undo any offensive moves that player might make as well as to beat out any defensive strategies that player appears to be executing. That's called tracking your opponent.

Like challengers and supporters, there's a relationship between your players and those they track. There's also a relationship between tracked players and other players farther downfield who may be in the heat of action. Failure on the part of your player to anticipate when the person he or she is defending might receive the ball and to prepare to challenge that player when necessary can give the opposition the opportunity they need to score.

Once again, it's a matter of understanding and appreciating the opposition's strategy. A strong player who can kick from midfield may receive a back pass that then may be set up or even kicked in for a goal. The player who's tracking the ball recipient must be able to anticipate such actions and act accordingly.

How do you prepare players to handle these situations? All players must concentrate and be engaged in the game *at all times*. This can be especially difficult for young players in backfield positions, especially when the ball spends a lot of time at the other end of the field.

Playing Tip

Coaches having trouble keeping younger players' minds on the game might want to have them play "Sports Reporter" during practice. Have each upfield player give a running commentary on the action downfield and what it might mean to the game. It's not a memory test, but by verbalizing what they're seeing, the young athletes may better be able to analyze and anticipate when their skills will be needed. Make it fun and it could be something they carry with them to actual games.

The Perils of Restarts

According to experts, as many as 50 percent of all goals are scored as a result of restarts—those interruptions in action that result in corner kicks, free kicks, goal kicks, and penalty kicks.

Restarts are dangerous for several reasons:

◆ Restarts interrupt the action, thus the momentum of the game. Since soccer is a game learned and played on the fly, most players are not at their best when starting from a dead halt. Restarts can affect players' speed, comprehension, control, and involvement in the game.

◆ Because of restarts' penalty nature, all kicks and throw-ins are unobstructed. In most cases, players can't get closer than 10 yards to the person with the ball. This gives the team with the ball an enormous advantage.

◆ Restarts may occur from anywhere on the field, but often take place at or near the defenders' goal. The ability to take careful and considered aim at the goal or to carefully set up a more complex play is a tremendous advantage to the offensive team—it's like being able to hit a golf ball off a tee rather than attempting to smack it while it's in the air.

Yellow Card _____

Restarts can become even more dangerous with teams that have a restart specialist. These individuals have a unique ability to help their team score on the restart plays. Some players can throw the ball a great distance, launching it into the danger zone like a rocket. Some have the ability to hit direct shots on goal with great power and/or accuracy. Some teams have players who can kick or throw the ball great distances. If a foul occurs 50 to 60 yards from goal these players can still kick it into the danger zone.

Too many coaches and players underestimate the potential impact restarts have on scoring goals. Perhaps that's why such a high percentage of goals are scored that way.

Playing Tip _____

Remember the concept of "territory." Keeping the ball in the opponents' defensive zone end farther away from your goal can pay big dividends. This will increase your chances of scoring and decrease the opponents' ability to get close to your goal. If they don't get close to your goal, they'll be less likely to score.

In all such cases, a good response to a restart involves the following:

◆ Having and following an effective strategy.

◆ Being able to smoothly transition between different roles, such as challenger, supporter, and balancing player.

◆ Concentrating on the action throughout the game.

◆ Anticipating and responding to the on-field challenges.

◆ Being able to turn the tables, seize the ball, and score when the opportunity presents itself.

Teams that can do even some of those things will reduce the number of goals scored against them while increasing their own ability to score. And that's what you've been trying to teach them all along.

The Least You Need to Know

◆ Like it or not, goals are scored as the result of errors in defensive play.

◆ Goals occur when an offensive player inadvertently allows a defender to seize the ball.

◆ Improper relationships between the challenger and ball carrier and supporter and challenger can result in a loss of advantage and a goal.

◆ Failure to adequately track an assigned player downfield could result in a goal.

◆ Nearly 50 percent of all goals occur during restarts like free kicks, corner kicks, and throw-ins.

Chapter 20

Beyond the Game

In This Chapter

- ◆ The intrinsic side of coaching
- ◆ How to do a self-appraisal
- ◆ Taking the enjoyment of soccer to another level

By the time you reach this chapter, you'll have been steeped in soccer tradition and history. You will have developed a new appreciation for what you now know to be the most popular game on the planet. And you will know how a sport that looks so simple can become so complex.

You should have mastered the skills of youth coaching, or at least gotten your feet wet. You should have learned to apply defensive and offensive strategies to their fullest effect and greatest impact. And you should better understand the unique and wonderful properties of the goalkeeper in today's game, or at least be a little less baffled by their performances.

You should have learned all of that and a hundred other things. If you've practiced diligently what we've preached, then your team already has taken the field by storm. They've no doubt executed some heroic moves and surprisingly effective strategies that caused the fans—not to mention your young players' parents—to sit up and take notice. You may even have guided them to a winning season, which makes you as much of a hero as each of them are.

Now What?

So what's next? How do you follow that act? How can you keep the momentum going so that your young athletes continue to practice and enjoy "the beautiful game" as they get older and even more capable.

First, ask yourself the following key questions:

Did I do the right thing by my players?

You should have learned early on in this volume that different kids at different developmental stages play soccer for different reasons. Young kids play soccer because they like *playing* and receiving adult approval for it. Just encouraging kids to have fun while playing the game means you've done right by them, regardless of whether they win or lose. Remember the phrase: "We lost, we won. Either way, we had fun." If you coach youth soccer, that should be your mantra.

Did I coach my team developmentally, helping them learn the techniques in ways that they could master?

Too many well-meaning volunteer coaches simply don't know how to coach, much less teach. They tell the kids what to do, maybe even show them, and then leave them to their own devices as if, like baby ducks, nature was going to somehow miraculously teach them to swim. For some kids, that works. But most need skills development and guidance. Drop that ball and their interest will soon wane. And that will be the end of their soccer careers.

> **Time Out**
>
> Kids won't make an effort if they believe they are going to fail. If you can communicate to your players that you believe in their effort—especially among the younger players—you'll find them going through amazing transformations. That increased self-esteem will help them master the skills they need, become better players and, most importantly, enjoy the game more.

Did I expect the best from my players and teach them to expect the best from themselves?

With the right emphasis, part of what your players will learn is self-esteem and pride in their performance. It may sometimes be difficult to get them to do things the right way, but if you make it clear that you appreciate their effort, it won't be hard to get them to *try* to do the right things and to do so with zest and enthusiasm.

As coach, did I lead by example?

As head of the team and the presumed authority, your players and their parents will be looking to you for guidance. If you embody the characteristics you'd like your players to embrace, then chances are your example will help them take the game more seriously. Not only will that mean better performances, but also more satisfaction for all involved.

Don't Forget Your Role

You may have noticed that the questions we just asked have less to do with whether you taught your players proper form for a corner kick and more to do with the nature of your style both as a coach and as a human being. True, you're not the clergy dealing with thorny questions of faith and hope. But you stand the chance of becoming one of the most important adults in the lives of your players. You must understood and embrace this charge, or at least appreciate it, because, like it or not, you *will* have a profound impact on their lives.

No matter how casual your relationship with the team, or how coincidental your coaching assignment, remember that you have an obligation to do your best for your young athletes. In addition to making a promise, you also are setting an example as a concerned adult. The better job you do living up to that promise, the better coach you'll be. And the better coach you are, the more likely it is that you'll be able to coax maximum performance from your team on a regular basis.

Any team's success begins and ends with the ability and commitment of the coach. The less you talk about that truism and the more you act on it, the more successful your team will be.

Playing Tip

Coaches can never do enough to inspire and motivate players. Throughout the season you can build their motivation and self-confidence by sharing familiar quotes and inspirational phrases printed on plain paper that can be posted in their rooms on the refrigerator at home. Reach for the heart as well as the head and you can't miss.

Time Out

Don't forget your own professional development as coach. Even if you're a part-time amateur, you need to keep up with the latest techniques and learn from other coaches. Take the time and make the effort to improve your coaching skills through course-work, reading, and coaching "camps." You won't regret it.

Beyond Play

The goal of this volume is to help you be a better coach and do a more effective job in cultivating player performance. Another goal—and we were unabashed in making this point—is to help you help young athletes develop an appreciation for the game that far exceeds their interest in your team. You've worked so hard to get your players to where they are today—it would be a shame if it all would end there.

So how do nurture an appreciation for soccer? Here are a few ideas.

Encourage players to follow the pro teams.

As kids age, they may become less interested in playing. But if they've developed an appreciation for and understanding of the game, they should be even more interested in following professional soccer, even if their community doesn't have a professional team.

The easiest way to do this, of course, is on television. ESPN and other sports channels are featuring more and more professional soccer coverage, both from this country and abroad. Watching the experts is a good way to learn, of course. For those fans who also have been or are currently playing the game, the coverage should be even more exciting.

Televised pro games are good, but live games are even better. Depending on where you live, that spectatorship may be limited to the local high school or college team, or you may be lucky enough to live in a community large enough to support a semi-pro or pro squad. Regardless of the level, encourage your players to take advantage of the chance to watch older players in action—something that wouldn't have been a bad coaching strategy all along, by the way. Watching the teams from Paraguay and Panama vie for an international title on the tube is one thing; watching the local college team up close sweat and struggle is quite another.

You, as coach, should make a similar effort to see live and televised soccer games.

> **Playing Tip**
>
> The *crème de la crème* of live soccer, of course, is being able to go to the World Cup. If there is any chance for a young player to go to the World Cup, it should be strongly encouraged because it could be a once in a lifetime opportunity.

> **Playing Tip**
>
> Every state has at least one soccer organization and some have two. Check out Appendix B for a list of state and national associations.

Encourage their involvement in professional soccer groups and associations.

Some kids may be too young to get involved in soccer groups and associations, but their parents might be interested. Even something as simple as getting on the mailing list might be enough to keep them enthused until they're ready to get more involved or get on another team. Teams come in every variety imaginable, and many of them are tailored to the needs of various groups and have regional and local chapters.

Create an appreciation for soccer as a lifetime recreational activity.

Many youth players continue to play soccer as they mature, joining high school and college teams. Some even go on to play in semi-pro and pro leagues, while others just become rabid fans.

What many people fail to realize is that soccer can be considered a lifetime sport. A reasonably fit adult can play with his or her age group well into maturity. The action may get a little slower and the kicks a little shorter, but soccer is a wonderful aerobic activity. The team environment also promotes a sense of friendship and community outside the workplace and family that can prove to be invaluable in years to come.

What's important for young players to remember is that their soccer journey is just beginning. They have years, perhaps decades, ahead of them. If you can get even a few of them to pursue soccer in the ensuing years, then you've been a positive influence on your young charges.

And who knows? You may even get one or two of them to become soccer coaches, picking up where you eventually will leave off. In terms of personal success as a coach, you really couldn't ask for anything more, could you?

The Least You Need to Know

- A coach measures the intrinsic value of the work he or she has done not so much by skills learned as by appreciation for the game.

- Encourage players to follow the pro teams and learn skills and techniques from them.

- Share state and national soccer organization information with players to encourage continued play.

- Promote soccer as a lifetime recreational activity.

Appendix A

Glossary

advantage   The continuation of a play after the opposing team has committed a foul and the attacking team has penetrated deeply into the opposition's territory. The referee allows the play to continue in order to prevent the defending team from having an unfair advantage.

assistant coach   The coach who helps the head coach with a wide variety of duties.

assistant referee   The person who monitors the sidelines in order to determine if a ball is in bounds, if players are offsides, who last touched the ball, etc. The former name for this position was linesman.

back heel pass   A pass that is completed by hitting the ball with the back of one's heel.

back pass   A pass that usually occurs between a defender and a goalkeeper and moves in the direction of the player's own goal.

bicycle kick   A potentially dangerous pass due to body position. It involves jumping in the air and moving one's legs as if on a bicycle. Once completed, landing properly is necessary to avoid serious injury.

boots   The term used for soccer shoes or cleats in England.

box   This is either the box used for penalties or the term used to describe the action of the goalkeeper when he/she boxes or punches the ball.

caution   The same as a yellow card. It is used to designate dangerous or unsportsmanlike behavior on the field.

center spot   The place where kickoffs occur (in the center of the field).

chip shot   A shot used to try to score when the goalkeeper is out of the net or when a player passes the ball to a teammate by kicking it over the defense.

clearance   Kicking the ball away from the net by the defending team.

club   Teams in all age groups from South America and most of Europe belong to soccer clubs. Pro teams in Europe have professional level teams with amateur/youth teams—either Under-10 or Under-19 clubs—under them. In the United States the professional teams do not have this type of hierarchy. There are youth teams, amateur teams, and so on that belong to different clubs.

coach   The person who trains the team and is in charge of making decisions regarding plays and lineup.

coin toss   Similar to the ritual in American football, this is done prior to the start of the game. The winner of the coin toss gets to choose to defend or attack during either the first or second half of the game.

corner flags   Markers that determine the boundary of the playing field. They are used to determine where to do a corner kick as well as to determine if a ball has crossed the sideline or goal line.

corner kick   A kick that originates from either the left or right side of the field after the ball has gone out of bounds. The ball is kicked by the defending team to the attacking team after it has been cleared from the goal or the end line.

cross   A play that moves diagonally across the playing field. It occurs when a player kicks the ball to a teammate who is either in front of the goal or on the other side of the field from which the kicker is standing.

dead ball   A ball that is not in play but still on the playing field. The ball is dead prior to penalty, free, or corner kicks or when the ball is to be thrown in.

defender   A playing position in front of the goalkeeper. The objective of the defender is to stop the opposing team from making any goals or shots. The defender may cover a particular player or a specified area. Outside fullbacks patrol the left and right sides of the field. Those defending midfield are the central defenders.

direct kick   A free kick awarded to the opposing team when a player handles the ball, holds an opponent, or kicks or charges another player.

draw   A game that ends in a tie. It may also be used to define those chosen for a particular tournament.

dribble   The manner in which a player moves the ball across the playing field one small kick at a time, always retaining possession of the ball.

drop ball   If play has been stopped due to an injury or other reason, the referee will drop the ball at the sight of the stopped play to resume the action. A player may not touch the ball until it has bounced once.

end line   The goal line.

expulsion   Ejection from the game. The term red card is also used.

extra time   The same as overtime. It is the time needed for one team to score. Also referred to as "sudden death" and usually means a 15-minute period of play after the end of a tie game. At the end of the extra period, the team with the greater score wins.

final whistle   The whistle that signals the end of the half or game.

finish   The same as the scoring of a goal.

flagposts   The same as the corner flags.

formation   *See* system of play.

forward   Any of the several types of offensive players. The goal of the forward is to either make a goal or allow another teammate to score.

foul   Any play that is against the rules. The result of a foul is a free kick for the attacking team. The kick may be either direct or indirect, depending on the type of foul.

free kick   The kick that takes place after a defending player has made a foul. The attacking team kicks the ball and the kicker is given a 10-yard clearance prior to the kick.

game officials   The referee, assistant referees, and the fourth official.

goal   The scoring action, which is worth one point. It occurs when the ball passes under the goal posts and crosses the goal line.

goal kick   This occurs when the ball is passed over the end line by the attacking team and the goalkeeper kicks the ball.

goal line   The same as the end line. It extends from sideline to sideline and is the line that the ball must cross in front of the net to score a point.

goal mouth   This refers to the area in front of the goal.

goalkeeper   The player who defends the goal. The only player able to use hands within a specified area referred to as the penalty area. If the goalkeeper uses his hands outside of this area he is given a red card and the other team is then granted a free kick.

goalkeeper's box   The area directly in front of the goal that is tended by the goalkeeper. It is six feet square. A yellow card is awarded to any opposing player that causes a foul within this designated area.

golden goal This term refers to overtime and was initiated into the soccer world in 1996.

halftime Fifteen-minute break between the first half and the second half. May also be referred to as an interval.

hand ball When any player intentionally uses their hands to illegally touch the ball. Goalkeepers may touch the ball when they are in the penalty box, but may be guilty of a hand ball if they are outside of their designated area.

head shot or header Using one's head to pass the ball.

indirect kick A free kick. It is awarded when a player obstructs another player, plays in an unsafe manner, or in anyway interferes with the goalkeeper from releasing the ball. An indirect kick can also be given if a goalkeeper takes more than four steps before he releases the ball, takes too much time, or uses his hands once the ball has been kicked by another player once he or she has released the ball into play.

keeper The same as a goalkeeper.

kickoff The kick that signals the start of the game.

player-to-player marking A type of defense in which each player is responsible for covering a specified player on the opposing team.

match The same as a game.

midfielder A crucial player who is required to run the length of the field throughout the entire game. They are the direct link between the defending team and the attacking team. A midfielder must be able to run deep into the opponent's territory and transition from an attacking player to a defending player depending on which team controls the ball. A midfielder may choose to be either a defensive player or an attacking one.

net The same as goal.

near post The closest goalpost to the ball.

obstruction A block caused by a player using his or her body to obstruct another player. The result of an obstruction is an indirect free kick for the opposing team.

officials Also called game officials. They are responsible for the action on the field. They consist of two assistant referees, one referee, and a fourth official.

offside If a player is standing closer to an opponent's goal than the second to last opponent when the ball is in play, that player is considered offsides.

offside trap A play that is used by the defending team repeatedly to draw an attacking player offside. It occurs when the defending team causes the player to be offside by moving together away from the goal.

one touch   A play in which a ball is kicked after a player has touched it only once during a pass.

overlap   If a defending player becomes part of an attack by running on the right or left flank, that player is said to "overlap" the offensive players, or forwards..

overtime   The same as extra time. It occurs if a game is tied at the end of regulation time. A set period of time—usually 15 minutes—is designated as overtime to give both teams a chance to score the winning goal.

pass   The movement of the ball from one player to another using one's head or feet.

penalty arc   An area at the top of the penalty spot that is in the shape of an arc. If a player is attempting to make a penalty kick he must stand behind this arc.

penalty area   The area directly in front of the goal that is tended by the goalkeeper. It is an 18×44-yard area in which the goalkeeper is allowed to use her hands on the ball.

penalty kick   A free kick that takes place if a foul occurs within the penalty area. The kick takes place in the penalty area and the goal is defended by the keeper who must stand 12-feet from the goal line.

penalty-kick tiebreaker   A method used to break a tie by allowing five players on each team to attempt a penalty kick against the goalkeeper. It is also referred to as a shootout or penalty-kick shootout. If the tie is not broken after five attempts, the game goes into overtime.

penalty spot   If a defensive foul occurs in the penalty area, a player will attempt a shot from this spot, which is 12 yards from the goal.

punt   The kick that is made by the goalkeepers downfield by kicking the ball high in the air toward the opposition's goal.

red card   The same as expulsion or ejection. A red card is given when there is dangerous action on the field such as spitting or tackling a player from behind. Two yellow cards equal a red card.

referee   A game official who monitors the action of the game and is in charge of fouls and goals.

restart   The same as a free kick, a goal kick, kickoff, corner kick, or throw-in.

save   When a goalkeeper does not allow the ball to cross into the net either by blocking, catching, or parrying the ball.

semi-pro   A player who earns part of his income from playing soccer, but not enough for it to be the sole means of support. The player must have a regular job as well.

set piece   Commonly referred to as a dead-ball situation. It can be a goal kick, corner or free kick or throw-in.

shot at goal   A failed attempt at scoring or making a goal.

shutout   When a team prevents the opposing team from scoring any points.

side   Another term for team.

square pass   A lateral pass made by one player to a player standing next to him.

stoppage time   Commonly referred to as injury time, it is the time allotted to compensate for time lost due to disputes, injuries, and so on.

striker   A center forward who focuses on scoring goals.

substitute   A player who takes the place of another player at some point during a game. The number of substitutions differs with different leagues. Pro soccer allows three substitutions; youth soccer generally does not limit substitutions.

system of play   The pattern of the team at the onset of the game. One popular system of play is the 4-4-2, which means there are four players defending, four players in midfield, and two forward players. Goalkeepers are not counted in the formation.

tackle   A move that involves dispossessing a player of the ball by kicking it away.

through pass   A pass that travels between a minimum of two defensive players.

throw-in   This play occurs when the ball goes out of bounds and is thrown back into the field to the opposing team. This is the only time a ball may legally be touched by regular players with the hands.

tie   Also referred to as a draw. It is when both teams have the same score at the end of regulation time.

time wasting   This occurs when the team that is winning tries to delay the game by taking the allotted time during dead-ball calls. If noted by the referee a yellow card is given to the offending team.

touch line   Lines that run on either side of the field from goal to goal. The length of the line is between 100 to 120 yards depending on the league.

trainer   In the United States a trainer is an individual who keeps the players healthy and in good condition to play. In Germany a trainer is considered to be the coach.

trap   Capturing the ball with the head, chest, foot or thigh.

unsportsmanlike behavior   Player activity that is considered to be unruly, dangerous, and unfitting for an athlete.

volley   Action that describes a ball that is kicked while it is still in the air.

wing   A midfielder or center who plays on either the right or left side of the field.

World Cup   The world's largest single-sport event, the World Cup soccer championship is played every four years among the top soccer teams in the world and representing their respective nations.

yellow card   A disciplinary card that is issued as the result of dangerous or unsportsmanlike behavior. Two yellow cards issued in a single game equal a red card, which is an automatic expulsion from the field.

youth player   Any player who is between the ages of 4 and 19.

zone defense   A defensive tactic in which players defend areas of the field rather than a particular player.

Youth Soccer Organizations

The soccer world is filled with organizations designed to promote different aspects of youth and adult play in the United States. In addition to offering memberships, many of the following groups also offer valuable resources for novice and experienced coaches and administrators alike.

National Indoor Soccer Council (promotes indoor soccer league play)
1225 Broadmoor, Stanley, KS 66223
Phone: 1-800-877-3790 or 913-851-9898 ext 31
Fax: 913-851-3431

North American Soccer Association USASA, USYSA (for youth teams of players up to 19 years of age)
P. O. Box 511
North Tonawanda, NY 14120
Phone: 716-695-5801
Fax: 716-695-0855

Soccer Association for Youth
4050 Executive Park Dr., Ste. 100
Cincinnati, OH 45241
Phone: 1-800-233-7291 or 513-769-3800
Fax: 513-769-0500
www.saysoccer.org

Soccer in the Streets (an inner city program with local chapters)
149 S. McDonough St, Ste. 270
Jonesboro, GA 30236
Phone: 770-477-0354
Fax: 770-478-1862
www.sits.org

U.S. Amateur Soccer Association (for youth and adult players)
7800 River Rd. North Bergen, NJ 07047-6221
Phone: 1-800-867-2945 or 201-861-6277
Fax: 201-861-6341
usaussf@aol.com

U.S. Soccer Federation FIFA (the U.S. chapter of the Federation Internationale
de Football Association, an international soccer organization)
U.S. Soccer House
1801-1811 S. Prairie Ave.
Chicago, IL 60616
Phone: 312-808-1300
Fax: 312-808-1301
www.us-soccer.com

U.S. Youth Soccer Association Inc. (for ages 19 and below).
899 Presidential Dr., Ste. 117
Richardson, TX 75081
Phone: 1-800-4SOCCER or 972-235-4499
Fax: 972-235-4480
www.youthsoccer.org

Here is contact information for the youth soccer associations in every state.

Alabama Youth Soccer Association
19220 Hwy 280 West
Birmingham, AL 35242
Phone: 205-991-9779
Fax: 205-991-3736

Alaska State Youth Soccer Association
PMB 1187, 200 W. 34th Ave.
Anchorage, AK 99503-3969
Phone: 907-789-7826

Arizona Youth Soccer Association
1815 W. Missouri Ave., Ste. 101
Phoenix, AZ 85015
Phone: 602-433-9202
Fax: 602-433-9221

Arkansas State Soccer Association
1100 E. Kiehl Ave. Ste. 1
Sherwood, AR 72120
Phone: 501-833-0550
Fax: 501-835-2176

California Youth Soccer Association—
North
1040 Serpentine Lane, Ste. 201
Pleasanton, CA 94566
Phone: 925-426-5437
Fax: 925-426-9473

California Youth Soccer Association—
South
1029 S. Placentia Ave.
Fullerton, CA 92831
Phone: 714-778-2972
Fax: 714-441-0715

Colorado State Youth Soccer
Association
7375 E. Orchard Rd., #300
Englewood, CO 80111
Phone: 303-770-6440
Fax: 303-770-6958

Connecticut Junior Soccer Association
757 W. Main St.
New Britain, CT 06050
Phone: 860-224-2572
Fax: 860-826-4400

Delaware Youth Soccer Association
P. O. Box 5325
Wilmington, DE 19808
Phone: 302-731-4523
Fax: 302-731-8972

Florida Youth Soccer Association
8 Broadway Ave. Ste. B
Kissimmee, FL 34741-5172
Phone: 407-847-2001
Fax: 407-847-5974

Georgia Youth Soccer Association
3684 B-1 Stewart Rd.
Atlanta, GA 30340-2760
Phone: 770-452-0505
Fax: 770-452-1946

Hawaii Youth Soccer Association
1442 Kona St.
Honolulu, HI 96814
Phone: 808-951-4972
Fax: 808-955-5513

Idaho Youth Soccer Association
2419 W. State St., Ste. 2
Boise, ID 83702-3167
Phone: 208-336-5256
Fax: 208-367-9044

Illinois Youth Soccer Association
1655 Arlington Heights Rd., Ste. 201
Arlington Heights, IL 60005
Phone: 847-290-1577
Fax: 847-290-1576

Indiana Youth Soccer Association
5830 N. Post Rd., Ste. 215
Indianapolis, IN 46216
Phone: 317-377-3405
Fax: 317-377-3428

Iowa State Youth Soccer Association
5406 Merle Hay Rd., Ste. 300
Johnston, IA 51031-1209
Phone: 515-252-6363
Fax: 515-252-7676

Kansas State Youth Soccer Association
8220 Travis Rd., Ste, 201
Overland Park, KS 66204
Phone: 913-648-6434
Fax: 913-648-0564

Kentucky Youth Soccer Association
443 S. Ashland Ave., Ste. 201
Lexington, KY 40502
Phone: 606-268-1254
Fax: 606-269-0545

Louisiana Soccer Association
2133 Silverside Dr., Ste, G
Baton Rouge, LA 70808
Phone: 225-766-0577
Fax: 225-766-0623

United Soccer Federation of Maine
35 Farvue Ave.
Bangor, ME 04401
Phone: 207-990-0662
Fax: 207-990-0662

Maryland State Youth Soccer
Association
303 Najoles Rd., Ste. 109
Millersville, MD 21108
Phone: 410-987-7898
Fax: 410-987-8707

Massachusetts Youth Soccer
Association
30 Great Rd.
Acton, MA 01720
Phone: 978-287-5207
Fax: 978-287-5212

Michigan State Youth Soccer
Association
23077 Greenfield Rd., Ste. 510
Southfield, MI 48075
Phone: 248-557-8220
Fax: 248-557-8216

Minnesota Youth Soccer Association
11577 Encore Circle
Minnetonka, MN 55343
Phone: 612-933-2384
Fax: 612-933-2627

Mississippi Youth Soccer Association
P. O. Box 13066
Jackson, MS 39236-3066
Phone: 601-982-5198
Fax: 601-982-5297

Missouri Youth Soccer Association
1811 Sherman Dr., Ste, 10
St. Charles, MO 63303-3976
Phone: 636-947-8442
Fax: 636-947-7626

Montana Youth Soccer Association
P. O. Box 1757
Kalispell, MT 59903-1757
Phone: 406-752-1776
Fax: 406-752-5015

Nebraska State Soccer Association
5616 S. 85th Circle
Omaha, NE 68127
Phone: 402-596-1616
Fax: 402-506-0660

United States Youth Soccer Nevada
55650 W. Charleston Blvd., #13
Las Vegas, NV 89146
Phone: 702-870-3024
Fax: 702-258-8381

New Hampshire Soccer Association
1600 Candida Rd., Ste. 2
Manchester, NH 03109
Phone: 603-626-9686
Fax: 603-626-9687

New Jersey Youth Soccer Association
P. O. Box 848
Hightstown, NJ 08520
Phone: 609-490-0725
Fax: 609-490-0731

New Mexico Youth Soccer Association
2300 Candelaria NE, Ste. 110
Albuquerque, NM 87107
Phone: 505-830-2245
Fax: 505-830-2247

Eastern New York Youth Soccer
Association
49 Front St., No. 2
Rockville Center, NY 11570
Phone: 516-766-0849
Fax: 516-678-7411

New York State West Youth Soccer
Association
P. O. Box 12
Corning, NY 14830
Phone: 607-962-9923
Fax: 607-962-0525

North Carolina Youth Soccer
Association
P. O. Box 29308
Greensboro, NC 27429
Phone: 336-856-7529
Fax: 336-856-0204

North Dakota Youth Soccer
Association
3022 Walnut St.
Grand Forks, ND 58201
Phone: 701-775-2942

Ohio South Youth Soccer Association
25 Whitney Dr., #104
Milford, OH 45150
Phone: 513-576-9555
Fax: 513-576-1666

Ohio Youth Soccer Association—North
P. O. Box 367
Richfield, OH 44286
Phone: 330-659-0989
Fax: 330-659-0993

Oklahoma Soccer Association
P. O. Box 35174
Tulsa, OK 74153-0174
Phone: 918-627-2663
Fax: 918-627-2693

Oregon Youth Soccer Association
4840 SW Western Ave., Ste. 800
Beaverton, OR 97005
Phone: 503-626-4625
Fax: 503-520-0302

Eastern Pennsylvania Youth Soccer
Association
2 Village Rd., Ste. 3
Horsham, PA 19044
Phone: 215-657-7727
Fax: 215-657-7740

Pennsylvania West Soccer Association
855 MacBeth Dr., No. 2
Monroeville, PA 15146-3332
Phone: 412-856-8011
Fax: 412-856-8012

Rhode Island Youth Soccer
Association
116 Eileen Dr.
North Kingstown, RI 02852
Phone: 401-885-0379
Fax: 401-885-9110

South Carolina Youth Soccer
Association
121 Executive Center Dr. No. 140
Columbia, SC 29210
Phone: 803-798-5425
Fax: 803-798-5425

South Dakota State Soccer Association
3701 Freda Circle
Sioux Falls, SD 57103
Phone: 605-371-2255
Fax: 605-371-2636

Tennessee State Soccer Association
161 Second St. NE, Ste. 2
Cleveland, TN 37311
Phone: 423-559-1150
Fax: 423-476-9993

North Texas State Soccer Association
1740 S. I-35 Ste. 105
Carrollton, TX 75006
Phone: 972-323-1323
Fax: 972-242-3600

South Texas Youth Soccer Association
P. O. Box 1370
Georgetown, TX 78627
Phone: 512-863-4969
Fax: 512-869-4785

Utah Youth Soccer Association
4476 S. Century Dr., Ste. A
Salt Lake City, UT 84123
Phone: 801-268-3365
Fax: 801-268-3415

Vermont Youth Soccer Association
P. O. Box 90
Williston, VT 05495
Phone: 802-859-9601
Fax: 802-859-9602

Virginia Youth Soccer Association
2239 G Tacketts Mill Dr.
Woodbridge, VA 22192
Phone: 703-494-0030
Fax: 703-551-4114

Washington State Youth Soccer
Association
33710 9th Ave. S. Ste 8
Federal Way, WA 98003
Phone: 253-476-2237
Fax: 253-925-1830

West Virginia Soccer Association
P. O. Box 3360
Beckley, WV 25801
Phone: 304-252-9872
Fax: 304-252-9878

Wisconsin Youth Soccer Association
10708 Hayes Rd.
West Allis, WI 53227
Phone: 414-545-7227
Fax: 414-545-7249

Wyoming State Soccer Association
7202 Bomar Dr.
Cheyenne, WY 82009-2017
Phone: 307-637-2304
Fax: 307-637-2305

Soccer Resources

Soccer on the Web

Coaching

Coaching Association of Canada
www.coach.ca/Tchart_e.htm
Canadian coaching site.

Coaching Soccer.net
www.coachingsoccer.net
A member of the coaching.net network.

National Soccer Coaches Association of America
www.nscaa.com
U.S. coaching site.

Soccer Tip of the Day
www.erols.com/soccertip/
A soccer tip for every day of the week.

Tournament Locator
www.eteamz.com/soccer/tournaments/
Hosted by eteamz, this database lists tournaments for all ages around the country and the world.

Rules

AskTheRef.com
www.asktheref.com
Ask a referee about soccer rules and regulations.

FIFA Laws of the Game
www.fifa.com/fifa/handbook/laws/index.laws.html
When in doubt, consult the laws.

Fitness and Health

Conditioning
www.performancecondition.com/soccer/
Q&As on soccer conditioning.

Soccer/Sports for Girls

Girls' Soccer World Online
www.girlsoccerworld.com
A soccer site just for girls.

Women and Girls in Sports
www.feminist.org/sports/sports.asp
Promoting sport for women and girls.

Women's Sports Foundation
www.womenssportsfoundation.org
A site promoting women's and girls' participation in sports of all kinds, including soccer.

U.S. National Teams

National Soccer Hall of Fame
www.soccerhall.org
Where legends live on.

Sam's Army
www.sams-army.com
Unofficial fan club of the U.S. National Soccer Team.

U.S. Soccer Federation
www.ussoccer.com
Gateway to information on U.S. Men's and Women's national teams and a host of other information on U.S. soccer.

Major League Soccer

Major League Soccer
www.mlsnet.com

Chicago Fire
www.chicago-fire.com

Colorado Rapids
www.coloradorapids.com

Columbus Crew
www.thecrew.com

Dallas Burn
www.dallasburn.com

D.C. United
www.dcunited.com

Kansas City Wizards
www.kcwizards.com

L.A. Galaxy
www.lagalaxy.com

New England Revolution
www.revolutionsoccer.net

New York/New Jersey MetroStars
www.metrostars.com

San Jose Earthquakes
www.sjearthquakes.com

U.S. Women's Professional Soccer

Women's United Soccer Association
www.wusa.com

Atlanta Beat
www.theatlantabeat.com

San Jose CyberRays
www.bayareacyberrays.com

Boston Breakers
www.bostonbreakers.com

Carolina Courage
www.carolinacourage.com

New York Power
www.nypower.com

Philadelphia Charge
www.philadelphiacharge.com

San Diego Spirit
www.sandiegospirit.com

Washington Freedom
www.washingtonfreedom.com

Media

CNN/Sports Illustrated Soccer
www.cnnsi.com/soccer
CNN and SI teamed up on this soccer site.

ESPN Soccer
soccernet.espn.go.com
The major sports cable network's soccer site.

Soccer America
www.socceramerica.com
Online version of popular soccer magazine.

Success in Soccer Online
www.successinsoccer.com
Success in Soccer's online site.

UK SoccerNet
www.soccernet.com
A popular British soccer site.

Books

Coaching

Coerver, Wiel. *Soccer Fundamentals for Players and Coaches*. New York: Prentice Hall, 1986.

Fortanasce, Vincent. *Life Lessons for Soccer: What Your Child Can Learn On and Off the Field*. New York: Fireside, 2001.

Hargreaves, Alan. *Skills and Strategies for Coaching Soccer*. Champaign, Ill.: Human Kinetics, 1991.

Learmouth, John. *Soccer Fundamentals: Basics Skills, Drills, and Tactics for Beginning Players*. New York: St. Martin's, 1994.

Maisner, Larry. *Ramp Up Your Soccer Tactics with Disguise and Surprise*. Youth Sports Publishing, 2002.

McAvoy, Nelson. *Teaching Soccer Fundamentals*. Champaign, Ill.: Human Kinetics, 1998.

McGettigan, James P. *Soccer Drills for Individual and Team Play*. Parker, 1987.

Simon, J. Malcolm and John A. Reeves, eds. *Practice Games for Winning Soccer*. Champaign, Ill.: Human Kinetics, 1997.

Simon, J. Malcolm. *Soccer Restart Plays, Second Edition*. Champaign, Ill.: Human Kinetics, 1999.

Conditioning

Bompa, Tudor O. *Total Training for Young Athletes*. Champaign, Ill.: Human Kinetics, 1999.

Brown, Lee E, ed., et al. *Training for Speed, Agility, and Quickness*. Champaign, Ill.: Human Kinetics, 2000.

Gambetta, Vince. *Soccer Speed.* Gambetta Sports Training Systems, 1998.

Luxbacher, Joe, Joseph, and Jim. *Conditioning for Soccer.* New York: McGraw-Hill/Contemporary Books, 1997.

Westcott, Wayne and Avery D. Faigenbaum. *Strength and Power for Young Athletes.* Champaign, Ill.: Human Kinetics, 2000.

Games, Drills, and Strategies

Caligiuri, Paul. *High Performance Soccer: Techniques and Tactics for Advanced Play.* Champaign, Ill.: Human Kinetics, 1996.

Garland, Jim. *Youth Soccer Drills.* Champaign, Ill.: Human Kinetics, 1996.

Harvey, Gil and Clive Gifford. *Passing and Shooting.* Edu Dev, 1997.

Luxbacher, Joe and Joseph. *Soccer Practice Games: 120 Games for Technique, Training, and Tactics.* Champaign, Ill.: Human Kinetics, 1994.

Kentwell, Richard G., ed. *Dutch Soccer Drills: Game Action Drills.* New York: McGraw-Hill/Contemporary Books, 1998.

———. *Dutch Soccer Drills: Individual Skills.* New York: McGraw-Hill/Contemporary Books, 1998.

McGettigan, James P. and Barbara S. *Complete Book of Drills for Winning Soccer.* New York: Prentice Hall, 1980.

———. *Soccer Systems and Strategies.* Champaign, Ill.: Human Kinetics, 2000.

Reeves, John A. and J. Malcolm Simon. *The Coaches Collection of Soccer Drills.* Champaign, Ill.: Human Kinetics, 1989.

Schmidt, Colin E. *Advanced Soccer Drills.* Champaign, Ill.: Human Kinetics, 1997.

Goalkeeping

Luxbacher, Joseph A. and Gene Klein. *The Soccer Goalkeeper: Techniques/Tactics/Training.* Champaign, Ill.: Human Kinetics, 2002.

Miller, Jonathan. *Soccer Goalkeeping.* E D C Publications, 1998.

Phillips, Lincoln. *Soccer Goalkeeping: The Last Line of Defense, the First Line of Attack.* New York: McGraw-Hill/Contemporary Books, 1996.

Welsh, Alex. *The Soccer Goalkeeping Handbook: The Essential Guide for Players and Coaches.* New York: McGraw-Hill/Contemporary Books, 1999.

Kids

Buston, Ted, *et al. Soccer Skills: For Young Players.* New York: Firefly, 2000.

Clark, Brooks. *Kids' Book of Soccer: Skills, Strategies, and the Rules of the Game.* New York: Citadel Press, 1997.

Crisfield, Deborah W. *The Everything Kids' Soccer Book: Rules, Techniques, and More About Your Favorite Sport!* Avon, Mass.: Adams Media, 2002.

Fischer, George. *The Illustrated Laws of Soccer.* Nashville, Tenn.: Ideals Children's Books, 2001.

Gibbons, Gail. *My Soccer Book.* New York: HarperCollins Juvenile Books, 2000.

Lineker, Gary. *DK Superguides: Soccer.* New York: London: DK Publishing, 2000.

Miller, Marla. *All American Girls: The U.S. Women's National Soccer Team.* New York: Pocket Books, 1999.

Remkiewicz, Frank. *Soccer Scrapbook for Boys and Girls.* Berkeley, Calif.: Peaceable Kingdom, 2001.

Scott, Nina Savin. *The Thinking Kids Guide to Successful Soccer.* Brookfield, Conn.: Millbrook, 1999.

Rules

American Youth Soccer Organization *et al. The Official American Youth Soccer Organization Handbook: Rules, Regulations, Skills, and Everything Else Kids, Parents, and Coaches Need to Participate in Youth Soccer.* New York: Fireside, 2001.

Kira, Gene. *Understanding Soccer: Rules and Procedures for Players, Parents, and Coaches.* Valley Center, Calif.: Apples & Oranges, 1993.

Mason, Bill and Larry Maisner. *The Rules of Soccer Simplified.* Youth Sports Publishing, 2000.

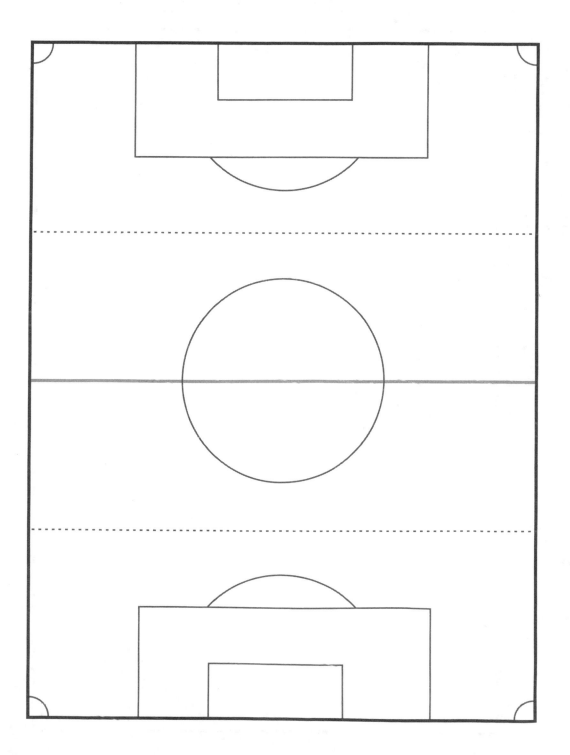

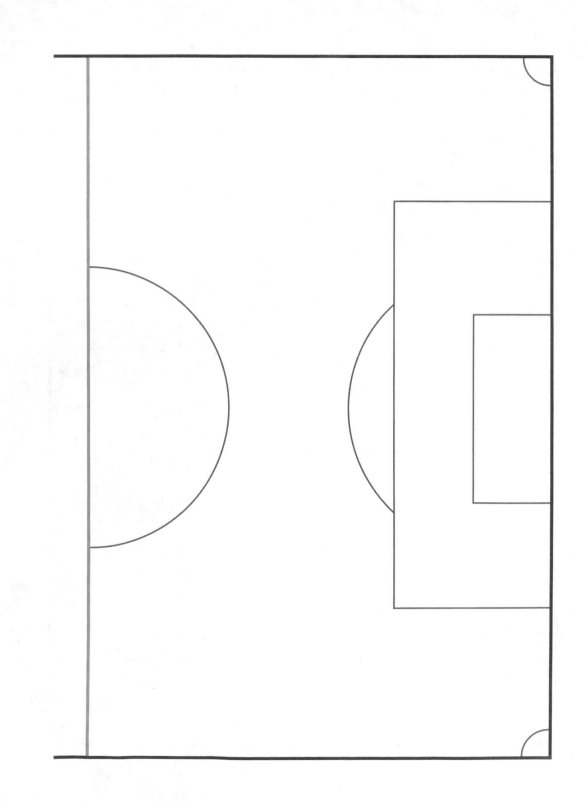

Index

A

administering pain relievers, 10
age groups, league organization, 14-15
American football, 20
amount
    defenders, 148
    games per seasonal half, 80
analyzing matches, 202
    field positions, 202-203
    opposition, scouting, 203
        defense, 203-204
        offense, 205-207
appreciation (soccer), nurturing, 42, 228
    lifetime recreational activity, 229
    pro teams, following, 228
    professional groups/associations, 229
assistant coaches, 63
associations
    becoming involved, 229
    NSCAA, 39
    state, 22
asthma, 119
athletic stress, 120-121
attacking
    balls, 154-155
    team defense, 212
attendance, 43
attitude
    players, 44
    positive, 42, 45

B

backward passes, 166
balanced diet, 123
    hydration, 124
    nutritional supplements, 124
    pre-game meals, 125
    ratios, 123-124
balanced strategy, 202
ball carriers, pressuring, 221
ball control, 96-97, 111-112
balls, 8
    attacking, 154-155
    intercepting, 155
    keeping in play, 12
    out of bounds, 185-186
    possession, 219-220
banana kick, 191
Basic Headball, 112-113
block tackles, 157
body parts, 11
breaks, 81
budgets (team), 61-62
Builders coaching style, 35-36
Bull in the Ring, 112

C

carbohydrates, 123
cardiac conditions, 119
castle strategy, 196-197

catches (goalkeepers), 110, 175-176
   chest, 176
   collapse dive, 177
   diamond catch, 178
   full-extension, 178
   one-on-one catches, 180
   overhead catches, 178
   scoop, 180
central defenders, 149
challengers, supporting, 222
chatterer parents, 57
cheerleader coaching style, 33
chest catches, 176
chip shots, 169
cleated shoes, 9
clothing (players), 8-9
clubs, 22
coaches
   appearance, 45
   caring, 23
   childhood memories, 29-30
   contracts, 41-42
   culture role, 23
   defined, 28-29
   developmental, 38-40
   effective teaching, 226
   efficiency, 45
   effort, 46
   enthusiasm, 24
   equipment, 10
   feedback, 45
   flexibility, 46
   goals, 16
   improvement, 46
   inner coach, cultivating, 30-32
   knowledge, 23
   leading by example, 227
   open-minded, 46
   philosophy, 38
   player expectations, 226
   player respect, 45
   positive/winning attitude, 45
   practice introduction, 82
   preparations, 45
   repetition, 46
   responsibility, 46
   right thing, 226
   role, 227
   statement, 59
   styles, 33
      Builders, 35-36
      Cheerleader, 33
      Commander, 34-35
      Tactical Technician, 34
   teaching, 24
   team concept, 46
coaching staff, 63
   assistant coaches, 63
   gear wranglers, 64
   head coaches, 63
   line judges, 63
   phone tree leaders, 64
   refreshment captains, 64
   team managers, 63
collapse dive, 177
combination drills, 101
combination kicks, 191
Commander coaching style, 34-35
commandments (teamwork), 51-52
commitment (contracts)
   coaches, 41-42
   players, 43-44
concentration, 207
concept discussions (practice), 82
concussions, 120
Cone Races, 115
cones, 9
conserving energy, 208
contacts, list of, 60
contracts
   coaches, 41-42
   parents, 64-66
   players, 43-44
cool downs, 85, 114-115

cooperation. *See* teamwork
corner kicks, 186-188
  defending, 194-195
  executing, 193-194
cover (defensive), 153-154
coverage, 221
Crablegs, 109
critic parents, 57
critical contacts, 60
cultivating inner coach, 30
  appropriate levels, 31
  knowledge, 31
  leading by example, 31
  player involvement, 32
  skills, teaching, 32
  strategies, teaching, 32
culture (social), 20-21
  clubs, 22
  coaches, 23
  leagues, 22
  national regions, 22
  players, 21
  state associations, 22
  teams, 21

D

defenders, 13, 133, 148
  amount, 148
  central, 149
  defense, 148
  defensive midfielders, 150
  outside fullbacks, 149
  types, 149-151
defense, 148
  attacking the ball, 154-155
  ball possession, 219-220
  challengers, supporting, 222
  corner kicks, 194-195
  coverage, 221
  defensive support/cover, 153-154
  development, 159
  goalkeeper support, 183

  goals, 218-219
  interceptions, 155
  offensive pressure, 152-153
  opponents
    tracking, 154, 222-223
    scouting, 203-204
  player-to-player, 151
  strong strategy, 202
  tackling, 156
    block tackles, 157
    funneling, 157
    hook sliding tackles, 159
    sliding tackles, 158-159
    toe pokes, 157
  team, 212
    attacking, 212
    funneling, 213
    goalside space, 213
    passing, 214
    patterns, 214
  zone, 151
defensive area (fields), 131
defensive midfielders, 150
dehydration, 124
designing practices, 81
  coaches introduction, 82
  concept discussion, 82
  cool downs, 85
  games, playing, 84-85
  pre-practice activity, 82
  skills development, 83-84
  warm ups, 83
  wrap ups, 86
developing skills practices, 83-84
development coaching, 38-40
diabetes mellitus, 119
diamond catches, 178
diet (balanced), 123-125
  hydration, 124
  nutritional supplements, 124
  pre-game meals, 125
  ratios, 123-124
direct kicks, 189-190, 195-196

disciplined environments, 42
discount sporting goods stores, 9
distraction plays, 191
Double Ladders, 112
Doubleday, Abner, 19
dribbling, 90-92
    curves, 93
    drills, 108-109
    goalkeepers, 184
    incremental, 92
    offensive tool, 165
drills
    combination, 101
    cool-down, 114-115
    dribbling, 108-109
    heading, 112-113
    juggling, 111-112
    passing, 110-111
    shooting, 113-114
    teamwork, 53
    warm-up, 104-107
drinks and food, 10

E

Eastern region, 22
effort, 46
elbow pads, 9
energy
    conserving, 208
    parents, 56
equipment
    balls, 8
    cleated shoes, 9
    coaching, 10
    cones, 9
    first aid supplies, 10
    food and drinks, 10
    miscellaneous, 10
    shin-guards, 9
    shirts, 8
etiquette (teams), 58
exercise. *See* fitness
expenses, 61

F

feedback, 45
feet, passing positions, 94
field positions
    analyzing, 202-203
    team offensive, 211-212
fields, 6, 131-133
first aid supplies, 10
fitness
    balanced diet, 123
        hydration, 124
        nutritional supplements, 124
        ratios, 123-124
    healthy lifestyles, 122
    physicals, 118-120
    pre-game meals, 125
    stress, 120-121
fixed costs, 61
flexibility, 46
flood strategy, 193-194
food and drinks, 10
forward area (field), 131
forward passes, 166
forwards, 13, 133, 162-163
fouls, 12
four corner arcs (field), 131
four pillars of soccer, 72
    performance, 75-76
    physical traits, 76-77
    tactical mastery, 74-75
    technical aspects, 73-74
Foxes and Rabbits, 109
free kicks, 189, 191
full-extension dives, 178
fun warm ups, 106-107
fundamentals
    dribbling, 90-92
        curves, 93
        drills, 108-109
        goalkeepers, 184
        incremental, 92
        offensive tool, 165

heading, 98-99, 112-113
juggling, 111-112
learning, 90
passing, 94
    chip shots, 169
    drills, 110-111
    entire body, 94
    foot position, 94
    heel passes, 168
    juggling, 96-97
    offensive tool, 165-167
    outside foot passes, 168
    push passes, 167
    receiving, 95-96
    skill levels, 170
    types, 166
receiving, 165-167
shooting, 100-101, 113-114
teaching, 88-90
funneling, 157, 213

G

game day, 86
game playing practices, 84-85
games
    amount per seasonal half, 80
    length, 11
    results, reviewing, 85
    schedules, 59
    tactical mastery, 74-75
gear wrangler, 64
gloves, 9
goal kicks, 191-192
goalkeepers, 13, 133
    catches, 175-176
        chest catches, 176
        collapse dive, 177
        diamond catch, 178
        full-extension dive, 178
        one-on-one catches, 180
        overhead catches, 178
        scoop catches, 180

defense support, 183
elbow pads, 9
gloves, 9
kicking, 183-184
near post saves, 182
positioning, 181-182
regular players, compared, 174-175
saves, 175, 180-181
goals, 11
    ball carrier pressure, 221
    ball possession, 219-220
    challenger, supporting, 222
    coaching, 16
    fields, 131
    opposition, 222-223
    preventing, 218
    problems, 218-219
    restarts, 223-224
    shooting, 170-171
    teaching change, 207
goalside space, protecting, 213
good coaches
    caring, 23
    enthusiasm, 24
    knowledge, 23
    teaching, 24

H

hammers, 149
head coach, 63
Headball Tennis, 112
Headbanger, 113
heading the ball, 98-99, 112-113
Headshots, 113
health
    balanced diet, 123
        hydration, 124
        nutritional supplements, 124
        ratios, 123-124
    concussions, 120
    conditions, 119
    lifestyles, 122

pain free, 120
physicals, 118-120
pre-game meals, 125
stress, 120-121
profiles, 60
heat illness, 119
heel passes, 168
history (soccer), 19
immigrants, 18
physical education classes, 18
pre-soccer United States, 17-18
hook sliding tackle, 159
hurdler's stretch, 104
hydration, 124

I

increasing popularity, 19
indirect kicks, 190, 196-197
inner coach, cultivating, 30
appropriate levels, 31
knowledge, 31
leading by example, 31
player involvement, 32
skills, teaching, 32
strategies, teaching, 32
inswinger corner kicks, 187
intellectual teamwork, 51
interceptions, 155
introducing coaches, 82
involving players, 32
isolation strategy, 197

J–K

Jacknife, 114
jerseys, 8
juggling, 96-97, 111-112

kicks
banana, 191
combination, 191
corner, 186-188
defending, 194-195
executing, 193-194
direct, 189-190, 195-196
free, 189, 191
goal, 191-192
goalkeepers, 183-184
indirect, 190, 196-197
inswinger, 187
long, 191
outswinger, 188
power, 190
short pass, 188
knowledge
fields, 131-133
players, 133-134

L

large group exercises, 84
Laws of the Game, 19
leading by example, 227
leagues, 22
organization, age groups, 14-15
learning skills, 90
length (games), 11
licensing, 39
lifestyles (healthy), 122
lifetime recreational activity (soccer as), 229
Lombardi, Vince, 37
Long Field Lope, 114
long kicks, 191
Long Legger, 114

M

managing teams, 58
budgets, 61-62
parents, 58-60
markers, 164
mastery (tactical), 74-75

match analysis, 202
    field positions, 202-203
    opposition, scouting, 203
        defense, 203-204
        offense, 205-207
meals (pre-game), 125
midfield, 131
midfield boot, 184
midfielders, 13, 133, 163
    defensive, 150
    offensive, 163
Midwest region, 22
miscellaneous equipment, 10
mock games, playing, 84-85
Musical Rotation, 107

N

Naismith, James, 19
National Coaching School, 39
national regions, 22
National Soccer Coaches Association
    (NSCAA), 39
near post saves, 182
necessities (playing)
    balls, 8
    fields, 6
    outfits, 8-9
new experiences, 5
no-hand rule, 11
NSCAA (National Soccer Coaches
    Association), 39
number 3 ball, 8
number 4 ball, 8
number 5 ball, 8
nutritional supplements, 124

O

obesity, 119
offense
    chip shots, 169
    midfielders, 163

opposition, scouting
    attack strategies, 205
    direct/indirect approach, 205
    forward functionality, 206
    patterns, 205
    scoring, 206-207
passing shots, 167-168
passing, teaching, 170
pressuring, 152-153
shooting the goal, 170-171
strong strategy, 202
systems of play, 163-165
team, 210
    field positions, 211-212
    strategies, 211-212
    teamwork, 210-211
tools, 165-167
offensive midfielders, 163
one-on-one catches, 180
open-minded coaches, 46
opponents
    scouting, 203
        defense, 203-204
        offense, 205-207
    tracking, 154, 222-223
orange cones, 9
out of bounds, 185-186
outfits (players), 8-9
outside foot passes, 168
outside fullbacks, 149
outswinger corner kicks, 188
overhead catches, 178

P

pacer parents, 57
packing order, 21
    clubs, 22
    coaches, 23
    leagues, 22
    national regions, 22
    players, 21
    state associations, 22
    teams, 21

pain relievers, 10
parents
    as critics, 57
    energy, harnessing, 56
    planning for, 58-60
    strategies, 58
    types, 56-57
    volunteer supporters, 62-64
passing, 94
    chip shots, 169
    drills, 110-111
    entire body, 94
    foot position, 94
    heel passes, 168
    juggling, 96-97
    offensive tool, 165-167
    outside foot passes, 168
    push passes, 167
    receiving, 95-96
    skill levels, 170
    team defense, 214
    types, 166
peel out strategy, 195-196
Pele, 6
phantom parents, 57
philosophies
    coaching, 38-40
    four pillars, 72
        performance, 75-76
        physical traits, 76-77
        tactical mastery, 74-75
        technical aspects, 73-74
    play, 70-71
    sports, 71-72
    teams, 59
phone tree leader, 64
physical teamwork, 51
physical traits (players), 76-77
physicals, 118-120
planning
    parental involvement, 58-60
    practices, 80-81
    strategies, 130

play formations. *See* systems of play
player-to-player defense, 151
players, 21
    attendance, 43
    attitude, 44
    attributes, 4
    coaching expectations, 226
    contracts, 43-44
    defenders, 133, 148
        central, 149
        defensive midfielders, 150
        outside fullbacks, 149
        types, 149-151
    forcing inside, 156
    forcing out of bounds, 156
    forwards, 133, 162-163
    fouls, 12
    goalkeepers, 133
        catches, 175-178, 180
        defense support, 183
        kicking, 183-184
        near post saves, 182
        positioning, 181-182
        regular players, compared, 174-175
        saves, 175, 180-181
    healthy lifestyle, 44
    involving, 32
    knowledge of, 133-134
    markers, 164
    midfielders, 133
        defensive, 150
        offensive, 163
    number on field, 12
    physical traits, 76-77
    positions, 11, 13-14
    respecting, 45
    stoppers, 149
    strikers, 162
    sweepers, 149
    welfare, 42
    wingers, 162

playing
    balls in play, 12
    body parts, 11
    fouls, 12
    goal, 11
    length, 11
    mock games, 84-85
    necessities
        balls, 8
        fields, 6
        outfits, 8-9
        new experiences, 5
    number of players, 12
    out of bounds, 185-186
    philosophy, 70-71
    popularity, 19
    positions, 11, 13-14
    responsibility, 5
    restarts, 186
        corner kicks, 186-188
        free kicks, 189-191
        goal kicks, 191-192
        throw-ins, 192
    rewards, 5
    technical aspects, 73-74
    tiebreakers, 12
    timeouts, 12
    World Cup, 20
playing games practices, 84-85
plays. *See* strategies
Pockets, 114
popularity, increasing, 19
positioning goalkeepers, 181-182
positions, 11-14
    defenders, 13, 133, 148
        central, 149
        defensive midfielders, 150
        outside fullbacks, 149
        types, 149-151
    feet, 94
    field
        analyzing, 202-203
        team offensive, 211-212

forwards, 13, 133, 162-163
goalkeepers, 13, 133
    catches, 175-178, 180
    defense support, 183
    kicking, 183-184
    near post saves, 182
    positioning, 181-182
    regular players, compared, 174-175
    saves, 175, 180-181
markers, 164
midfielders, 13, 133
    defensive, 150
    offensive, 163
ready to play, 90
stoppers, 149
strikers, 162
sweepers, 149
wingers, 162
positive attitude, 45
possession (ball), 219-220
power kicks, 190
practices
    breaks, 81
    coaches introduction, 82
    concept discussion, 82
    cool downs, 85
    designing, 81
    games, playing, 84-85
    planning, 80-81
    pre-practice activity, 82
    schedule, 59
    skills development, 83-84
    teaching change, 207
    warm ups, 83
    wrap ups, 86
pre-game meals, 125
pre-pass touch, 95
pre-practice activity, 82
preparations, 45
pressuring
    ball carriers, 221
    offense, 152-153
preventing goals, 218

pro teams, following, 228
professional soccer associations, 229
professional soccer groups, 229
protecting goalside space, 213
psychological characteristics (performance), 75-76
push passes, 167

Q-R

ready to play position, 90
reasons (playing soccer), 5
receiving the ball
    drills, 110-111
    offensive tool, 165-167
    passes, 95-96
recruitment, 4
red cards, 12
refreshment captain, 64
Region I, 22
Region II, 22
Region III, 22
Region IV, 22
regions (national), 22
regulation fields, 6
repetition (coaching), 46
replay tag, 107
respecting players, 45
responsibility
    coaches, 46
    players, 5
restarts, 186, 223-224
    corner kicks, 186-188
    free kicks, 189-191
    goal kicks, 191-192
    throw-ins, 192, 197-198
reviewing game results, 85
rewards (players), 5
rotation, 107
Round Robin, 111
rules
    Laws of the Game, 19
    no-hands, 11

S

saves (goalkeepers), 175
    near post, 182
    scoop, 180-181
schedules, 59
scoop catches, 180
scouting opponents, 203
    defense, 203-204
    offense, 205-207
screamer parents, 56
secondhand sporting goods stores, 9
self-esteem, 72
self-fulfillment, 72
self-worth, 6
Set and Shoot, 114
shin-guards, 9
shirts, 8
shoes (cleated), 9
shooting, 100-101
    drills, 113-114
    goals, 170-171
short pass corner kicks, 188
short passes, 184
shots (passing)
    chip shots, 169
    heel passes, 168
    outside foot passes, 168
    push passes, 167
signing contracts
    coaches, 41-42
    players, 43-44
simple strategies, 144
skills
    dribbling, 90, 92
        curves, 93
        drills, 108-109
        goalkeepers, 184
        incremental, 92
        offensive tool, 165
    heading the ball, 98-99, 112-113
    juggling, 111-112
    learning, 90

passing, 94, 170
   chip shots, 169
   drills, 110-111
   entire body, 94
   foot position, 94
   heel passes, 168
   juggling, 96-97
   offensive tool, 165-167
   outside foot passes, 168
   push passes, 167
   receiving, 95-96
   skill levels, 170
   types, 166
  receiving, 165-167
  shooting, 100-101, 113-114
  teaching, 32
skills development practices, 83-84
sliding tackles, 158-159
small group exercises, 83-84
social culture, 20-21
  clubs, 22
  coaches, 23
  leagues, 22
  national regions, 22
  players, 21
  state associations, 22
  teams, 21
social playing field, 71
Southern region, 22
space, creating, 211
sports philosophies, 71-72
square passes, 166
staff (coaching), 63
  assistant coaches, 63
  gear wranglers, 64
  head coaches, 63
  line judges, 63
  phone tree leaders, 64
  refreshment captains, 64
  team managers, 63
state associations, 22
statements (coaches), 59

stoplight, 107
stoppers, 149
Straight Shooter, 114
Strategic Thinker coaching style, 34
strategies, 130
  balanced, 202
  castle, 196-197
  defining, 142-145
  distraction plays, 191
  field knowledge, 131-133
  flood, 193-194
  isolation, 197
  peel out, 195-196
  player knowledge, 133-134
  simple, 144
  strong defensive, 202
  strong offensive, 202
  systems of play, 134
    3-5-2, 139
    3-6-1, 140
    4-2-4, 137
    4-3-3, 136-137
    4-4-2, 134
  teaching, 32
  team offensive, 211-212
  throw-ins, 198
  triangle, 197-198
  zone in the goal, 194-195
stress, 120-121
stretches
  hurdler's, 104
  toe touches, 106
  tripod, 105
strikers, 162
strong defensive strategy, 202
strong offensive strategy, 202
styles (coaching), 33
  Builders, 35-36
  Cheerleader, 33
  Commander, 34-35
  Tactical Technician, 34
supplements (nutritional), 124

support
   challengers, 222
   defensive, 153-154
   teams, 46
sweepers, 149
systems of play, 133-134
   3-5-2, 139
   3-6-1, 140
   4-2-4, 137
   4-3-3, 136-137
   4-4-2, 134
   offense, 163-165

T

tackling, 156
   block tackles, 157
   funneling, 157
   hook sliding tackle, 159
   sliding, 158-159
   toe pokes, 157
tactical mastery (game), 74-75
Tactical Technician coaching style, 34
tactics, 130
   defense, 212
      attacking, 212
      funneling, 213
      goalside space, 213
      passing, 214
      patterns, 214
   offense, 210
      field positions, 211-212
      strategies, 211-212
      teamwork, 210-211
teaching
   change, 207-208
   effectiveness, 226
   fundamentals, 88-90
   passes, 170
   skills, 32
   strategies, 32
   teamwork, 53

team managers, 63
teams, 21
   assembling, 4
   beyond players, 46
   defined, 50
   etiquette, 58
   managing, 58
      budgets, 61-62
      parents, 58-60
   philosophy, 59
   tactics
      defense, 212-214
      offense, 210-212
   welfare, 42
teamwork, 50-51
   commandments, 51-52
   defined, 50
   offensive, 210-211
   principles, 51
   training drills, 53
   value, 214
technical aspects (play), 73-74
throw-ins, 192, 197-198
tiebreakers, 12
timeouts, 12
toe pokes, 157
toe touches, 106
tools (offense), 165-167
tracking opponents, 154, 222-223
training drills, 53
trapping, 97
triangle strategy, 197-198
Triple Play, 110
tripod stretch, 105
tsu-chu, 19
types
   defenders, 149-151
   forwards, 162-163
   parents, 56-57
   passes, 166

U–V

uniforms, 8-9
U.S. Soccer Association's National Coaching
  School, 39
Up the Ladder, 112

variable expenses, 61
volunteer supporters (parents), 62-63
    contracts, 64-66
    positions, 63-64

W–X–Y–Z

warm-up exercises, 93, 104
    fun, 106-107
    hurdler's stretch, 104
    toe touches, 106
    tripod stretch, 105
Western region, 22
wingers, 162
winning attitudes, 42, 45
World Cup, 20
wrap ups, 86

yellow cards, 12

Zigzag, 108
Zigzag Tag, 109
zone defense, 151
zone in the goal strategy, 194-195

DATE DUE   0603

JUL 1 6 2003

796 MUC
Muckian, Michael
   Complete idiot's guide
TIV   31887000850290

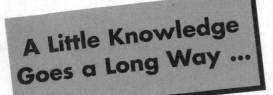
A Little Knowledge Goes a Long Way ...

Check Out These
Best-Selling
COMPLETE IDIOT'S GUIDES®

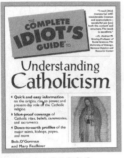

Understanding **Catholicism**

0-02-863639-2
$16.95

Learning **Spanish** on Your Own
SECOND EDITION

0-02-862743-1
$16.95

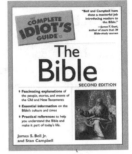

The **Bible**
SECOND EDITION

0-02-864382-8
$18.95

Feng Shui
SECOND EDITION

0-02-864339-9
$18.95

Playing the Guitar
SECOND EDITION

0-02-864244-9
$21.95 w/CD-ROM

Personal Finance in Your **20s & 30s**
SECOND EDITION

0-02-864374-7
$19.95

Creating a **Web Page**
FIFTH EDITION

0-02-864316-X
$24.95 w/CD-ROM

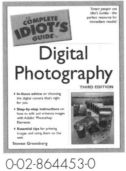

Digital **Photography**
THIRD EDITION

0-02-864453-0
$19.95

Windows XP

0-02-864232-5
$19.95

More than *400 titles* in *26 different categories*
Available at booksellers everywhere

ALPH